the Zoo on the Road to Nablus

the Zoo on the Road to Nablus

A Story of Survival from the West Bank

AMELIA THOMAS

PUBLICAFFAIRS
New York

Library of Congress Cataloging-in-Publication Data

Thomas, Amelia.
    The zoo on the road to Nablus : a story of survival from the West
Bank / Amelia Thomas.
        p.   cm.
    ISBN 978-1-58648-489-7 (hardcover : alk. paper)
    1. Zoo animals—Qalqilyah. 2. Qalqilyah—Description and
travel. I. Title.
QL77.5.T46   2008
590.73'56953—dc22
                                                            2008006806

First Edition
10 9 8 7 6 5 4 3 2 1

A Robin Red breast in a Cage
Puts all Heaven in a Rage...
A dog starv'd at his Master's gate
Predicts the ruin of the State.

Joy and Woe are woven fine,
A Clothing for the soul divine;
Under every grief and pine
Runs a joy with silken twine.

—*Auguries of Innocence*, William Blake

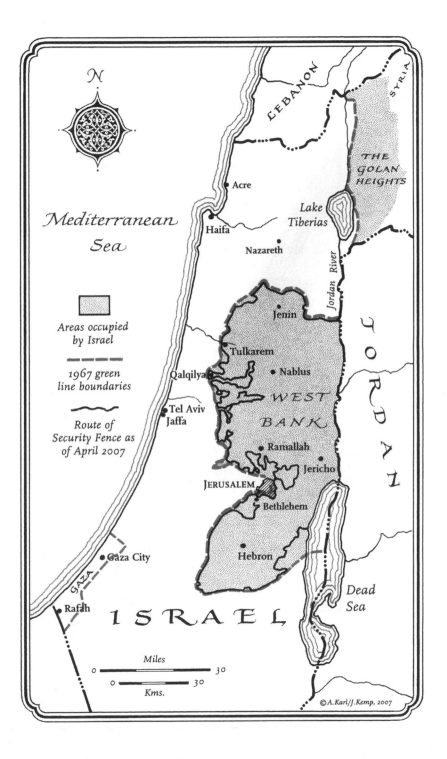

N

Mediterranean
Sea

Areas occupied
by Israel

1967 green
line boundaries

Route of
Security Fence as
of April 2007

LEBANON

SYRIA

THE
GOLAN
HEIGHTS

Acre

Haifa

Lake
Tiberias

Nazareth

Jordan River

Jenin

Tulkarem

Qalqilya

Nablus

WEST
BANK

JORDAN

Tel Aviv
Jaffa

Ramallah

Jericho

JERUSALEM

Bethlehem

Gaza City

GAZA

Hebron

Rafah

ISRAEL

Dead
Sea

Miles

0   30

0   30

Kms.

©A.Karl/J.Kemp, 2007

QALQILYA ZOO

Slaughterhouse

Stables for dying horses and donkeys

Wahib the camel and his "wife"

Shetland ponies

Hay barn

Dr. Sami's laboratory

Wolves

Dubi the hippo and his peacocks

Addax

Ostriches

Cameroon sheep

The hyena

Fateen the baboon

Zebras and goats

PLAYGROUND

Future quarters for Rambo and Bussi

Porcupine   Badger

Holi, Rad, and Rabir, the lions

Chika the leopard

Rama the leopard

Baboons   Vervet monkeys

Baboons   Baboons

Crocodiles

Quail

Owls

AREA RESERVED FOR DR. SAMI'S FUTURE AVIARY

Gift shop

Mushi the bachelor bear

The Syrian bears

Tortoises

Snakes

Men's WC

Mosque

Mansur's electric train ride

PLAYGROUND

To the site of the future amusement park

©A. Karl/J. Kemp, 2007

SCHOOL

SCHOOL

Dr. Sami's carnivore
department

Berber sheep,
chickens,
and geese

Ruti's night
shelter

Ruti's giraffe
enclosure

N

Fufu the ibex
and the hog deer

Dr. Sami's
office

Steps

Large
tree

GRASSY
AREA

Museum
of Every-
thing

Natural
History
Museum

PLAYGROUND

MUSEUM
COURTYARD

Agri-
cultural
Museum

Peacocks

Pigeons

Empty
swimming
pool

MAIN AVENUE

PICNIC

GROUND

Men's
WC

Friends'
Restaurant

To
Qalqilya
Souk

Fountain

Amjad
Daoud's
ticket office

Abu Shir's
Office

Main
Gate

Introduction
September 2005

Meet Your Brothers.
Take Them to Your Hearts,
and Respect Them.
—SIGN ABOVE THE GATE OF THE SIXTEENTH-CENTURY PUBLIC ZOO OF
EMPEROR JELAL-ED-DIN-MUHAMMAD, "AKBAR THE GREAT"

*T*he Municipal Zoo stood in a derelict district of the once prosperous farming town of Qalqilya. The road stretching away was deserted except for a garage, from which came a rhythmic clanking and the sharp drone of a welder. Paint peeled from a shabby signpost above the entrance, bearing the remnants of a cheerful procession. Lions, a camel, and dancing bears followed a high-stepping giraffe. To either side was bolted a broken neon "ZOO" sign. Power cables hung in vines from a deserted stadium flanking the approach, its walls pitted with fist-wide pocks.

The main gates were padlocked; a side door stood ajar. Mosquitoes whined in the hot September sun. Inside the ticket booth, a toothless old zookeeper snoozed on a plastic chair, clutching a walkie-talkie suspended from a curling wire. The air was still and smelled of petrol and spoiled hay. A spluttering car drew up. Its

1

engine died with a cough, and a plump, spry figure in a tweed jacket climbed out. He hummed, swinging an old leather briefcase, and walked through the open gate.

Qalqilya is a compact town of almost fifty thousand. At its heart is the souk, dense and throbbing. Veiled ladies squabble for meat, bleach, and stockings in alleyways enveloped by a haze of rotten fruit and clogged drains. Radiating from the souk run arteries of dusty homes that together form a tight, breathing band around the town center. The last of Qalqilya's farms and garden nurseries range out beyond, contained by the circular path of the Wall. In places a series of staggered razor-wire fences, in others a thirty-five-foot face of concrete, the Wall cuts a gray swathe through farmland that once undulated down the hill into Israel.

The entrance to town, prefaced by a checkpoint, is marked by smoldering rubbish dumps and a sprinkling of the poorest smallholdings. At its mouth are the police station, a manufacturer of playground equipment, and a miniature cement mosque striped yellow and white, surrounded by flowerbeds of pansies and marigolds. The road straightens into a wide main street, lined with shops piled high with furniture and second-hand fridges. At the bottom is a junction where a white-gloved policeman directs lazy traffic. The traffic lights are often broken. To the left is the souk and the Municipal Council offices. To the right a straggle of shops selling paint, exhaust pipes, and sacks of grain; a food distribution bureau; and, further along, the zoo. The road leads on to Nablus through a second checkpoint, which is rarely open.

A canopy of plane trees shaded the zoo's entrance. Pipes sprouted from a fountain's dry, pebbled terraces. Somewhere a big cat roared in warning or protest. Above the snoring keeper a single fly buzzed erratically, turning sharp angles over his upturned face. It alighted on a vibrating bottom lip. The old man snorted, and awoke. A chubby tweed figure stared down at him. The keeper's cross-eyes widened. "Dr. Sami!" he exclaimed, involuntarily thumbing a button on the walkie-talkie. His voice boomed down the zoo's tinny tannoy system, reverberating from rusty megaphones. It mingled with the wails of a muezzin summoning the faithful to midday prayer and the shrill alarm hoot of a monkey. Dr. Sami waved cheerfully and disappeared up the main avenue, past lines of concrete cages.

Dr. Sami Khader was the only zoo veterinarian in the Palestinian Territories. Portly and clean-shaven, he wore a nylon shirt, tight around the armpits, with an African-print tie in bold shades of orange, black, and gold. His jacket was patched at the elbows, his briefcase scuffed. A generous belly protruded over stay-pressed trousers. His thick black hair was peppered gray at the temples. His face was soft, unlined, and his eyes twinkled.

A tall, sullen man, with a turtle's slack neck and bulging eyes, stepped from the Friends' Restaurant next to the empty fountain. He wandered to an office marked "Manager" with a smeared plastic sign, drawing deeply on a Victory cigarette, and stepped inside. The office was windowless, draped on all sides by heavy curtains. The walls were tongue-and-groove pine, thickly varnished toffee brown. A rattling fan circulated cigarette smoke evenly throughout the room. One poster showed an impish Yasser Arafat waving to a crowd; another, a glossy white tiger. An old concertina of postcards—"Qalqilya: Ambitions and Achievements"—displayed a dull array of municipal buildings, each with a Palestinian flag fluttering on top. A drum of rat poison perched on a shelf. The tall man bolted the door behind him.

The zoo manager, a small, terse figure puffing impatiently through a packet of Alla cigarettes, was stationed behind a vast, empty desk. Angry lines were carved across his forehead, above heavy eyebrows and a thick mustache. A homemade tattoo, heart-shaped and bleary, decorated his right forearm. His eyes were a distant blue. He nodded, then went back to scowling into his newspaper. The tall man sat down on a vinyl sofa that ran the length of the room and examined the glowing tip of his cigarette.

An old electric clock on the desk dealt out digits. Eventually, a rap came at the door. The tall man rose to open it.

"As-salaam al-lekum, Abu Shir," said Dr. Sami, stepping in. "Any news about the carrots?"

"Al-lekum as-salaam," replied the zoo manager gloomily, without looking up from his newspaper. "I have not had the time."

Dr. Sami nodded to the manager's sullen assistant. Mr. Eesa gave a sallow smile and flicked away an inch of ash.

"I see." He turned back toward the door. "A foreign journalist is coming today."

The manager dropped his newspaper.

"Dr. Sami?" Abu Shir called as the vet departed, hastening up the avenue, "Dr. Sami?"

Dr. Sami chuckled and kept on walking.

◆　　　◆　　　◆

Zoo animals have frequently found themselves at the center of human conflicts. During the Franco-Prussian War of 1870, the inhabitants of Paris's Jardin Zoologique were ordered slaughtered and handed over to butchers' shops. World War II saw Rosa the hippopotamus bombed to death in her pool at Berlin, along with seven Indian elephants. Berlin's aquarium was hit dead-center. Gasping fish mingled with shards of glass and cascaded in torrents down grand, empty staircases. In Wroclaw, German soldiers shot the lions, bears, and elephants. The rest, including a rare Amazon manatee and three chimpanzees trained to take tea, died of cold and starvation. In 1812, the czar's magnificent animal collection was slain when Napoleon's troops surrounded Moscow. In modern

Sarajevo, the last animal at the zoo, a brown bear, finally starved after surviving for seven months on the bodies of its companions.

Iraq, once home to the world's first zoological garden at Ur, watched an international public, inured to bombs ripping through mosques and markets, lament a rare Bengal tiger shot dead by a drunken American soldier. Far away, fundraisers rallied to save what remained of Baghdad's once impressive collection. Though a sign on the gate requested "No Alibaba," the zoo had largely been looted. Among the survivors, too intimidating or ugly to warrant theft, was Mandor, a Siberian tiger whose coat hung shy of his ribcage.

In Afghanistan, Kabul Zoo, inaugurated in more progressive times by the royal family and zoologists of the university, was decimated by the Taliban. Its elderly keeper was taken from his hut and shot one winter night. Many of the zoo's creatures had been maimed or killed during the civil war; others were slaughtered for food or succumbed to hunger and freezing winters. Then came international forces and another wave of destruction. In Kabul, they discovered Donatella, a bear whose nose had been slashed by the Taliban, and Marjan, a pitiful blind lion who roused the sympathies of the world, while children died of hunger in the Afghan mountains.

Qalqilya's was the last Palestinian zoo. A zoo in Jericho had opened its doors briefly and without fanfare in the 1990s before draining its coffers dry and disappearing as quietly as it began. Another, in Gaza City, had been attempted in 2004, but its prize lion cub was stolen within a week and the enterprise brought to a halt.

Not far from the Mediterranean beaches of Gaza, sandwiched between the seething Rafah and Brazil refugee camps, there had once been one more modest zoo, which contained at its peak more than eighty specimens. In May 2004, Israel Defense Forces Operation Rainbow tanks rolled in and flattened it. The unlucky ones—the pheasants, ducks, emus, and lovebirds—disappeared easily beneath the tanks' treads. The more fortunate got away. A gazelle, crushed and quaking, was plaster-cast and treated for shock. A rock wallaby cowered in a nearby basement. Fifty parrots, macaws and African grays, disappeared entirely; soldiers claimed to have set them free. Seven creatures survived unscathed, including a twenty-foot python recovered alive from the rubble, a raccoon, and an ostrich. The zoo's tiger, wolves, foxes, and jaguars were never seen again.

In Gaza, parents still whisper tales to restive children of creatures that roam the camps in dead of night, searching for young, disobedient prey. Legends endure of ferocious leashed wildcats, heaved in by heavies and racketeers to extract protection money from recalcitrant members of an already impoverished population.

Qalqilya Zoo was founded in 1986 with help from Israeli zoologists, vets, and wildlife workers. A year later, the first Palestinian intifada erupted. Riots, strikes, and demonstrations showering Israeli military forces with Molotov cocktails spread across the region as Palestinians rallied to the call for an independent homeland. In 1988, some began a nonviolent protest movement, withholding taxes from the Israeli government. Many were imprisoned or their homes demolished. In 1989, a Tel Aviv bus on its way to Jerusalem was hijacked and driven over a precipice. Fourteen passengers perished. In the West Bank and Gaza, Palestinian death squads killed hundreds of their own, labeled collaborators with Israel. By 1992, almost two hundred Palestinian children had been killed for hurling stones at Israeli troops.

The zoo sat out the storm. In September 1993, as the hard-wrought Oslo Accords were signed between Israeli and Palestinian leaders, promising a measure of independence for a region to be administered by the Palestinian Authority, an uneasy calm settled on the West Bank. The zoo profited and grew. Visitors began to return. Palestinians and Israelis spent summer afternoons wandering its shady lanes, eating at its Friends' Restaurant and feeding peanuts to its inhabitants. Optimism was in the air. Israeli professionals ventured back, bringing new animals. But for most Palestinians, little changed in the wake of the Oslo Accords. Discontent simmered on for seven years. Finally, the second, "Al-Aqsa," intifada erupted in September 2000, named after Jerusalem's holiest mosque.

This time, Palestinian suicide attacks across the border in Israel increased in frequency and ferocity. Retribution was harsh, and punishments often collective. Qalqilya became paralyzed by military roadblocks, and visitors from neighboring towns disappeared. By the end of 2000, the zoo's Israeli friends no longer came. Inflation soared as quickly as unemployment. Though the zoo slashed its ticket prices and opened its gates every day, its avenues emptied.

In 2001, week-long curfews heralded the end to Qalqilya's scout groups, youth clubs, and soccer practice. By 2003, the zoo's visitors had dwindled, from a reliable weekly five thousand to less than two dozen a month. It was now the sole source of entertainment for the town's children. There had never been a cinema or theater. There was no river and no access to the sea, though from the higher slopes of the town it could be seen twinkling tantalizingly on the horizon. The mountains, the beaches, Jerusalem: All were a world away. At the zoo, no international teams of animal behaviorists were sent to lend a hand. No donations were received.

By 2005, Qalqilya Zoo had survived the lean years. It was half a decade since the Al-Aqsa intifada had ushered in violence. Arafat was dead and gone, and with him widespread support for the politically dominant Fatah party. Suicide attacks had slowed to a trickle, and conditions for Qalqilyan civilians had eased slightly. There were no more curfews, though Israeli jeeps still embarked on daily patrols of the town's streets, and nighttime arrests remained commonplace. A few dozen workers were reissued permits to cross the border into Israel

But the town had lost faith in the governance of Fatah. It was time for a change, and the only major opponent was Hamas.

In May 2005, Qalqilya voters elected the very first Hamas Municipal Council in the Palestinian Territories, and clean men with clipped beards moved into the council buildings on Market Street. "Strength. Honesty. Credibility," boasted their motto. Hastily, the last of the town's allies backed away.

◆　　◆　　◆

Dr. Sami greeted the journalist at the ticket office.

"Welcome," he said. "Please come this way."

He began a tour of the zoo, first heading north up the zoo's main avenue, past the dry fountain, the restaurant, and a dusty playground. At the top, he introduced Ruti, his prize giraffe. An impassive silver-haired keeper trailed casually a few footsteps behind. Along the back wall ranged the herbivores: Fufu, a sleek, bearded ibex, another of Sami's favorites. Four piebald Shetland ponies. An irritable camel. A collection of sheep.

"The people want to see something in every cage," Sami explained, "so I filled them with whatever I could find."

Halfway along, the path cut left across the playground to a narrow central boulevard that bisected the zoo. A row of cramped, bare quarters contained the smaller animals. A porcupine. A gaggle of fat geese. Five tawny owls. Pigeons. A plump, solitary badger taking a dust bath in the sunshine.

At the boulevard's eastern end, a crowded stretch of avenue led back down toward the southern perimeter wall. It housed Sami's best exhibits. Three glossy zebras. Dubi, the hippo. A hyena, four wolves, and eleven miserable monkeys. Three ostriches, two pairs of crocodiles in an oily pool. A glaring emu. Four hirsute Syrian bears. A pair of leopards, curling against the bars of their tiny separate cells. And Holi, Rad, and Rabir, three handsome young lions who yawned and kept watch from a spartan cage no more than forty feet square. Dr. Sami shook his head, whistling through his teeth. He pointed out some tortoises and moved along. The silver-haired keeper followed. "That," hissed Sami, "is head keeper Yail Misqawi." He tutted. "One day I'll run away to Africa."

The park clock struck midday. A young father appeared, leading a dawdling little girl through the zoo. He hoisted her up to tap on the grimy glass of a snake tank. Sami led the way back across the zoo, toward a squat, two-story building. "Watch your step," he warned. "Ladies' latrines." A swarthy construction worker emerged, zipping up his trousers, and coughed phlegmily.

Dr. Sami climbed iron stairs up to his first-floor office and fiddled with a lock. He glared down at the keeper, who lingered, kicking at a patch of dead grass, then bustled inside and firmly shut the door.

The office floor was littered with cages of chirruping budgerigars, finches, and canaries. Two more sat on a table in the corner near the window.

"No money for a computer," Sami said. "Instead, a live screen saver."

The vet set an old kettle on to brew and seated himself at a desk scattered with papers, books, and bric-a-brac. Binders, feathers, and scraps of medical equipment lay about the small room. Against one wall, a squat cabinet held old boxes and bottles of medicines, and the empty cases of missiles and ammunition shells that once tumbled down on the zoo. On top, a monkey skeleton squatted, smoking a cigarette. Mounted on the wall above it were two stout, crudely made rifles. "When the troubles began," Dr. Sami said, "our anesthesiologist from Israel would no longer come." He had pleaded, even securing for the vet a "Certificate of Permission" from the local council, but the elderly Dr. Motke Levinson would not relent. What use, he asked, was written permission if someone shot you before you could pull it from your pocket?

"So I had to do something myself," Sami said. He took one of the long-barreled wooden rifles from the wall. "Made here, in the city," he fondly turned the heavy object over in his hands, "to my own design."

The larger gun bore a metal nameplate, "Dido." The other was decorated with a sticker of a squirrel turning a somersault. In place of bullets, each fired syringes, which Sami had tailored to fit with flights of hen feathers. Propelled by a small carbon dioxide canister, the larger gun had an anesthetic range of ten yards. But for times when canisters were scarce, he had come up with another alternative.

"Watch."

He pushed a sharp syringe into Dido's barrel. Putting his lips to the head of the rifle, he aimed and puffed. The syringe shot out and stuck firmly in a cork notice board on the opposite wall. "Thirty foot capability," he said contentedly. "My own invention."

Dr Sami settled down behind his desk. "A very important point. If we open our minds, we can achieve many things." He took a small dispenser from his desk drawer. "If we do not," he deposited two sweetener tablets into his mug, "nothing."

Steam rose from two mugs of Butterfly Brand tea as he arranged a rainbow of felt-tipped pens in a Dammam Modern Poultry Company penholder.

Sami had tended to the animals of Qalqilya Zoo for five years, arriving in early 2000, just months before the outbreak of the second intifada. Since then, he had witnessed violence and hardship ebb and flow. He took a sip of tea and cleared his throat.

"In this place," he noted, "there are many problems."

Politics, he said, deprivation, and military, civilian, and suicide attacks. Lawlessness, isolation, and corruption. The incompetence of his staff, without qualifications, training, or discipline. "These people," he lamented, "will be the death of me." His wages, unchanged since his arrival at the zoo, so low that he supplemented them by running his own private clinic each evening in town.

"And this man, Abu Shir." The zoo manager, once a farmer, then a laborer and a ticket clerk at the zoo, before his mysterious promotion, overnight, to manager. "He will be here soon," he whispered, "because he will worry he is missing something. This man likes to talk about himself too much."

The absence of open borders, Sami resumed, the lack of money. Few connections, making it all but impossible to replenish lost stocks. "We are treated like animals," he concluded with a dry smile.

"Why, then, bother at all?"

Dr. Sami fell silent, his smile fading. He stared down at his desk.

"Every country has a zoo," he answered at length. "Tell me. Why shouldn't we?"

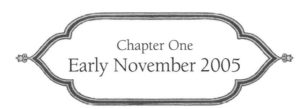

Chapter One
Early November 2005

Kullu am wa antum bi-khair.
May you be well throughout the year.
—Arabic saying

Ruti stood alone in her favorite dusk-time spot, her head resting on the tall fence at the top of the main avenue. Evening light shifted through the whorling dust. She selected a mouthful of dry leaves from an overhanging branch, tugging gently with her tongue, and considered the scene. She chewed and watched with interest. All along the avenue, bright strings of light bulbs draped the deciduous trees. Red, yellow, and electric blue, they popped and fizzed, as quick isosceles bats emerged, flitting from branches above. A long trestle table stretched along the avenue, bristling on either side with folding chairs. Plastic tablecloths, embossed to resemble lace, flapped in the breeze. Crowds of hungry men, congregated in conversation beside the ticket booth, made their way to the table. They sat elbow-to-elbow and poured orangeade into plastic cups: Zookeepers, postmen, city sweepers, clerks, and officials, puffing cherry-scented narghiles and pointing at the bright white bow of a new moon.

Ruti swallowed and turned. The snack had woken her appetite. She moved silently toward the doorway of the night shelter. Behind her sprawled a whitewashed school, its windows dark and empty. She splayed her front legs, squeezed her eyes tight, and plunged her face into a pile of sweet, grassy hay.

It was the fifth of November, the welcome end to Ramadan, and Eid ul-Fitr, the Feast of Breaking the Fast, was in full swing. Some, Dr. Sami's wife among them, were preparing for a second, six-day fast in the hopes of garnering an extra dose of spiritual advantage. Others were relieved to be back to normal after being deprived during daylight hours of food, water, coffee, cigarettes, and unkind and lascivious thoughts for a long, torturous month.

Forty miles south, in the ancient, labyrinthine Arab quarter of Jerusalem's Old City, the streets echoed with the call to prayer from the Al-Aqsa mosque, Islam's most hallowed after Mecca and Medina. Floodlit lanes milled with festive Muslim families down from Nazareth or maritime Acre, all decked out in their best new outfits. Little girls wore frilly white frocks, pink ribbons, and polished patent shoes. Young boys, walking hand in hand with their parents, sported smart nylon suits of brown and sky blue, their ties straight and hair slicked back with brilliantine. A makeshift fair had been set up on a scrubby patch of wasteland; a wooden Ferris wheel, its limbs creaking, hoisted bucket loads of squealing children up over its peak. Two teenage boys raced unbridled horses, sparks flying, up and down Al-Mujahideen Street past the stout wooden doors of the Monastery of the Flagellation. Groups of ten-year-old tearaways battled each other with spluttering plastic Kalashnikovs, gifts from friends and relatives to celebrate the arrival of the holidays.

Qalqilyans were celebrating, less ebulliently, at home. Few had been granted permits to join parties in neighboring cities or the congregational prayers at Jerusalem's Noble Sanctuary. Nevertheless, the mood was convivial, and the smell of food wafted temptingly along on the evening breeze. On each corner, young boys submerged patties of mashed chickpeas into dark vats of bubbling oil. Trays of glazed pastries, dripping with honey, gleamed in the windows of bakeries, their surfaces jeweled with luminous green pistachios. Newspaper cones of large, meaty fuul beans were handed out to the poor. Even the stray cats, after a month of privation, had rich pickings. Rubbish bags overflowed with the remnants of yesterday's dinners. At the zoo, six hundred municipal employees settled down to steaming plates of lamb stew with rice, served on gaily patterned plastic plates with a battalion of fizzy drinks, laid on by the new Municipal Council.

In the cooking tent, Dr. Hashem al-Masri, Qalqilya's deputy mayor, perspired as he dished up portions. Wajeeh Qawas, the mayor, ate his own Eid meal in a prison cell on the other side of the Wall. By the time of his election in May 2005, Qawas had spent three years in administrative detention, without trial, in Israel. No one was certain, when his overwhelming victory was announced, whether he had known he was in the running. Though barely forty years old, he had a heart condition. Each time a six-month jail stint came to an end, it was extended to another. His wife feared that the father of her five small children would not survive his unraveling sentence.

The zoo's avenues were alive with laughter from heavily loaded tables, but for some the air clung chill with the ghosts of Eids past. At the far end of the table, Abu Shir sat in unusually private contemplation, prodding distractedly at his food with a fork. At the opposite, a safe distance away, Dr. Sami took a mouthful of rich, gelatinous stew.

◆ ◆ ◆

Dr. Sami had not grown up in Qalqilya. He was raised from infancy in the Saudi Arabian town of Al-Hasar, sharing a dusty childhood home with his father, his mother, a dozen brothers and sisters, and his father's second young bride. His father was a refugee twice-over. For centuries, the Khader family had lived in

the ancient port of Jaffa, a short walk south from modern Tel
Aviv. Sami's parents, grandparents, and extended family had fled
Jaffa in 1948 when Israel's War of Independence—the *Nakba*, or
Catastrophe, as it was known to Palestinians—pitted surrounding
Arab countries against the fledgling state and uprooted hundreds
of thousands of Palestine's Arabs from their ancestral homes.
Some went to Lebanon, others to Egypt, Syria, or Iraq. A few of
Sami's great-uncles traveled, with tens of thousands of other
refugees, to Saudi Arabia. Many more flooded into the West
Bank, recently captured by neighboring Transjordan. The Khaders
settled together in the farming town of Qalqilya and quietly re-
built their lives.

The family remained in Qalqilya until the 1967 Six-Day War
once again saw pan-Arab armies battling Israel. Three hundred
thousand Palestinians, fearing for their safety, fled the West Bank.
Though a handful of Sami's relatives remained behind, refusing to
abandon their homes a second time, the Khader family scattered.
In June 1967, Sami's father and mother, with baby Sami and four
older brothers and sisters in tow, left for Saudi Arabia. Days later,
Qalqilya was captured and occupied by Israeli soldiers, and almost half its buildings destroyed.

Sami first returned to Qalqilya in 1984, aged twenty-one. He
was young, fresh from the dissection bench at King Faisal University, and was to be matched to a nice Palestinian wife. Sara was
sweet, pretty, and keen. They were married within the week and set
off back to Saudi Arabia. It was hard for a Palestinian to find work
as a veterinary surgeon or to establish his own practice; Saudis
preferred other Saudis to administer to their animals' needs. But
salaries for other professions remained far superior to those back
in the West Bank. By day, Sami worked his way up to a decent
salary in Dammam Modern Poultry, as branch manager and itin-
erant physician to sick chickens. By night, he pursued a private
passion for taxidermy, preserving the diverse detritus of the King

Faisal University veterinary department. In 1990, his lineage was secured by the birth of his first baby, a jewel they named *Uzhdan,* a new beginning.

Ten years passed. In Qalqilya, the mayor, Maa'rouf Zahran, decided to inaugurate a museum of natural history to complement his already successful zoo, which he would dedicate, for his efforts, to himself. He designated a narrow, empty lot on the eastern edge of the zoo and ordered the erection of three domed red-mud buildings, in traditional Palestinian style. Soon, he heard of Dr. Sami Khader, in town on his summer visit to the in-laws and hard at work stuffing a python to kill the time. The mayor, determined to secure both a museum curator and a dedicated veterinarian for his zoo with just one paycheck, invited Sami for a hearty lunch, and afterward they strolled the zoo's lanes. There Sami met Ruti and Brownie, two contented giraffes, and was immediately enchanted. A proposition was made, and hands were quickly shaken.

Sami's wife was thrilled at the prospect of returning permanently to her homeland. She missed her family and wanted her daughter to experience the delight she had felt, as a child, during long summers at play in its fields. Sami, too, felt his ancestors tugging at his shirtsleeves and secretly dreamed of his very own giraffes and a shrine to the art of taxidermy. In the last months of the twentieth century, the family came home.

Qalqilya was a backwater, an old-fashioned farming town, with a constant convoy of grocers' trucks bumping their way to the markets of Nablus, Hebron, and Jericho. For Sami, it held new promise and opportunity.

Barely a year later, the Al-Aqsa intifada erupted.

"You came, and the troubles began," accused his wife's relatives.

Together, Sami and his zoo were plunged into chaos and casualties. Plans for the Natural History Museum were put on hold. The red-mud buildings stood empty and unfinished. The mayor fled to safety across the border and was quietly considered a traitor. Herbivores died. Carnivores died. Amphibians, reptiles, and birds died. Sami collected the dead and went about stuffing, salting, and skinning them, so that no one would forget his victims of war.

"If it weren't for me," Sami told his wife, as she nursed a healthy baby girl, born at home the night before, "people might think the stories of these animals were only propaganda."

"We'll call her Hend, after my grandmother," his wife replied, gazing down at the slumbering newborn.

Slowly, a new collection of creatures began to pile up in the zoo's storeroom, as Palestinian animals mingled with their Saudi Arabian cousins.

◆　　◆　　◆

Ruti was Sami's most highly prized exhibit and his firm favorite. She had arrived in 1992 as part of a shipment of a half-dozen reticulated giraffes sent to Middle Eastern zoos by a game park in South Africa. She had taken up residence at Qalqilya Zoo, young and coy, and promptly set about bewitching her audiences. She batted lustrous eyelashes, flirting for treats of unpeeled bananas and butter biscuits, and stooped so that visitors could scratch her nose with the blunt end of a pencil.

Presently, she was joined by a male. Donated as surplus from Jerusalem, Brownie was older and towered a good yard above her. He was unhandsome and lopsided. He walked with a shamble and feared children, pigeons, and lawnmowers. First, Ruti had pursued him around the enclosure, relentlessly nudging him toward the pleasures of the water trough or the hay net. Next, she had tried, without success, to rest her neck against his every time he stopped for a moment's rest. Then, finally, one dusk-time, after weeks of reticence, she had offered him the ultimate intimacy, a share of the best dry leaves from her overhanging branch. With this, an exhausted Brownie was won.

The name "giraffe" is said to derive from the Arabic *zarafa*, she who walks swiftly. The ancient Greeks called the giraffe *Camelopardis*, believing it to be a camel in leopard's clothing. In the second century, Oppian wrote of "the Pard of spotted back joined and united with the camel." Medieval Arabs blended the panther with the camel, or the camel with the hyena and the wild cow, in order to produce the giraffe. Others thought it had something of an ostrich in its lineage or had sprung from beastly sexual promiscuity at wayward watering holes.

Far back into the reaches of time, the first giraffes to set their cloven hooves on new territory have seized the imagination of history's publics. Three and a half thousand years ago, the female Pharaoh Hatshepsut, stepmother to Thutmose III who kept a menagerie among the dancing columns of Karnak, commanded that a giraffe be brought back from the land of Punt to entertain her pleasure garden visitors. In the fifteenth century, newly crowned Emperor Yongle thanked his lucky stars for the appearance of two giraffes from India, which, in Confucian China, were believed to be unicorns, heralding a munificent monarch whose governance must be obeyed.

In 1827, the first Nubian giraffe arrived in France, a gift to King Charles X from Muhammad Ali Pasha. She was walked from Marseilles to Paris under cover of darkness, in case rumors of a monster disrupted a restless population. Around her neck she wore an amulet inscribed with verses from the Quran. Installed in parquet-floored quarters at the Jardin des Plantes, she swiftly inspired *L'année de la girafe*. There was a waltz, a dinnerware pattern, soap, toys, toothpicks, a flu christened *la grippe de la girafe,* and a fashion for hairstyles so tall that well-to-do ladies were obliged to seat themselves on the floors of their carriages to be transported about town.

Meanwhile, in England, another of Ali Pasha's giraffes had an equally enthusiastic reception from King George IV. The king lovingly fed his pet only on the freshest of cow's milk, and when, to his dismay, she failed to thrive, ordered a wheeled contraption to be fitted to her, that she might be conveyed more comfortably about her enclosure.

Ruti and Brownie proved no exception to the rule, and crowds flocked to see the very first giraffes ever to reach Palestine. For many years the pair fared well, despite a barren paddock riddled with small, sharp stones that had to be picked out, occasionally, by the bucketful. In response to her celebrity, Ruti blossomed, dipping her head down over her fence to greet small children and rooting unashamedly for mints and toffees hidden in ladies' handbags.

Brownie did not join in. He let Ruti bask alone in her limelight and dawdled in the background, eyeing the crowds from behind her marbled flanks. But when the people trickled away and the evening air grew still, he walked by her side to the perimeter fence to pick leaves and survey the silent zoo. Sometimes, she let him lead her to the privacy of the tall, corrugated night shelter, where she chewed her cud with disinterest as he eagerly positioned himself at her rear. Finally in 2001, after many years of brief and ungainly nocturnal encounters, Ruti fell pregnant.

Giraffes have a gestation period of fifteen months, usually producing a single six-foot calf, and as Ruti's belly slowly swelled to carry the baby, Dr. Sami rejoiced. For over a year already, life had been looking bleak. There were curfews and power cuts. There were regular, mysterious night-time military incursions, often ending in a gun battle and a crop of arrests. Work was scarce. Thousands employed in industries across the border with Israel could no longer reach their jobs. Trade ceased, and prices rose. Who could afford a ticket to the zoo when there were hungry mouths to feed at home?

Then, one night in July 2002, two months before the baby's anticipated arrival, Israeli soldiers streamed into Qalqilya. It was hot, and they fired phosphorous flares into a starless firmament as they moved down Shanti Street. They forced open the doors of the town's principal boys' school to use as a makeshift base. The school's back windows, reinforced with chicken wire and stout iron bars, looked down, across a stretch of wasteland, onto the silent giraffe enclosure.

Suddenly, from the classroom command center, a soldier yelled and opened fire. Yards away, the noise startled the giraffes from their midnight browsing. Ruti looked up. Over the years, the enthusiastic fireworks displays accompanying births, Eids, and weddings had accustomed her to the noisier aspects of Qalqilya's aural landscape. Brownie had never grown used to it. He reared and bolted. Dashing back and forth as gunshot peppered the zoo's perimeter wall, Brownie lost his footing. He slipped and slammed hard into the shelter doorway. His head cracked against its metal lintel. He reeled, keeled over, and lay still.

◆　◆　◆

The crocodile, most famous of all crying creatures, is a sham. For centuries, it was believed to lure its unwitting victims by eliciting sympathy through false tears of sorrow. "The crocodile," recorded the English slaver Admiral John Hawkins, "doth cry and sobbe like a Christian body." Others, including the author of the "Voiage and Travaile of Sir John Maundeville," a fanciful guide for the Jerusalem-bound medieval pilgrim, thought the creature expressed genuine remorse after the kill. "Ben gret plentee of

Amelia Thomas

Cokadrilles," he wrote. "Theise serpentes slen men, and thei eten
hem wepynge." It is now accepted that crocodiles, though they
shed saltwater tears through lachrymal glands, do so only to prevent their eyes from drying out.

Not all bestial tears have been proven false. Charles Darwin,
in *The Expressions of the Emotions in Humans and Animals,* noted
that "the Indian elephant is said sometimes to weep," describing a
captured elephant that, when tied up, sank to the floor "uttering
choking cries, with tears trickling down its cheeks." "On a abbatu
l'élephant du Jardin des Plantes," Victor Hugo recorded in his 1872
diary, "Il a pleuré. On va le manger." 'They slaughtered the elephant at the Jardin des Plantes. He wept. He will be eaten.' Beavers
weep when denied the company of their fellows. Horses cry tears
of pain. Some captive chimpanzees recognize, and try to console,
tears among humans. "A chimpanzee trained to carry water jugs,"
reported the *Minnetonka Record* on the eighteenth of January,
1907, "broke one and fell a-crying, which proved sorrow, though
it wouldn't mend the jug. Rats, discovering their young drowned,
have been moved to tears. A giraffe which a huntsman's rifle had
injured began to cry when approached."

The tears of the giraffe have been observed across the ages.
"Mute, dignified and majestic stood the unfortunate victim,"
recorded Victorian hunter and adventurer Captain William Corn-
wallis Harris, "occasionally stooping his elastic neck towards his
persecutor, the tears trickling from the lashes of his dark, humid
eye as broadside after broadside was poured into his brawny
front." "How can one look unmoved at this great noble creature,"
marveled another hunter, Frederick V. Kirkby, in 1896, "when,
hopeless of escape, he slackens speed and turns round to face you
squarely, without shrinking, without sound, without attempt at
revenge, whilst the great teardrops course one another down its
face, welling from soft, dark, languishing eyes that have not their

equal for beauty upon earth?" Victor, a fifteen-year-old giraffe mortally injured at a British zoo in the 1970s, was observed by the public with tears rolling down his cheeks. Petronell Nieuwoudt, a giraffe expert at the Game Capture School in Faerie Glenn, Pretoria, swears it happens frequently.

Brownie died on the floor of his shelter as the hot night fell silent in a break between ammunition rounds. The next morning, Sami found Ruti standing close beside her mate. He gazed up at her face. She seemed to be crying.

The following day, Ruti refused to eat. For the rest of the week she declined even butter biscuits and bananas. She stood with her face to the wall in the far corner of the enclosure, refusing Sami's supplications. Tears traced the patterns of her neck. Seven days after Brownie's death, Ruti delivered a stillborn calf.

"Fifteen thousand dollars!" Abu Shir wailed to anyone who came within earshot. "Plus the price of Baby. Half size, half price. Twenty-two thousand five hundred!"

Sami felt his zoo slipping away. He had arrived with grand plans and great enthusiasm and was still learning daily. Those plans, he realized, would have to be set aside, on his dusty office shelf, until life returned to normal. But, as he spent days cajoling Ruti with fond words and licorice sticks, his resolve deepened. He would not accept defeat. The zoo would go on, and it would improve. It would prosper. And, one day, it would be International.

Still, he was irritated. "Our people are dying every day," he snapped at one keeper, who stood weeping in front of the fence. "Do you cry for them like you do for this animal?"

Eventually, Ruti recovered. Over time she grew particularly attached to Dr. Sami, who continued to greet her every morning with a treat hidden for their mutual pleasure inside his briefcase or the pocket of his tweed jacket. She was not the coquette she once had been but seemed plump and at ease. She began to take pleasure in her visitors—nowadays just a trickle—and once again let children feed her peppermints.

Nevertheless, Sami knew that a captive giraffe must have the company of her own kind to maximize her chances of a long and healthy life.

◆　　◆　　◆

At the Eid ul-Fitr banquet, evening melted into night. Men helped themselves to second and third portions and chattered on in high spirits. Dr. Sami mopped up his stew juices with a thick wad of pita and chuckled as his neighbor recited a joke. At the far end of the table, one plate was untouched. A lump had risen to Abu Shir's throat, making it impossible to eat. He sat hunched over his chair, brow knitted, struggling to banish the memory of another Eid and a woman in a rose-patterned scarf.

It had happened on the first day of Eid ul-Ahda, the Feast of Sacrifice, several years before. Flocks of unaccompanied children from Qalqilya and its neighboring villages had arrived at the zoo, enticed by the prospect of free holiday entry. Most were teenage boys, happy to have escaped the strictures of school, high and raucous on an overdose of heavy Arab sweets. Following his morning rounds, Dr. Sami had returned home to spend the day with his family, while Abu Shir stayed on to drink coffee with the keepers. Only the most slothful of the zoo's inhabitants dozed on in the sunshine as the boys shared food and playful punches.

An hour after the vet's departure, news slipped in through the gates that a military patrol had entered the city from the check-point that once led east to Nablus. The boys scattered. Some turned left and rushed home to tell their families of the impending incursion. Others, ignoring the warnings of the keepers, dashed off to the right to confront the tanks. Armed with fistfuls of stones, the boys ducked along back streets, while barbequing families hastily bundled up their picnic baskets and bolted their front doors.

As the convoy rolled along Qalqilya's streets, an eerie silence descended. Colored paper streamers fluttered nervously in the breeze. The only sound was an occasional yell, followed by a scuffle and the futile clank of stone on armored metal. The convoy kept on rolling. Inside the zoo, the keepers waited. Abu Shir sat in the sunshine, fearing the worst. Though he never knew the real purpose of these incursions, he'd seen enough of them to know that they rarely ended without trouble. He lit a cigarette and sucked on it solemnly, listening to the rattle of gunfire a few blocks away.

Suddenly, a woman appeared at the front gate, her bright rose-patterned headscarf slipping back to reveal disheveled strands of black hair. Her coat was made of wool, too hot for the day. "My name is Suha al-Gazawi," she breathed. "Have you seen my son?" She described him: his long, curly hair, his sweatshirt, jeans, and red satchel. "He is fourteen."

Abu Shir was quite certain he recalled the boy, one of a dozen picnicking in the shade of a willow tree next to the playground.

"He went that way," he told the boy's mother, pointing right, toward the main road.

"I've heard news," she whispered. "A boy was shot for throwing stones at the tanks."

"I am sorry I don't know more. I will listen out for news."

The woman thanked him and hurried away.

Less than two hours later, a funeral was held for a teenage boy in Qalqilya's cemetery. The sun had retreated behind a cloud, and crowds of Qalqilyans abandoned their festivities to attend. Abu Shir entered the packed graveyard and looked around for familiar faces, pushing his way forward through the throng. Then, he saw the rose-patterned scarf. The slim figure was slumped, weeping, against an old man's shoulder. She had known, he thought. Abu Shir elbowed his way to the front of the crowd and caught the woman's eye. He frowned, in what he hoped was a gesture of sympathy, and she attempted a smile. He fought back tears. He felt something inside him lose hope and wither.

Close by, men clustered around a makeshift wooden stretcher bearing the small, shrouded figure of fourteen-year-old Mahmoud al-Gazawi. Abu Shir stepped forward to join them and hoisted the stretcher easily onto his shoulder.

Bills bearing Mahmoud's last school photograph adorned Qalqilya's lampposts for a while, until newer posters replaced them. The town consoled his mother for her loss. Her neighbors trooped daily down the main street to sit quietly in the mourning tent. "He's with God now," said one. Others reminded her that Allah afforded children and martyrs a very special place in paradise.

But such comments offered Suha little comfort. God had taken her Mahmoud on the very same day he had once spared Ismael, son of the prophet Ibrahim.

◆   ◆   ◆

Dusk fell over the Qalqilya municipal dinner. Partygoers sat back, loosened their belts, and sipped thick, cardamom-scented coffee brewed in brass pots topped with crescent moons. A baboon whooped into the chill night. Ruti disappeared into her night shelter. A breeze rustled through the empty playground, stirring a swing on its hinges. Silence seeped in. Abu Shir lit a cigarette.

"It is said," he suddenly addressed a man across the table, "that a cornered cat fights like a lion." The man smiled politely and helped himself to some more coffee.

"But," Abu Shir inhaled deeply on his cigarette, "it is still just a cat."

The man looked at him uneasily and turned back to his neighbor.

At the opposite end of the feast, Dr. Sami rose and dusted down his jacket. "Five Star," he concluded, as he shook a barrage of extended hands, "Tip-top, First Class. International. Wait and see." He headed to his car. Eid ul-Fitr, says the Quran, is a time for reconciliation. Feuds and disagreements are settled during its long, languid days. Mornings begin with prayers, thanking Allah for fortitude in the face of hunger throughout the month before and looking forward to new, bright prospects.

But who could think of reconciliation or conceive of a brighter future, when life invariably got worse each time it seemed to be getting better?

Dr. Sami felt that he might be the only one. He was a natural optimist. He had made telephone calls. And he had a plan.

Chapter Two
Mid-November 2005

Lions at play, free as their jungle homes;
tigers crouching, springing, gambolling, with
as little restraint as on the low plains of their
native India—such is the dream of everyone
interested in zoology.
—LONDON DAILY NEWS, 1869

T he society of the wild Hamadryas baboon, an Old World monkey with its ancestry carved from the Arabian wastes, ensures every member knows its place. Each dominant male, caped in silver fur, red-faced, sharp-nosed, and glaring, composes his harem of up to two dozen females, who divide their days between scrupulous grooming and foraging for dinner. Two or three harems together form a family clan, within which males, all blood relatives, are careful to avoid improper advances on each other's wives. Several clans amass to become a band, and then at sunset, bands swell to a vast troop on the rocks and cliff faces of their desert home. Young males inherit females from their fathers. Kinship and clan allegiances are all-important. Safety lies in numbers.

Females, too, have their own indomitable hierarchy that guarantees peace within the harem. One central female, the most beautiful or fecund, is matriarch, and is accorded the closest shelf on the rock to her mate. Her daughters enjoy higher social standing among the ranks of peripheral ladies. Only if a female of lower status exhibits delusions of grandeur will the male intervene, nipping at her neck to chivvy her back to her rightful place. In the wild, with an immense territorial range, this unambiguous system works perfectly. In ill-conceived captivity, baboon society can crumble into catastrophe.

By nature, baboons are social, curious creatures, placid toward humans when kept well, and with a keen interest in the world about them. At Qalqilya, cramped into damp, bare cages thick with wire mesh, devoid of diversion and natural sunlight, they were unhappy. Only one male enjoyed a harem of two small females. Two others lived partitioned with a single partner. They were bored, dissatisfied, but generally docile.

The eighth baboon was a five-year-old male named Fateen. A massive, unbecoming creature with sharp yellow incisors and huge, strong limbs, he presented a particular problem to the vet. Though born in captivity, confinement did not rest easily on his broad shoulders. Fateen lived a life of crushing tedium, frustration, and years without range, mate, or distraction.

Alone and unaware of observation, he would calmly watch armies of ants march in neat columns up and down his cage walls. The occasional ladybird that hurtled its mistaken way into his enclosure was ejected carefully on a calloused palm. But when people were about, the baboon's inexpressible desire to swing, lunge, forage, and scramble, which tormented him to the core, found its outlet in what Sami had read was "hyper-aggression." Fateen detested humans. Sami had never dared introduce him to another monkey. Instead, fearing for the safety of others, he had sentenced Fateen to a lifetime of solitary confinement.

One rainy Tuesday morning, when a gaggle of minor civil servants arrived on an official tour of the zoo, Dr. Sami could not resist pausing in front of Fateen's cage to demonstrate his aberrant behavior.

"Take this," Sami began, reaching into his jacket pocket for a boiled sweet. Nervous, sensing impending peril, a thin Municipal Works officer reached out to take it. "Now offer it to the monkey. Hold it tight and do not move."

With trepidation, the spindly visitor crossed the low barrier separating the cage from the footpath. Fateen sat regarding him with suspicion, as the official poked the treat an inch inside the bars. Instantly, the baboon reared up from his concrete perch and careened howling toward it.

"Yaaaaaah!" Dr. Sami responded.

The visitor, his eyes closed tight, whimpered a fond farewell to his fingertips. But Sami's bellow was enough to send Fateen reeling back in a spluttering fit of rage, flinging himself about, rattling his bars, and emitting ear-piercing screams.

Back on his platform, the monkey glowered and muttered wrathfully, the treat still untaken in the official's trembling hand.

"You see?" Sami said, satisfied. "He will not take it. He is a crazy man. Come, let me show you the leopards."

◆　　◆　　◆

Dr. Sami thought of himself as a man of vision. He was educated. He had known something of life outside the city walls. He had ambition and had worked hard to make the most of his lot. Most importantly, he knew what he wanted. He dreamed of transforming his small, scrubby domain, filled with ragtag animals, into what he referred to, frequently and with reverence, as an "International Zoo." In his mind's eye, he saw a well-laid-out, roomy series of large enclosures. He saw alliances with other international zoos. Gifts of new, prolific stocks of animals and the chance to consort with world-class veterinarians. He wanted an aviary instead of wire cages, lush grasses to replace dank concrete. A lake for the crocodiles, airy ranges for the carnivores, and a jungle of ropes, ladders, and clamber nets for all but the most lunatic of the monkeys.

Dr. Sami's plan could not begin with his eight Hamadryas baboons. There was no room yet to build the new monkey house they needed. Redemption, he believed, would have to begin with the Carnivore Department.

It had been a long hiatus. Five years of scraping by, with an indifferent Municipal Council that glossed over Sami's attempts at improvement and innovation, even when the town's troubles waned for a while. The council had been complacent, sure of its position, and had no need to strive for approval. Though Sami had tried, on several occasions, to ignite officials' enthusiasm for expanding and modernizing the zoo, for seeking new species and resuming plans for the Natural History Museum, his efforts had been ignored. Sami had understood that it was best to withdraw and wait.

Local elections the previous summer had stunned the council into silence. Its members were still gaping like goldfish as they made their way, carrying cardboard boxes, framed diplomas, and potted plants, out from the municipal offices on Market Street.

Their replacements had a lot to prove. New and controversial, they were eager to demonstrate their competence, their financial acumen, and their understanding of the people's material, spiritual, and recreational needs. Quickly, it was decreed that the Natural History Museum be completed. Workmen moved into the red-mud buildings, abandoned for years. Sami made sketches and plans. The council would get the glory; Dr. Sami would provide the scheme, the exhibits, and the labor at no additional cost. Sami was momentarily thrilled. At nights, at weekends, early in the morning, he slipped off to the zoo to design museum displays and preen his stockpile of taxidermized exhibits.

But, though he began to see one dream slowly realized, he knew that this alone would little alter his plan for Qalqilya Zoo's international future. His next, most crucial step was the Carnivore Department, a new area he had long proposed to fill a stretch of wasteland at the far end of the zoo. It would consist of vast new pens, ten or twenty times larger than the residents' current cages, landscaped with shrubs and grasses, ponds, boulders, and real trees. The lions, leopards, wolves, bears, and hyena would be moved to these happier carnivore quarters and would thrive there.

For this, however, the municipality would have to loosen its purse strings.

In his office, between daily patrols of the zoo's residents, he set about building scale Carnivore Department models from whatever he could find. Cotton wool trees colored green with felt pen, silver foil pools, and lollipop stick fences populated the world of his creation. Laboriously, head bent over his desk, he made papier-mâché contours in the miniature landscape and built pedestrian walkways from tiny pieces of gravel. He pored over the technicolor pages of a brittle *Visitors Guide to Berlin Zoo,* published in the 1980s with one hundred and thirty-six color photographs, though he had never been to Germany. He invited Abu Khaled, the redoubtable municipal engineer, to discuss how the imaginary enclosures would be built to international specifications.

Meanwhile, he went about his rounds as usual, tending to the sick, patching together as best he could the most ramshackle of the cages, and liaising with untidy, indolent builders, all messy overalls and bright woolen hats, who were slowly erecting his museum in the muddy courtyard beneath his office window.

Finally, it was time. He had done his research. He had prepared all the groundwork. He had consulted with the appropriate bodies. The Carnivore Department was ready to begin. All he needed now was one, crucial, consent.

◆ ◆ ◆

It was the fifteenth of November, 2005, Independence Day, marking the occasion in 1988 in Algiers when the National Council had declared the establishment of the State of Palestine. On that day, the declaration had concluded, the Palestinian people stood on the threshold of a new dawn. In the years that followed, the day had been accompanied by an air of festivity, with firecrackers, bonfires, and parties in backyards.

Seventeen years later, celebrations had dwindled. But on a quiet street corner, in a sunny first-floor bedroom looking out onto the Wall and the fallow fields beyond, Dr. Sami awoke in high spirits. Today, an old friend was coming to call.

"Please do not worry," he had reassured Dr. Motke Levinson some weeks ago over a crackling telephone line. "It is safe now. Very safe."

"But what about permission?" a wary voice had returned, "Shall I ask the army?"

"No, no." Dr. Sami cleared his throat. "There are plenty of people coming to Qalqilya these days. Plenty. Please," he pressed on, "pay us a visit. Unofficially; just for fun."

Several telephone calls later, Dr. Motke gave in and agreed to meet Sami at the mouth of the town, just beyond the military checkpoint. He drove the familiar road toward Qalqilya, past skull-capped youths thumbing rides to a local settlement, and pulled up onto a patch of muddy ground. He waited. On the opposite side of the road, a soldier sat guarding a ramshackle watchtower. Farmers, their donkey carts half-filled with produce, trundled past across potholes. Motke adjusted the car's climate control and looked wearily at the red road sign ahead. "Attention," it read. "By order of the Israeli government and Israel Defense Forces, it is illegal for Israeli citizens to proceed beyond this point." He sighed and eyed a bag of gaily wrapped gifts on the front seat.

Dr. Motke Levinson was gruff and overweight, with an elaborate gray mustache. He was now in semi-retirement. He hadn't much patience for politics, and, as the years advanced, cared for little beyond his everyday concerns. His grandchildren. His dogs. His new car. Anesthetist and occasional consultant at Qalqilya since its founding days, he had grown fond of Sami Khader, who had appeared one day after Motke had dealt, for more than a decade, with conceited local vets who refused to admit they were ignorant of anything outside the farmyard. Dr. Sami had been a breath of fresh air. Arriving direct from the Dammam Modern Poultry Company, Sami had readily acknowledged the enormity of the task in front of him.

They first met when Motke was called in to heal an addax. Dr. Sami was waiting for him at the gate.

"Hello," he said, "I am Dr. Sami Khader. In all my life, I have never worked in this job. So you will be my teacher, and, if you agree, I will be your student. Shall we take tea?"

No other vet at Qalqilya had ever offered Motke tea. They shook hands, and the relationship was cemented.

Across the road, an overloaded minibus taxi screeched to a halt. Motke watched as Dr. Sami climbed out. Close at his heels came Abu Shir. Sami passed two coins to the driver and waved. Motke raised one hand in a grim salute. Abu Shir dusted down the lapels of his stiff gray suit, dragged out especially for the occasion, and clambered glumly into Motke's spotless backseat.

"My friend!" Dr. Sami patted Motke's shoulder. "It's been too long!"

"Good to see you, Sami. How's the family?" He passed the bag of presents.

"Fine, fine."

"How's life, Abu Shir?"

"Hard."

Sami rolled his eyes. He heaved the gifts aside and glanced anxiously at his wristwatch. "Now," he said, "a very important point. We are late for the deputy mayor."

Qalqilya's souk was busy with shoppers as the long, gleaming car slid into a parking space outside the Municipal Council building, a tall structure squeezed tightly between an ironmongery and a butcher's shop, where plump chickens waited obliviously in baskets. Downstairs, dozens of clerks in tiny glass-walled compartments were busy signing, stamping, and sending on mountains of documents. The humid air was irrigated by frantically whirring fans. Blithe secretaries swathed in robes and headscarves breezed in between, carrying stacks of typing. A cardboard cutout film star on the first-floor landing reminded employees that smoking was harmful to their health. Above him, a huge framed aerial photograph showed the wall that chopped a jagged circle from Qalqilya's farmland.

On the fourth floor, Nidal Jaloud, international relations officer, had his own room. A window swagged with gold-trimmed curtains looked onto the street. On his table sat the day's *Al-Quds* newspaper and a leather-bound edition of John Grisham's *A Time to Kill*, in French. A baroque hat stand occupied one corner; a tidy cupboard full of files stood in another. An air conditioning unit hummed on the wall above it. Beside the window, an assistant in a pale yellow shirt worked at a smaller desk.

Nidal Jaloud was compact and well kept. He exchanged his delicate gold-framed spectacles for silver, tucking the first pair into his breast pocket. A young secretary arrived carrying a tray of mint tea. "Mademoiselle," he jumped to his feet, "merci beaucoup." The girl blushed, the edges of her face blending hotly with her cerise headscarf. She hurried out of the room. "Arab ladies," he sighed to his assistant, stirring sugar into his tea and leaning back in his chair. "So beautiful, yet so invisible. I wished to visit the ladies of Paris, but, alas," he sipped delicately, "c'etait seulement une rêve."

A clatter of footsteps drifted up from the stairwell. Nidal Jaloud squinted out through the office door and then leaped to his feet, quickly re-exchanging his silver frames for gold. Out on the landing, Dr. Motke paused to catch his breath. The stairs were steep and the vet recovering from the exertion. "Our VIP! And just in time! Please, *mon ami*, come this way."

Dr. Motke was ushered up a final flight of stairs and into the immense, refrigerated offices of the deputy mayor.

Deputy Hashem al-Masri was a large, imposing figure, sporting a brown tailored suit, gold watch, and close-trimmed beard. As the group entered, he rose coolly to his feet. Motke, in a faded gazelle-print t-shirt and safari waistcoat, wiped his brow and offered his hand.

"As-salaam al-lekum," said the deputy mayor. "Welcome. Sit."

Motke sank into a chair nearest to the desk. Nidal Jaloud, Abu Shir, and Dr. Sami quickly assembled themselves in a single row. An ancient, wizened employee entered, totted up heads, and disappeared.

For several moments, the group sat in silence. The deputy, like a huge, tidy praying mantis, was quiet, poised, tightly wound. His chair was tucked so far under his desk that he appeared to be about to burst out from it. Beside a gently wheezing Dr. Motke, Nidal Jaloud adjusted the chain on his spectacles. He secretly cared little about the zoo, deeming it a tiresome drain on resources. But, as one of his scant areas of official business, he was obliged to demonstrate a modicum of interest. At his elbow, Abu Shir pulled out a packet of Alla cigarettes, laid them on a low table, and regarded them balefully. The old employee reappeared with a tray of coffee.

"Mr. Deputy Mayor," Sami cleared his throat, "Dr. Motke Levinson is a very important old man. He has come to request that we begin work on the Carnivore Department." He glanced encouragingly at Motke, who raised an eyebrow and folded his arms across his wide stomach.

The deputy mayor reached for his cigarettes. With relief, Abu Shir, itchy from his suit and uncomfortable in the grandeur of the mayoral offices, did the same. Everyone turned expectantly to Dr. Motke.

Motke thought for a moment. "To keep a zoo alive," he began cautiously, "you need to keep moving. You have to expand, refresh, find places from which you can renew your inventory."

Hashem al-Masri regarded him solemnly. "We have no female lions," he replied, inhaling deeply on his cigarette.

"And the biggest problem for your zoo," continued Dr. Motke, "is that animals are very costly. I don't know if you have the resources."

"We have the resources."

Nidal Jaloud glanced aghast at the deputy mayor. He opened his mouth, then closed it again, and said nothing.

"But anyway," said Motke, "most zoos today aren't selling animals. They are giving them away. You see, more and more zoos all over the world are members of an association—"

"An international association," interjected Dr. Sami.

"—and when you're a member," said Dr. Motke, "the zoos swap animals with each other or donate them as gifts."

The deputy mayor arranged five pencils in precise parallel lines. "You have," he asked, "an idea of how we can become a member?"

"Well," Dr. Motke hesitated. "That's a difficult question. The standards here are nowhere near high enough."

The deputy mayor adjusted a pencil that had rolled slightly askew.

"But you have," he took a sip of coffee from a minuscule patterned cup, "an idea?"

"The association's standards," said Dr. Motke patiently, "are very exacting. They are all written down. You could," he added, "look them up."

Abu Shir nodded sagely and flicked ash from his cigarette. Dr. Sami tapped one foot lightly on the floor. The deputy mayor straightened a stack of paper on his desk. "It is not impossible," he said "to meet these standards."

"Nothing's impossible," agreed Motke.

The deputy nodded faintly and glanced out of his window to the souk, where his brother was undoubtedly doing a brisk trade. A pharmacist-turned-veterinarian, his brother had a tiny surgery tucked away in a passageway opposite the municipality building. It was usually filled with old men, squeezed in among cans of flea spray and vitamin powders, gossiping and drinking coffee. The deputy, too, was a pharmacist. He had found himself sitting in this grandiose office quite by accident. And now, instead of the orderly, methodical business of mixing pills, he was expected to solve the ills of a penniless town, along with its ailing zoo.

"By the way." Dr. Motke, warming to the subject, interrupted his reverie. "What are the connections today between Qalqilya Zoo and Emmen Zoo, in Holland? Emmen Zoo is one of the best in the world."

The deputy mayor frowned. "We have no relations."

"Years ago, there was a connection between Qalqilya and Emmen. It's the most beautiful zoo in Europe, and quite wealthy. Perhaps it's possible for you to ask for help from Emmen Zoo."

The deputy frowned again. "We haven't any," he replied enigmatically, "but they accepted to cooperate with us. To keep the relations which there were. But until now, there are none."

Dr. Motke glared. "I also believe," he turned to Dr. Sami, "that to get goodwill from other zoos, you must become involved in educational programs for schoolchildren. This is one of the very, very basic lines of running a zoo. Remember, they're not only for the amusement of the people. Education is extremely important. And of course, a good education program brings acclaim, more visitors, international relations."

At the mention of international relations, Nidal Jaloud perked up. But the others seemed less interested. Deputy Hashem al-Masri was gazing out of the window again, and Abu Shir appeared to have drifted off into a daydream.

"We need many kinds of females," the deputy mayor suddenly announced. Abu Shir and Nidal Jaloud both jumped. "For breeding."

"But you don't have space," said Motke. "On the other hand," he conceded, "there's nothing worse than an empty cage."

"I filled one with chickens," said Dr. Sami.

Dr. Motke thought for a second. "I do know someone," he considered, "who's looking for a home for some Berber sheep."

"I can move the chickens."

"I'll take a look to see if the place is right."

"I'll make it right."

There was a long silence. Sami took a deep breath.

"So, Mr. Deputy Mayor," he asked encouragingly, "what is your belief about the Carnivore Department?"

The deputy mayor exhaled through his nose and then gathered his pencils together in one strong fist. He nodded. Sami beamed. Nidal Jaloud muttered something indistinguishable, in French. Abu Shir glanced surreptitiously at his watch.

"All right," said Dr. Motke, sitting forward in his chair, "now I'd like to see the zoo." He turned to the deputy mayor. "You must also continue your connections between Qalqilya Zoo and the Israeli zoos. You should write letters."

"Yes," said the deputy mayor, unconvincingly.

"I know it's not easy, but it's a start."

Dr. Hashem al-Masri nodded. It was not easy. He was acting head of a council that had yet to acknowledge that Israel had the right to exist. He could hardly start spinning off friendly letters to Israeli zoo managers. "You are a good man," he said gloomily to Dr. Motke, "for peace," and dropped his five pencils neatly back into their pot.

◆　　◆　　◆

The zoo's avenues were quiet as Motke's car pulled up outside the gates. Three small boys on bicycles gazed at it in admiration.

A tall, aquiline man with a thin moustache and a cardboard tube waited in the shadow of the plane trees.

"Aha," nodded Dr. Motke, hoisting himself out of the car.

Abu Khaled grinned. "It's been a long time," he said. The men shook hands heartily.

Abu Khaled, a structural engineer, was the original architect of the zoo and its manager for the first decade. In 1996, he had been promoted to the municipal engineering department, leaving the path clear for Abu Shir's unlikely ascent into the managerial ranks. Now he was once again involved in zoo matters, engaged as renovations project engineer to turn Dr. Sami's grand international plans into blueprints and structural diagrams.

Amiable and generally smiling, he was a perpetual source of infuriation for Sami, since he was, and had always been, more concerned with aesthetics than with animals. Each time he arrived at the zoo with a smart new set of architectural plans, Sami set about scribbling on top of them, marking areas that should be enlarged, widened, deepened. At Abu Khaled's next visit, however, the engineer's carefully drafted pen lines, even and symmetrical, had remained stubbornly in place. He had the organized mind of a collector, thought Sami, but a collector was the wrong sort of person to plan a zoo.

Clapping Motke on the back, Abu Khaled unrolled a sheaf of papers from the cardboard tube and drew him over to a rickety picnic table. They sat down. Unlike Sami, Abu Khaled spoke fluent Hebrew, the product of his early years as an engineer in Israel. Soon, he and Motke were deep in discussion. Abu Khaled pointed out small, mystifying annotations to his set of plans. At Motke's elbow, Sami struggled to keep up. After a few minutes, he lost the thread entirely.

"Dr. Motke," he interrupted Abu Khaled in mid-flow, "don't you think this pool," he tapped the plan with a red ballpoint and glanced at the engineer, "is too small for the crocodiles?"

It was one of their longest-running battles. From the very start, Dr. Sami had conceived a grand Crocodile Island to replace the shallow, sand-edged trough in which the creatures now spent their languorous days. Crocodiles, in close confinement, could become nasty. One of his males had already lost several toes as the result of a spat, and he feared tensions would escalate unless something drastic was done. Conditions, moreover, were not right for breeding. "We have lost more than fifty eggs already this year," continued Sami, "because the sand is not deep enough. It must," he turned again to Abu Khaled, "be deeper."

Sami's ideal Crocodile Island would be lush and roomy, with a deep sand beach. Wooden footbridges would thread across an expansive pool edged with tropical plants, providing visitors with an impressive suspended view of the reptiles. For Abu Khaled, such a large island disrupted the simple line of his wide main boulevard. Each time they met, Sami took out his red ballpoint pen and changed the shape of the whole avenue, creating in its place a square with Crocodile Island at the center. But, when Abu Khaled returned, it was back to its original, streamlined form, the crocodiles confined to a convenient sliver running up the middle of the avenue.

"Yes," Motke agreed. "It must definitely be bigger. And the sand must be deep enough for them to bury their eggs."

Dr. Sami shot Abu Khaled a cutting look. "Please note," he said, turning to the engineer, "'Crocodile Island must be bigger. And deeper.'"

Abu Khaled nodded graciously but quickly rolled up his plans before Sami could take to them with the red pen.

"All right," said Motke, consulting his watch, "I haven't got much time."

Striding ahead, Motke set off north up the main avenue. Sami trotted anxiously behind. At the top, to the left of Ruti's night shelter, they stepped through a hole in the old perimeter wall and entered the rubble-strewn wasteland that stretched to the back of the boys' school on Shanti Street.

"This will be my Carnivore Department," explained Sami. He was certain the old vet would disapprove. Despite the school's fortifications, he knew there was a chance that schoolboy missiles, launched at his prize specimens through malevolence or exuberance, might harm or even kill one of them. But it was this area or nothing, the only disused space at the zoo big enough for a new, larger set of cages. Motke looked around.

"Lions. Leopards. Wolves," listed Sami. "Bears. The hyena. The hippo. They'll all go here. And," he added dreamily, "a pair of tigers."

"Fine," said Motke. He glanced up at the school. At a high-barred window, a young face appeared, shrieked, then disappeared. "But," he considered, "why move the hippo? All he needs is a deeper pool." Abu Khaled smirked and drew a thick line across part of his plan. Sami ignored him. He nodded obediently. "Of course. Please, Dr. Motke, follow me."

Making their way further through the zoo, Motke, Sami, and the engineer reached a rocky enclosure inside which Abdel Raouf Joadi, the elderly cross-eyed zookeeper, was diligently cleaning with a dribbling hosepipe, brush, and bucket. Two dozen bantam chickens scratched in the dirt. Dr. Sami stopped. "Here is where we could put the Berber sheep." He watched Motke's face as the vet surveyed the enclosure. Motke nodded. "Yes, this seems to be good enough. I believe the zoo has four sheep that need new homes."

"Are there males and females? Both sexes?"

"How should I know?" Motke snapped. "Either you want them or you don't."

"Every time Dr. Motke comes," Sami beamed and nudged Abu Khaled, "he brings a nice surprise."

Hurrying on past wolves, ostriches, and zebras, Dr. Motke drew up at the saddest, shabbiest area of the whole zoo. He heaved a sigh and shook his head, glancing at Fateen. "Now. What about the monkeys?"

The new Monkey House, the second phase of Sami's plan, depended on the successful completion of the Carnivore Department. It meant razing the area currently dominated by the miserable series of old carnivore pens. In their place would be constructed one huge, roomy playground for the Hamadryas baboons, and, in among them, his three pretty Vervet monkeys.

On the plains of Africa, baboons and Vervets could live quite comfortably side by side. When there was adequate food, space, and shelter for all, they shared foraging grounds, the delicate Vervets spending time in the trees and the baboons on the ground. It was only when resources were scarce that their coexistence might be stretched to unpleasant limits. Then, to avoid becoming prey, the smaller monkeys would have to resort to life in the treetops, snapping away just the topmost twigs.

"I want to put them all together. Like nature." Sami pointed to Fateen, who looked up from examining a bubble gum wrapper and glared at them with mistrust. "Except for him."

"Why not that one?" asked Motke.

"He is a mad monkey," said Sami, tapping the side of his head.

Motke narrowed his eyes. "Why do you think he is," Motke tapped his head in imitation, "mad?"

Abu Khaled suppressed a snigger. Sami glowered.

"Because he is dangerous. Very vicious. He will try to bite you if you offer him food."

Motke looked at the monkey's cage. The cement floor was damp. There was nothing, except for the bubble gum wrapper, for distraction. "Sami," Motke said sternly, "if you lived in a house like that, wouldn't you try to bite the hand that feeds you?"

"He is not normal."

"His life is not normal."

Sami looked down at his hands.

"In the wild, monkeys get along perfectly well in large groups, even many males together," said Motke. "If you give him the right home, this monkey can live quite happily with anything you decide to put in with him. It is better for him than being alone."

"But—" Sami began.

"In the wild," said Motke firmly, "there are no mental institutions."

Sami was quiet for a moment. "Yes," he brightened, "I believe it will be very nice. And maybe then," he continued cautiously, "we can also get some more monkeys. A different breed. Every time people come, they see the same monkeys. It's not interesting for them."

Dr. Motke frowned. Fateen went back to his wrapper.

"Perhaps some chimpanzees," Sami continued.

"You'll never get chimpanzees. Not in a million years. You might as well," Motke muttered to himself, "ask for a unicorn."

It was difficult enough for Sami to acquire any monkeys at all. The only group of Hamadryas baboons interested in reproducing were the three members of the small harem. But while normally tranquil and agreeable, each appearance of a baby baboon had yielded a bloodbath.

The first baby, born one evening to the subordinate of the two females, did not last the night. As the zoo slumbered, the young mother picked up her tiny, wide-eyed offspring and flung it about the cage by its slender tail. All that was left, by the time the first keeper arrived the next morning, was a little sack of fur, broken and bloodied. Then the three baboons had turned on each other.

The second time, Sami had managed to rescue the baby, injured but alive, and tentatively planned to take it home to nurse. Over the years, Sara Khader had grown used to being the wife of a zoo veterinarian. She knew that from time to time, her husband would return bearing some creature or other that needed special care. For more than a year, Fufu, the baby ibex, had lived in their house, making puddles on her rugs and chewing the potted plants. Nowadays, Sara kept only the plastic kind, just in case.

But she drew the line at monkeys. They seemed, to her, grotesque: small, mean caricatures of people with disgusting habits and alarming human expressions. She was willing to coexist with an odd assortment of creatures, both living and dead, but had made it clear from the outset that there would be no monkeys while she was in residence.

The baby baboon died before the end of Sami's working day, its injuries too great to overcome. For Sami, it was a disappointing loss; for his wife, a lucky escape.

Sami's three female Vervet monkeys had, in contrast, once bred willingly and copiously. Their babies, clinging to their mothers' velveteen stomachs, were well-fed and content, all fathered by the ladies' two virile male companions. Years ago, in a slim period of peace, Dr. Motke had taken to re-homing the zoo's abundant young, selling them off for one hundred dollars apiece to wildlife parks and petting zoos in Israel. Then, he heard from a colleague that a zoo was on the lookout for a fertile adult male. The fee would be five hundred dollars in cash, payable on delivery. Though money mattered little to Dr. Sami, Abu Shir was excited. A deal was struck. Motke was to come the next week, armed with carrying cage and tranquilizer dart, to whisk the monkey off to its new life.

All went well the following Monday morning. Motke took aim and hit the small gray creature with a wave of anesthetic in the inner thigh. It drifted off to sleep and was transferred, with ease, to a nicely padded transportation cage. Sami saw the monkey off, sadly, at the gate, and went about his business.

An hour later, a call came in. In transit, between Qalqilya and its new home, the monkey, under anesthetic, had expired. Dr. Motke was mystified. It was the first time that had happened in his entire career—and to a young, healthy animal. What, he asked Sami, would he like him to do now? Bring back the body or donate it to veterinary students at the university?

Motke returned with the dead monkey. The payment would not be made, since the goods had not been delivered. Abu Shir was mortified.

Within a fortnight, the other young Vervet male was found dead in its cage. Sami was left with three fertile females and little hope of fulfilling their biological imperative.

But sometimes, animals appeared from unlikely quarters. One of Sami's adult Hamadryas pairs, insular as an old married couple, had come from a private park in Nablus, where the pair had been procured from the wild and kept since babyhood. Once they matured into uglier, stronger adolescents who could bite and bare their teeth, interest in the creatures waned. There they led a miserable, immured existence until their owner finally decided it was time to let them go.

On a summer's morning in 2003, Dr. Sami went to collect the two baboons. The journey to Nablus went smoothly. He had acquired an official document from a local doctor, certifying that he was in need of urgent medical attention at the town's hospital. Sami glanced at the paper, which detailed his complaints. "I am a very sick man," he chortled, hauling himself onto the ambulance stretcher and reclining for authenticity. The eighteen-mile journey took two and a half hours, and at eight o'clock, he was deposited deep in the heart of Nablus.

Sami was met at the park by an old, sun-withered worker. Together they picked their way across the remains of a recreation area. Charred carcasses of mattresses and ancient, crippled couches lounged around an empty swimming pool. Several inches of soupy rainwater had collected in its bottom. Dead, bloated frogs floated among chunks of fluffy polystyrene.

The baboons were kept in a dilapidated metal shack at the back of the park, with the remains of their last meal scattered dismally around them. Crouched in a dark corner, huddled together, they issued petrified barks as Dr. Sami produced his trusty homemade rifle. He took a deep breath and shot each, *Phht . . . Phht*, peremptorily in the buttock. Examining the cage's rusty padlock, the old man scuttled off, reappearing with a pair of wire cutters. Together they loaded the woozy creatures into a wheelbarrow. With one finger, Sami checked the male baboon's wrist. "Very nice." In an afterthought, he draped the huge creature's inert arm around his companion's slumbering shoulder.

"Lucky man," said Dr. Sami.

"Lucky lady," agreed the old man.

Sami had arranged to borrow a vegetable wagon to transport the sleeping animals back to their new home at Qalqilya Zoo. It waited outside the abandoned park, two homemade wire crates taking the place of cucumbers and cauliflowers. The hefty male baboon was lifted in first and, once secured, the female slid in snugly beside him. Checking their vital signs once more and satisfied that all was well, Dr. Sami climbed into the driver's seat, turned around, and started out for home.

At the first checkpoint, Sami passed with the usual formalities. First, he handed over his documents—a letter from the mayor, a receipt for purchase of the baboons, his identity papers—and received a curt nod from a fair, fresh-faced soldier. The soldier cast a scrutinizing glance into the back of the wagon. Sami heard a hoot of laughter. Several other soldiers sauntered over. "Monkeys," called Sami nervously, "for the zoo." The young soldier returned to the window and handed back his papers. "Have a nice day," he said, as he waved them through.

At the next two checkpoints, Dr. Sami was ushered along similarly, without delay. At the fourth, a long queue of traffic—civilian cars, merchants' vans, an ambulance—stretched out from a roadblock, at which two soldiers were slowly examining a taxi. Sami turned off the ignition and stepped out. He walked along the line of stationary vehicles.

"What's the problem?" he asked a driver.

The driver shrugged.

Sami returned to the wagon and settled himself in for a long wait. An hour later, he reached the front of the queue.

"Documents?" A face in reflective sunglasses barked out an order. Sami handed over his papers. The face disappeared.

Fifteen minutes passed. The face reappeared. "Get out of the vehicle."

Dr. Sami stepped down onto the dusty road.

"Open the back doors."

Sami walked uneasily round to the back of the wagon and swung open the doors. Inside her metal crate, the female baboon was beginning to stir. Sami glanced at her but said nothing.

"What's this?" asked the soldier, pointing to the cages.

"Baboons, for the zoo."

The soldier disappeared again, into a booth on the opposite side of the road. Sami waited. In any other place in the world, he thought, looking down the line at the dozens of motionless vehicles, drivers would stand on their horns. Irate passengers would confront the adolescent soldiers, demanding to see a superior. Here, they simply waited their turn.

For ten minutes, Dr. Sami stood in the strong afternoon sun.

The male baboon extended an arm and flexed his fingers. The soldier reappeared. "The monkeys can pass," he said, "but you can't. Go to the next checkpoint to the south."

"But" protested Sami, "my papers are all in order."

"Go," the soldier repeated, "to the next checkpoint to the south."

"What about my monkeys?"

The soldier held out his hand and motioned for Sami's keys.

"They will be waiting for you on the other side."

It was a brisk fifteen-minute walk to the nearest intersection, where Sami flagged down a ride from a lorry driver. As they crashed over potholes, Sami tried to push images of escaped, marauding monkeys from his mind. He concentrated on the road ahead until the checkpoint finally loomed into view.

This time, it went faster. Joining the pedestrian line, Sami negotiated the crossing in less than half an hour. On the opposite side, he hailed a taxi, its passengers levered in like sardines, and sped back to his wagon. It was parked, safely, in the sun. He waited. Ten minutes later, the same soldier, who Sami estimated was barely a day over twenty, strolled over and tossed him the keys.

Without a word, he turned and walked away.

Dr. Sami was relieved to find that the baboons, though drowsy, were not yet alert enough to attempt to struggle to their feet. They lolled in their hot cage in the back of the wagon like two elderly drunkards. Sami turned the key in the ignition, wound down the passenger window to allow some cool air into the stifling vehicle, and sped home to Qalqilya.

It took the new arrivals, whom he named Nora and Nira, time to get used to their new lodgings. At first, they were timid and cowered in a corner, issuing wild growls whenever a keeper approached. They spent much of the day grooming each other with obsessive thoroughness. In time, they adapted. Their cage, though small and dismal, was much roomier than the one in which they had grown up. The food was regular and of better quality. The drinking water was clean. Their quarters were hosed down daily, and, in place of silence, they heard the sounds of other animals. Smiling faces peered in through their bars. Voices called to them. Children waved and tossed popcorn.

◆　　◆　　◆

Dr. Motke's car pulled away from the zoo gates just as a clock in the ticket office, its face embellished with a gilt-edged image of the Kaaba at Mecca, chimed a falsetto four. His last call had been at the snake section.

"Who's in charge of the snakes?" he asked, glancing skeptically down the line of dark, grimy tanks.

"I am," said Sami.

"You have to do something about this."

"Yes. We don't have any sunlight inside the snakes' enclosures. It's a problem."

"So install some neon," said Motke, "and you need to clean those windows."

"We don't know what it is. It won't come off."

"It's dirt," replied Motke. "It will. And don't forget that monkey."

Hamadryas baboons react to poor conditions in captivity in a variety of ways. Some, like Nora and Nira, retreat within. Unnerved when boundaries are broadened, they develop strong interpersonal bonds to help them find comfort in their imprisonment. Many succumb easily to minor ailments. Stress-related immune deficiencies frequently develop, in time, into acute illnesses.

Other baboons, like the diminutive harem, appear to be functioning normally. Roles within their small hierarchies become highly defined, since power and personal space are crucial. Severe underlying psychological problems are only thrown to light when something unusual upsets the fragile balance of everyday life. Then, one member, or more, snaps beneath the strain. Aggression turns inward, escalates, and is vented against the rest of the usually peaceful group.

Finally, there are the angry few who fight throughout their lives against their captors. Mostly males, they retain forever a gnawing aggravation at being in a situation over which they have no control and from which they have no escape. But, even then, a simple sense of freedom, of community and purpose, will usually ease the load.

Sami checked his watch, confirming the hour. It was time to cross town, to open up the little backstreet clinic, with its tank full of bright goldfish and shelves stocked with gauzes and tinctures. He glanced, in turn, into each of the baboon cages. It was almost feeding hour, and the animals were restless. Though their surroundings were dreary, their appetites were still healthy. Fateen paced and issued a low, gurgling growl. Sami watched him. Perhaps there was hope for Fateen after all.

"Good afternoon, crazy monkey," said Sami brightly. "Enjoy your meal."

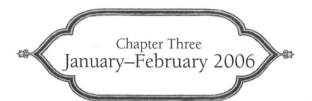

Chapter Three
January–February 2006

Who does more wrong than the one who tries
to create something like My creation?
—HADITHS OF AL-BUKHARI, VOLUME 9, BOOK 93

On the twenty-fifth of January, two cold and dismal months after Dr. Motke's visit, the first legislative elections in more than a decade were held in the Palestinian Territories. A few nights earlier, canvassers had come to Sami's door. "I give my vote to my wife," he told them, and they went away, puzzled.

At the zoo, Yail Misqawi, Qalqilya's head keeper, was oblivious to the drama unfolding outside its walls and went about his rounds with customary care. Humming lightly, he forked hay into the hippo's stall and raked sand over the zebra paddock. Then he looked in at the Syrian bears. He gasped. In the corner of their cage was something small, curled, and furry. A rat. He looked again. The rat wasn't moving, though he could see its belly slowly rising, slowly falling. Simka, the male, and Darling, his daughter, were tucked up asleep inside their night quarters. Marla, his mate, was chewing on a leftover morsel in the corner, ignoring the interloper. The keeper stared, in confusion and disbelief. How could a rat have infiltrated the bears? The bars were close-knit to prevent inquisitive fingers being nipped off. Yail Misqawi made a hasty tour of the enclosure. No holes in the fencing; no possible way for the nasty creature to have entered. And why was it asleep? Perhaps it was unwell, rabid even, and might bite Marla if she ambled over to examine it. A rabid rat would mean a rabid bear, and a rabid bear could mean a rabid zoo.

In a fit of panic, Misqawi fled. He sped across the zoo and took the slippery metal stairs up to Dr. Khader's office two-by-two. "Doctor! Doctor!" he panted. "Open up! There's a rat—a rat among the bears!"

Inside the office, Sami had just brewed his first tea of the morning and was settling down at his desk to enjoy it. It was grim outdoors, and he had been relishing a few moments' quiet with his feet against the squat two-bar electric heater that whirred and pinged beneath his desk. He heard the steps clattering up the exterior staircase. He listened as Misqawi banged and shouted at the door. He slowly got to his feet and took a sip of tea, carefully winding the tea bag's string around a spoon before extracting it, squeezing it twice against the side of the cup, and depositing it in the waste bin. Misqawi's alarm calls were usually for nothing.

Sami took his tweed jacket from the back of his chair, pulled it on, and straightened his tie. Glancing out of the window, he noticed it was still raining and remembered that he had forgotten his umbrella.

"Doctor!" came the frantic cry from outside again, "are you there?"

Sami stretched and went to the door. He turned the key in the lock.

Outside, Yail Misqawi was breathless and red in the face. "Come quick!"

Silently cursing the keeper, Dr. Sami followed across the damp zoo. They arrived at the bears and looked inside. Sami spun to face Yail Misqawi. "Stupid man!" he fumed. "That is a baby bear."

Sami immediately knew something was amiss. The pair of shaggy, honey-colored Syrian bears had managed to produce one small female cub in the thick of the intifada, and Darling had grown and thrived. But since then, Marla had remained barren.

Bears required somewhere quiet to nurse their young, and Sami blamed their lack of privacy. Strangely, the intifada had provided the perfect environment for Marla to suckle her baby unmolested. As artillery fell across the city and the zoo remained empty, Marla diligently tended to Darling. For once, no catcallers disturbed their solitude.

Syrian bears, though the smallest of their subspecies, can grow to two hundred pounds. Their babies, at birth, weigh less than ten ounces and are easily disguised throughout their gestation within their mothers' bulk. Sami had not noticed that Marla was pregnant. Now, her behavior made him fear for the baby. A mother bear, he knew, should perform a predictable pattern of tasks directly following birth. First, she should retire with her new baby to a dark, confined space. Then, she should enter a temporary state of hibernation, fasting and snoozing while the tiny creature suckles her milk. In the wild, during the long months of hibernation that follow the breeding season, this conserves a vital 15 percent of a mother bear's body weight. What she shouldn't do, thought Sami grimly, is abandon her baby in favor of breakfast.

As if suddenly aware she was being watched, Marla shot a glance up at the vet and keeper, then sniffed the air. With dread, Sami realized what might happen next. The most basic of instincts could start to take over if Marla felt her baby threatened by their presence. Even though she seemed to have shunned her vulnerable charge, a primordial compulsion lodged deep within her heart would tell her what she must do to protect it. Mother bears, along with mother rabbits, mice, monkeys, and many others, will consume their babies before allowing them to meet harm from outside.

Sami froze, motioning with his eyes for Misqawi to do the same. Marla lumbered to the baby bear and grasped it between her teeth. She stood watching the two men, the baby's legs wheeling helplessly.

"Bring food. Whatever you can find," Dr. Sami hissed at the keeper. "Don't move quickly. But hurry."

Yail Misqawi nodded. He took several delicate, elongated steps backward, then dashed off. Moments later, he returned with a cardboard crate filled with old fruit and vegetables.

"Now. Slowly. Gently," instructed Sami, "slide them in."

With sweat beading on his brow, Yail Misqawi unlatched the enclosure's low feeding hatch. Hands trembling, he pushed in a knobbly carrot, a red apple, and four limp leaves of lettuce, then slid it shut.

"Stay there," warned Dr. Sami. "Don't move."

For several moments, Marla was motionless. Then, in one quick motion, she dropped the baby and galloped to her food bowl. The baby yelped; Dr. Sami winced. "Now," he said, "go round to the back of the cage, and throw the rest of the food into the sleeping quarters. Make sure she notices."

Misqawi rose to his feet. Marla looked up, regarding him carefully, as he inched toward the back of the cage and disappeared from view. Sami heard the sounds of the outer cage door being unbolted, then of the keeper coughing and cooing. Simka, the male bear, called back in appreciation as it began raining food inside his bedroom. Marla devoured the last of her lettuce and listened to the dull squish of overripe tomatoes spilling out from the bears' sleeping quarters. Without a glance at her baby, the bear lolloped back across the cage and disappeared inside.

"Now!" yelled Sami, "Shut the door! Shut the door!"

Behind the enclosure, a gate banged shut and the puffing keeper reappeared, tugging at a lever to one side of the cage. A metal door slid sharply across the entrance to the bears' bedroom, confining Simka, Marla, and Darling within.

Dr. Sami breathed a deep sigh. "Very nice," he said. "Now, let's get this baby out of there."

It was barely ten o'clock when Sara Khader heard the sound of a key turning in the front door. She was busy in the kitchen, drying mint leaves to add to the flat, oily patties her family loved to devour. The girls were both at school, and neither usually came home for lunch until some time around two.

"Don't worry," announced her husband. She heard him stop to kick off his shoes before appearing with a small object wrapped in an old pink towel. "Baby bear. Mother didn't want it."

Depositing the bundle on one of the ornate armchairs that stood in a semicircle in front of the television set, Dr. Sami made for his balcony. His wife turned up the heating and continued cooking. Outside on the chilly balcony, Sami carefully constructed his homemade hatchery.

As soon as it was complete with thermostat, cover, and soft wool blanket, Sami fed the tiny bear cub a few drops of substitute milk from a rubber dropper. The baby sucked them up greedily. Then Sami hastened off again, first back to the zoo and on to an unchallenging afternoon of examining a goat's teeth, a budgerigar's skin complaint, and a sheep with foot rot at his clinic in town.

The town was still bustling with voters heading for the polls as the vet arrived outside his clinic. Sami watched with amusement from the window as cars paid for by the dueling parties ferried sick and elderly voters to the booths. One party, he knew, had distributed fuel coupons to those willing to transport people to the polling stations. Certain drivers, who had readily taken up the offer, were now busy driving voters for the opposition back and forth. Others had cashed in their coupons and decided to stay at home. Sami hurried through the evening's appointments, eager to see how his hapless arrival was faring in its makeshift bed.

That night, while news networks across the world monitored the first shocking exit polls, Sami stationed himself in his favorite armchair on the far side of the living room, half-watching the news. It would be a long night for reporters in Ramallah attempting to make sense of the patchy information trickling in from the Election Commission.

The day had passed in relative peace and quiet. In Nablus, some scuffles had broken out between rival parties; in Gaza, police fired into the air to control a crowd. But even the head of the Al-Aqsa Martyrs Brigade, who had vowed to disrupt the elections, turned up at a West Bank polling station to declare, "I'm voting like everyone else." Unlike everyone else, he was protected by a knot of thirty armed henchmen who, on being requested to check in their weapons before voting, did as they were told.

Beside Sami, the baby bear floundered in its hatchery. The tiny thing had had a rude awakening, and Sami hoped it would pull through. Every half hour or so, he fed the creature a few more drops of milk from a baby bottle. It suckled well, but he knew that such a delicate animal could succumb easily without the antibodies of its mother's milk. Sami browsed the television channels, but election news was being broadcast on every station. It seemed that the West's greatest fears were being realized: The religious hardliners were heading for electoral glory.

At some time around two-thirty the next morning, Sami's eyelids finally drooped, and he sagged in his chair.

At daybreak, he awoke with a start. Uzhdan was standing over him with a glass of orange juice. "They won, Daddy," she said, "and the baby's dead."

Sami didn't know exactly what caused the death of the baby bear. Perhaps the temperature inside the hatchery had dropped as he dozed beside it. Perhaps he hadn't offered enough or the right kind of milk. Perhaps if he hadn't nodded off, it might have pulled through.

Sami sighed, pulled the woollen blanket over the baby's inert body, and walked wearily to the bathroom to bathe before work.

◆　　◆　　◆

Dr. Sami had received no word from the deputy mayor and assumed the municipality had been too busy campaigning, and then celebrating, to think of his Carnivore Department.

Eventually, a week after Election Day, he went to Abu Shir.

"What are they waiting for?" he complained. "Good weather?" It was raining and had been for some weeks.

"Ah," replied Abu Shir. He looked reluctantly down at his desk. "Perhaps this will tell us something." He picked up an envelope bearing the municipality's green, spread-eagle crest, concealed beneath a stack of newspapers.

"When did that arrive? What does it say?"

"I do not know." Abu Shir shook his head mournfully. "I do not know."

Sami sank onto the vinyl settee as Abu Shir tore open the envelope and unfolded its contents. The manager squinted and put on his reading glasses. He crossed the room to turn on the neon light. It buzzed hesitantly into illumination. He sat back down and lit a cigarette. He rubbed his face with both hands and adjusted his glasses. "By order of Deputy Mayor Hashem al-Masri," he read, "we are pleased to inform you that funds for Qalqilya Zoo's improved Carnivore Department have," he paused and glanced at Sami, "been released." Sami leapt up in jubilation. Abu Shir looked worried. "It will mean a lot more work," he considered, "but I am glad they agreed to my plan."

Sami glanced down at the manager, then snatched up his jacket and hurried away.

The workmen turned up three weeks later. They were lazy and needed some encouragement, which Sami tried to provide by demonstrating his vision.

"The lions will be here," he said, gesturing to an old oil drum, then to a spiny gorse bush, "and the bears' swimming pool over there." The workers stared at their shoes or up at the rain clouds.

Abu Shir plied them with tea. When all was quiet at the Carnivore Department, Sami could bet there were workmen propping up the rental narghiles at the Friends' Restaurant, listening to one of the manager's long, meandering tales of woe.

"Like an amputated limb," he overheard Abu Shir saying to a rapt crowd. Sami knew this story of Abu Shir's family farm very well. "Gone, but still felt." Sami decided to take tea in his office.

On sunnier days, the workmen spluttered into action. Ruti looked on with curiosity as the wasteland behind her enclosure began slowly to be cleared of old tires and twists of rusty metal. She nudged and nibbled at the laborers who moved in to remove quantities of rubble and stones. They fed her tugged up clumps of grass and the nettles and dandelions that grew between the rubbish. One man gave her a carrot from his lunchbox, and she slurped it up happily.

Sami found Nabil Baron, the municipality's debonair new chief engineer, outside the zoo manager's office on a moist Thursday morning. The office was locked, and the lights were off. Baron was looking at his reflection in a pane of glass. He brushed a fleck from his suit lapel and carefully patted down his hair.

"How long will this project take to complete?" Sami asked.

"Two months," Baron assured him, flashing a dazzling smile as a chauffeur helped him into his car, sleek and black with smoked-glass windows. "Please tell Abu Shir I stopped by."

Sami walked alone from the office through the drizzle, toward his Carnivore Department. In his mind's eye, bears already paddled in a vast swimming pool. Rabir, the largest lion, stood proudly on a boulder, surveying his domain. The old hyena lounged on a soft patch of grass and gnawed on a rib cage. A mother tiger, a baby gamboling between her legs, licked her mate's forehead. He paused, his breath blowing a hot cloud into the dreary air, and smiled. A screech rattled over the tannoy system. "Dr. Sami Khader! Municipal visitor! Please proceed to your office!" Sami scowled. The laziness of his keepers never failed to astound him. The zoo entrance was barely one hundred yards from where he stood. You could be sure that there were at least three employees huddled with ticket clerk Amjad Daoud in his booth, around a struggling two-bar heater. Yet no one could drag themselves away to deliver an official guest. Things would be different, he thought dourly, when this became an international zoo.

Sami turned to see his municipal visitor tiptoeing cautiously up the avenue, avoiding small puddles and patches of mud spiked with twigs. Nidal Bakir was a youngish man with a brown wool suit, a long brown wool coat, and a chilly expression, an engineer whose responsibility, he announced, lay in "agriculture and the protection of regional plants." He had been sent to discuss planting arrangements for the grassy areas that Sami had proposed, "like nature," inside the new carnivore enclosures. Sami shook Bakir's cold, smooth hand and took him up to his office for tea. It seemed appropriate that Bakir should deal in wildflowers, shrubs, and plants. With his level stare through steely eyes and calm, unnerving temperament, he was almost reptilian. Sami could easily imagine him slithering about in the long grasses.

Mr. Bakir sipped his hot tea. "I have held this position for nine months now," he droned. "Before this, I completed a master's degree at a university in America. I am very international. I am looking forward to working with you on the replanting of the zoo."

Bakir actually found his job rather dull. At present, in a climate of what Nidal Jaloud, back at the municipality, called "confiscation et isolation," agriculture was far from flourishing. Except for the flowerbeds at the entrance to town, there were precious few regional plants to protect. Still, his was a good, steady job—a "grassroots" position, he liked to joke to his international friends—one that he expected to move swiftly beyond.

Sami drained his cup and jumped to his feet. "Shall I show you around?"

Bakir arranged his lips into a smile but remained in his seat.

"There is someone very nice," tempted Sami, "who would like to join us."

Outside, the rain had stopped. Abu Shir had arrived at work and stood in the middle of the avenue, apparently inspecting a tree. "As-salaam al-lekum, Abu Shir," said Sami. "How are you today?"

"Cold," said Abu Shir, staring at the tree trunk. They passed by.

Further along, they came to a large pen enclosing three Nubian ibex, two hog deer, and a sprinkling of goats. A dainty beige form, with four white socks and stubby horns, was perched atop a pile of rocks, pressing its chocolate muzzle against the fence.

"Halloo, Fufu!" Sami called through cupped hands.

Fufu sprang down from her rock and danced across the enclosure to the gate.

It was rare for the zoo's animals to display any hint of affection for their guardians, when generally they received such scarce return. But Nubian ibex, a hardy species still surviving wild in the deserts of the Middle East and North Africa, respond well to socialization. "Once a tame ibex was dragged in for our admiration: another time an oryx," said T. E. Lawrence of his time among the Bedouin in 1917. Their comfort level with humans might, some say, explain their dwindling numbers, since ibex feel no fear of the hunters who pursue them for their skin and the males' handsome, curving horns. In the wild, they have now joined the ranks of the "critically endangered." In captivity, they breed well.

Two years ago, Fufu's mother had abandoned her at birth, blankly ignoring the plaintive bleatings for milk and reassurance. But the tiny creature had spirit and was doggedly undeterred by the setback. First, she tried the other mothers, who sniffed her, then nudged her away. Then, she ran clumsily, her cottontail wagging, toward Sami. She suckled on his finger, expecting breakfast. He picked her up, cuddling her against his jumper, and went for the powdered baby milk. She drank eagerly, and he took her home.

Bottle-fed for her first intrepid months as she explored the Khader household, she had become, along with Ruti, Sami's firm favorite. Where Ruti was his sister and his equal, Fufu was a much-loved child. Tickled, coddled, and generally made much of by Sami and his daughters and tolerated valiantly by Sara, Fufu would forever regard Sami as kin.

"I do not know if she thinks I am father or mother," Sami liked to joke. Either way, Fufu was eager to be at his side whenever possible.

Bakir grimaced as Fufu trotted to catch up with them. A pair of small children squealed and giggled as the little ibex stopped to sniff the air, but when the braver child gingerly extended one hand, Fufu skipped off. Though she loved Sami unconditionally, Fufu seemed ambivalent toward other human beings. Bakir returned the indifference tenfold.

Fufu pressed close to Sami's heels as the men headed to the Carnivore Department, peopled by glum, waterlogged workmen. While the rest of the world saved labor wherever possible, the people of Qalqilya were doing just the opposite. Rather than acquiring legions of bulldozers and cranes, cement mixers and hammer drills, the zoo's hired hands refused modern conveniences. They were men skilled in other fields: carpenters, electricians, the odd schoolteacher or professor. Sent in batches, in weekly rotation, their wages were paid by the United Nations so that as many men as possible could take home a pay packet once in a while. It made sense to eke out the work as long as possible.

Sami regarded the building site. It had almost been cleared of rubbish, and the first foundation's trench was slowly being dug by a pair of middle-aged men with a shovel and a wheelbarrow between them.

"Very nice," he murmured.

He turned to Bakir. "Here's where the lions will live," he said, gesturing to one side of the muddy vacant lot. "I am happy to hear your plans for planting the cages."

Bakir sniffed. He shifted his weight, tapping muck from the toe of one shoe. "And I am happy to discuss them with you," he tapped again, "as soon as there are some cages to plant." Behind them, Fufu nibbled unsuccessfully on a stick poking out of the mud. "I have many good ideas," elaborated Bakir, "but I am a very busy man."

Quickly, they toured the remaining area, Dr. Sami pointing out a further string of invisible boundaries. Every now and again, Mr. Bakir nodded and forced a gracious smile. He glanced up at the sky, which was clouding over. It looked like rain again.

"Come," attempted Sami as he felt his visitor's enthusiasm waning. "Would you like to see a leopard?"

"The leopard," said Bakir, "would be toward the exit?"

"You're right," replied Sami.

"Please, lead the way."

With Fufu still skittering behind, Dr. Sami and Nidal Bakir walked in silence through the empty zoo. Most animals had taken shelter from the weather. Only a solitary wolf remained outside, turning tight circles.

At the leopard cages, Sami clambered over the low railings. Bakir watched, transfixed with horror, as Fufu nibbled at a neat ornamental hedge. Rama, the male, growled petulantly. "You see this leopard? Just a grumpy old tomcat," Sami said. Rama pressed his head against the bars, eyes squeezed shut. Sami inserted one finger into the big cat's mouth and prized it gently open.

"One tooth missing," he pointed. "Too many sweets. But wait," he looked up in dismay, "what is this? He is in the wrong cage. He should be next door; his wife should be here. Why are they changed around? This is stupid work!"

Nidal Bakir glanced at the two cages, identical except that the male's rightful domain contained an old scratched tire suspended from the ceiling by a chain. Both were pitifully small and barren. He said nothing.

"Yail!" Sami bellowed. "Yail!"

Seconds later, as if from nowhere, the keeper scurried to the scene.

Yail Misqawi was forty-two years old, but his thick silver hair added almost a decade. He had worked for the zoo for six years. He loved his job, and he loved the animals, though the pay was poor, and words of praise or gratitude from his superiors were thin on the ground. Long ago he had been a welder across the border, where, he recalled, the money had been good and opportunities for work bounteous. Here at home, it was quite the opposite. But in these uncertain times, at least he felt secure, hidden away behind the zoo's high walls.

Misqawi was a diligent worker. He never arrived late, never took days off sick, and usually did as he was told to the letter. Sami found this thorough lack of imagination hard to swallow. Wherever Sami went, it seemed, Misqawi was hovering just footsteps behind, shadowing his every move. Sometimes, if the vet spun around quickly enough, he could trip theatrically over the keeper in a show of exasperation. Misqawi needed instruction, specific and comprehensive. Otherwise, he would arrive back at Sami's office, time and again, with the same light tap-tap-tap at the door, until all possible angles of even the most straightforward task had been covered.

"Yail Misqawi, why are these leopards in the wrong houses?" Sami didn't bother to wait for an answer. "Put them back where they belong."

The keeper nodded and immediately went to work. He opened the connecting hatch between the two cages, first coaxing Rama back into his own cage with the help of some loud, quizzical purring, then prodded Chika, the female, with an old stick. Chika snarled, waved a paw menacingly at Rama, and stayed put. Sami shook his head in despair.

"Very well then, Doctor," Bakir said. He gave Fufu who, emboldened, was now attempting to chew his shoelaces, a surreptitious kick. "I will be back when there is something to see."

"Next time you'll bring plans? Ideas?"

"Do not worry. I will do an excellent job on the plantings. It is easy work compared, for example, to my master's degree from America." Mr. Bakir nodded. "I can see myself out."

Sami watched Bakir's retreating brown form and heaved a sigh of exasperation. Fufu licked his hand. Behind him, Yail Misqawi let out an excited purr and rattled his stick. The keeper would be the death of him. The man had no common sense.

◆　　◆　　◆

Throughout zoological history, zoos' upper echelons have often run into difficulties with their keepers, though none so much so as in the case of the mercurial Matthew Scott. Scott's rise to power began in 1861, when, somewhere in the thick of the Ethiopian brush, a mother elephant was pursued and shot dead by a big-game hunter. Her calf, as big as a pony and clinging shivering to its mother's tail, was captured alive. The baby was sold to a Bavarian animal dealer, who, in turn, sold the creature on to the Jardin des Plantes. With haste, the management swapped him for a rhinoceros and shipped him to London Zoo, where he arrived in 1865, dirty, thin, and covered in weeping sores. His name was Jumbo, and Scott was his only friend.

Like the giraffes of Qalqilya, Jumbo and his new "wife" Alice, the zoo's old she-elephant, soon became star attractions. Jumbo recovered his health and attained a magnificent fifteen feet. He posed for photographs and gently took treats from the cupped hands of awestruck children. His tremendous bulk coined the term "jumbo" itself. It was not long before he became a national treasure. But as he entered the thick of adolescence, the scent of spring on the breeze saw him restive, angry, unpredictable. And in that certain season, only Matthew Scott could control him.

Scott was a canny fellow with a long face and longer moustaches who was wholeheartedly disliked by the managerial ranks at the zoo. He offered elephant rides to pretty ladies and pocketed the takings. He showed no respect to his superiors, well aware that he was the only one who could control the great beast. By 1882, the zoo authorities could take no more. Jumbo was a liability and Scott a nuisance. Though it pained them take so drastic and unpopular a step, Jumbo had to go.

It happened that precisely at that moment, the great American showman Phineas T. Barnum was on the lookout for a new star attraction. Having heard tales of the splendid Jumbo, he offered the zoo ten thousand dollars, sight unseen, and they gladly accepted.

The British public was not so easily appeased. "All British children," wrote the editor of the *Daily Telegraph* in an urgent telegraph to Barnum, "distressed at elephant's departure." "Fifty millions of American citizens," came the cool reply, "anxiously awaiting Jumbo's arrival."

But, in what the public took to be a show of supreme patriotism, Jumbo wouldn't budge. For days, he refused to enter his shipping crate, and no end of enticements could induce him to set foot outside the zoo's gates. Not, at least, until the day Matthew Scott received his own hearty tender from Barnum, offering him the lucrative opportunity to join his charge in a new life overseas. Scott accepted. That day, without fuss or bother, Jumbo stepped into his shipping crate. The pair set sail for America, to live together in comfort and celebrity, in their own circus carriage decked out in scarlet and gold.

Then, one Ontario night in 1885, the elephant was hit by a runaway freighter while crossing the tracks on the way back to the circus train. Jumbo died, feeling about with his trunk in his final moments to grasp Scott's hand. Scott, disconsolate and obsolete, disappeared from history. But Barnum determined to make the most of the situation. He ordered the mighty pachyderm stuffed by an enthusiastic young taxidermist named Carl Akeley, who packed the skin so tight that the finished effigy was a full foot taller than the original. Crowds flocked, with morbid fascination, to see the dead elephant for themselves.

At Qalqilya, too, there was a skilled taxidermist. Sami hoped that the preserved remains of Brownie and his stillborn calf would inspire the same enthusiasm.

◆　　◆　　◆

The first texts detailing the tricks of the taxidermy trade date back to the sixteenth and seventeenth centuries, to the works of Pierre Belon and Giovanni Petro Olina, who penned scientific treatises on the preservation of dead birds. Methods were rudimentary and results short-lived: The treatment of skins was confined largely to baking and salting. The hazardous addition of arsenic aided the preservation process, as, later, did bichloride of mercury. Most specimens were kept in the "cabinets of curiosity" of the rich. Iguanas were so distorted in the stuffing, their poses improvised to such an extent, that they kept alive a belief in monsters well into the eighteenth century. Preserved crocodiles were hung from the vaults of churches as proof of the Bible's Leviathan with the "eyes of the morning" and of God's victory over Lucifer.

By the early nineteenth century, when European hunters started to return home with exotic spoils, each taxidermist had developed his own secret method of preservation. Skins were treated and then taken to upholsterers to have them sewn up and filled with rags. Thousands of startled stags' heads soon adorned ancestral homes the length and breadth of the continent. They, in turn, proved inspiration for a generation of passionate Victorian collectors who would pounce upon every rare insect, bird, and mammal in sight, with the enthusiastic aim of pinning it, spearing it, shooting it, and stuffing it. In the last years of the nineteenth century, German taxidermists developed a system of casting the creature's body in ceramic before topping it off with the thoroughly treated skin. Specimens could enjoy a longer shelf life than ever before. Taxidermy was here to stay.

Today, it has evolved into an art form whose practitioners shudder at the term "stuffed," favoring the more neutral "mounted." After a modern taxidermist has been at work, little of what remains is a creature's flesh and bone. Like skilled morticians, they are experts at concealment and replacement and at preserving the radiant appearance of life. Eyelids are replaced by molded clay. Soft nose and mouth tissues are recreated from epoxy or wax. The bodily structure, or "manikin," is created from polyurethane foam and mirrors every muscular contour of the living beast.

Such methods and materials, however, remained out of Dr. Sami's reach. He went about stuffing his subjects the old-fashioned way.

The first casualty he ever attempted was a zebra, after a teargas attack in 2001 left four dead.

"Five thousand dollars," lamented Abu Shir as he stood over the corpses. "Times four."

"These animals don't have gas masks," replied Sami. "We will feed the meat to the leopards."

Until now, the largest creature he had ever attempted was an ancient caracal, so the challenge was quite fresh. But what he needed was a dedicated place to toil. So far, he had improvised on his balcony, soaking skins in washing-up bowls meant for plates and cups and sorting bones into Tupperware boxes. His wife, tolerant of his unusual obsessions, had turned a blind eye. She might not be so forgiving if he returned home with a zebra in the throes of rigor mortis.

So Sami set to work, quickly transforming an empty room at the back of the zoo, beside the supplies barn and slaughterhouse, into a laboratory worthy of Victor Frankenstein. The room was windowless. Someone, not Sami, had chalked a skull and cross-bones onto the heavy, black-painted metal door. Inside was part charnel house, part operating theater. Medieval implements lay on every available surface, and beneath a chaotic work bench, piles of grayish femurs in descending sizes were stacked on polystyrene tiles. Bits of snakeskin, gristle, and fur speckled the floor. A series of clear plastic pipes, coiled in various thicknesses, were stained crimson.

On the far side of the room, a grizzled antler poked forlornly from an old oil drum containing an oozing black liquid. Next to it, in the corner, a stained sackcloth covered something grim reclining in an old enamel bath. A strange chemical smell hung in the air, over a darker, deeper smell of rot and decay. But Sami saw none of the gloom and ghastliness. For him, the workshop was his inner sanctuary, a place to wipe away the cares of the world. Here was his escape, his refuge. His secret chance to play at creator, to grant immortality to his subjects.

When the zebra was complete, its legs stuck out at comical angles like a gastric, upturned cow. Its jaws were open, and its blue glass eyes astonished. Next came others. A spider monkey that had died of fright. An oryx and a hyena. A crocodile, two deer, and an ostrich, killed by shrapnel. Until one morning in July 2002, Sami was faced with his biggest project of all: Brownie, the fully grown, male giraffe.

◆　◆　◆

Until recently, Brownie and his calf had stood side by side, gathering dust in the tall supplies barn outside Sami's laboratory. Cobwebs stretched between Brownie's ears. His neck was lumpy, he had developed an underbite, and his glass eyes stared out into the barn's gloom. Then, in the summer of 2005, the municipality had ordered the Natural History Museum's shell hurriedly completed, and the giraffe was winched down into it. There he now stood, in the museum's central, circular antechamber, whose ceiling had been patched up above him.

Pale winter light struggled through drizzle onto the museum's mud roof. Workers huddled on the steps lining its courtyard, in whose middle sat the squat dome of an island, surrounded by an empty water channel. The courtyard had been planned by Abu Khaled as an amphitheater, with a stage where the island now stood, on which plays could be performed on balmy summer evenings. But, rumor had it, the municipality objected to such frivolity, where men and women might come into close contact. So plans were altered, and the stage was transformed into an island. The amphitheater's staggered stone steps were planted with shrubs, and a waterfall feature installed.

Sami and Fufu squelched along the cardboard walkway to the front door of the largest mud structure and peered inside. "Mr. La'aba!" Sami called. "Are you there?" Within seconds, Muhammad La'aba appeared. An owlish man with small wire-rimmed spectacles perched on his nose, he swiped his wool hat from his head, wiped his hands down the sides of paint-spattered dungarees, and proffered one for shaking.

"How is work going?" Sami asked his Natural History Museum foreman.

"Not bad, not bad," he smiled, nervously welcoming Dr. Sami in through the doors.

Fufu would not follow.

Inside, Sami's masterpiece was almost complete. "It will be a scientific museum," he told all who came to inspect the progress, "the very first of its kind in the whole of Palestine." The building consisted of a series of interconnected domed rooms, dark, windowless, and slightly moist. Every ostrich, every mummified screaming bat, every badger, rabbit, crocodile, and lion in the whole place had been stuffed by his own hand.

He intended his museum to be a place of education, and to that end had procured a series of posters in English, Arabic, and French diagramming the various systems—respiratory, digestive, circulatory, nervous, and "l'appareil Genital"—of the human body. Beside them, in a cabinet near the door, anemic fetuses floated peacefully in stoppered glass jars. "Most are abnormal. Mutated," Sami noted, glowing.

Next to Brownie and his baby stood the partial remains of a third giraffe, who had expired soon after its birth at an Israeli zoo. Although Sami found it nearly impossible to obtain livestock from Israel, he had been more successful at procuring the dead. The baby giraffe, however, had undergone a particularly rigorous autopsy, and Sami had been surprised to receive, all packed up in a box, only the head and neck of the unfortunate infant. "What to do with just the head?" he had pondered.

Making the best of a bad specimen, he mounted the baby giraffe's grinning head on a pedestal. It now rose, like a furry Venus, from a varnished tree trunk, its neck garlanded in a rainbow of fake flowers.

Across the room, a variety of splayed animal skins were stapled to the wall. A grim assortment of native scorpions lay pinned down beneath a glass case. A deformed baby sheep, with four legs but two heads and two tails, perched on a shelf. A bunch of desiccated roses lay on the floor in front of the cupboard full of jars.

The next room had been painted deep blue and had the stifling air of an underground cave. Here, Sami had separated the "Domestics" and the "Carnivores." At one end of the room, a stack of stiff ibex, goats, and geese waited patiently to be incorporated into a lifelike scene; a painter was hard at work stippling grass and imitating running water. His colleague screwed insensate feet to rocks and plaster promontories.

At the opposite end, a cavernous pair of wire-and-plaster jaws, painted a lascivious red, roared out from the ceiling and floor.

La'aba pointed proudly. "It is nearly finished," he said.

Dr. Sami nodded with satisfaction. "The rest of the large beasts are to be inserted inside the mouth." On a rocky hillside behind the jaws, a stuffed hyena chewed at a bloodied chunk of leg from a supine zebra. Sami gestured to an old desk fan, next to which was a lightbulb, painted red, and some strips of cloth. "Then, connect my bush fire."

A narrow corridor led off to one side of the jaws, past two glass cases containing the remnants of two baboons, one skeletal and one stuffed. "This one," Sami pointed out to Mr. La'aba, "was the very first animal in the zoo. He lived here from 1986 until just last year. A very important creature." The moribund baboon had finally met its maker at a great age. It was ragged and moth-eaten, with a variety of scuffs and scars. In an attempt to protect the modesty of visiting schoolchildren, Dr. Sami had removed a crucial part of the baboon's anatomy, which, previously, had dangled long, proud, and fiery red. Opposite the baboons, a hairy leg protruded from an otherwise empty wall.

Rounding the next corner, Sami inspected the work in progress on a massive steel spider web, slung along one side of the corridor. It harbored a malicious hair-and-metal spider, the size of a hyena.

"Children will like it, I think," said Sami.

Beyond was an archway comprised of sun-bleached skulls, beneath which odd fragments of teeth, ribs, and vertebrae were being set, mosaic-fashion, into the cement wall. "Abandon hope," the skulls sighed, "all ye who enter here."

At the end of the corridor, the penultimate room housed an immense, riveted metal snake, its scales painted alternately silver and gold. Around it was arranged a colony of stuffed snakes of different sizes, shapes, and degrees of flexibility. La'aba, surveying Sami's face anxiously, was relieved to see a smile of satisfaction.

"Put the facts on poison here," Sami pointed, "and the information on deadly snakebites there."

At the snake's tail end, a workman battled away with a pile of metal scales and a spray can. He paused to look up at Dr. Sami. "Don't stop working," commanded Mr. La'aba importantly. "We haven't got all day."

Further along stood the final section of the museum, which would house the remainder of Sami's skeletal collection, including that of his huge, prized African python. "Six hundred and thirty ribs," breathed Dr. Sami, as much to himself as to the anxious foreman. "Three whole months to assemble." The collection ranged around the last of Dr. Sami's mutant visions: a massive reclining monkey skeleton, its arched rib cage rising from the floor, its beaming skull emerging from the far wall.

"Please note," Sami added sternly, "we must find a case for the snake, or people will be stealing the ribs."

Several tiny monkey skulls had already been set, like pale-faced demonic dolls, into the wall. Other creatures still needed to be assembled. Presently, they intermingled into calciferous cross-breeds in bags and boxes stacked against the bone-indented walls.

"I am satisfied with the progress," said Sami. Next month, he thought, it would be ready for its grand public debut. "Maybe," he joked, "the president himself will come to the opening."

Fufu was still waiting by the museum door when Sami emerged. She bleated and nuzzled his palm. He had one final task to complete before heading to his clinic. Several of his glossy brown Cameroon sheep had delivered lambs, and the nursing ewes had to be checked to ensure they were better mothers than Fufu's. If not, as frequently happened, Sami would take the hungry babies home to bottle-feed. With Fufu by his side, he strolled through the zoo to the slaughterhouse. He dragged open the slaughterhouse's huge corrugated doors and walked through, avoiding the dark puddles. Fufu, hesitant in the white-tiled hangar with its strange smell, its cleavers, and its rusty hooks, trotted close behind.

Out at the back was a quiet stable, where coffee-colored babies bleated and burrowed, shielding themselves from the chill. Their mothers stood quietly chewing hay, placid, warm, and content as a row of middle-aged women at the hairdresser. Sami picked up the lambs and looked them over, one by one. They were bright-eyed and struggling. Tonight there would be no new additions to the Khader household. His wife would be glad, Uzhdan disappointed. Sami let the last lamb, still unsteady on its long legs, drop clumsily back into its stable. He picked up his briefcase. "Come, Fufu," he said, shivering.

Sami pushed open the iron door to his laboratory and set a kettle on to brew. Fufu hovered outside as Sami prodded at a carcass in a bucket and checked the glue on a severed ostrich head. The kettle whistled. Sami fetched a tea bag. He took his box of sweeteners from his satchel, dropped two pellets into his tea, and offered Fufu a slice of shortcake.

Chapter Four
March 2006

At a time when people have no bread,
the menageries must be destroyed.
—*ENCYCLOPÉDIE*, 1751–1772

he common hippopotamus leads a double life. It must browse on land for great quantities of vegetation—a hundred pounds or more—each day, but spend much of its time underwater to keep from drying out. It belongs to the pachyderms, meaning "thick skin," but loses water, through a paper-thin epidermis, three times faster than other mammals. It appears ungainly on dry land, but can outrun a human being. It may hold its breath, submerged, for five minutes. Prehistoric flaps cover the nose and ears, making them watertight; calves are born and suckle underwater and swim toward the light to take their first breath. In the wild, lions attack fewer humans than hippos do. More people are killed by hippos each year than are run over by London buses.

The name stems from the ancient Greek words *hippos* and *potamius*, meaning "riverine horse," and the animal's split personality confused and fascinated the people of antiquity and beyond. Herodotus thought that the hippo had "the mane and tail of a horse, visible tusks, and a voice like a horse's neigh." In a seventeenth-century translation of his *Historia Naturalis*, Pliny the Elder said that "when he setteth forward to any field for his releefe, he goes alwaies backeward, and his tracts are seene leading from thence, to the end, that against his return he should not be forelaied, nor followed by his footing." The hippo was believed to sweat blood. Thomas Babington Macaulay called it "the ugliest of the works of God."

Ancient Egypt, too, noticed the dichotomous nature of this hulking creature that milled the waters of her Green and Blue Niles. In one incarnation the hippo was Seth, god of chaos and wild desert storms, who fought underwater against his nephew, Horus, for the throne of Egypt. In another, the hippopotamus became Tauret, goddess of childbirth and creation, a pregnant hippo cow with breasts that swept the floor. George Washington's false teeth were carved from hippo tusks. Obaysche, the first hippo to reach Europe since Roman times, inspired the "Hippopotamus Polka," which took nineteenth-century salons by storm. After World War II, a hippo named Knautschke became a celebrity, one of only ninety-one survivors of an original two thousand inhabitants at the Berlin Zoo.

The hippopotamus, the largest living artiodactyl, is a dangerous vegetarian with a baritone bellow that can reach a hundred and fifteen decibels. Its famously languid yawn is actually a threat of violence. Its inch-thick hide can withstand a bullet shot, but it has no enemies except others of its own species. Its great teeth are capable of crushing a limb like a matchstick, yet it uses them only for pulverizing grass. And, so long as its simple needs for browsing and bathing are met, it is easily kept in captivity.

Suzanne, a journalist on assignment from Germany, pulled a camera from her satchel and snapped a picture of Dubi, Qalqilya Zoo's fifteen-year-old hippopotamus.

"Wait," said Dr. Sami. "Dubi!" The hippo heaved his great bulk around and ambled to the fence. "Eftah, Dubi!" shouted Sami. "Eftah! Eftah!" Dubi obliged, opening his great mouth to expose thick, yellow teeth. He yawned, gurgling. Suzanne took a picture.

"You see?" beamed Sami. "All the animals here listen to me."

Dubi had arrived at the zoo not long before Sami himself, in 1999. A zoo-born adolescent male, he had been rejected by the rest of his Israeli herd, or "bloat." He was bitten, nudged, and attacked and eventually transferred from Israel to Qalqilya. The alternative, said his original keepers, was suffering or death. Now, they smiled with satisfaction, he could look forward to twenty-five years of undisturbed browsing in his Palestinian home, with just a few strutting peacocks and their dizzy chicks for company.

No one can quite decide whether hippos are gregarious or solitary and how far they will push their claims to territory. Scientists have described the hippo as "socially schizophrenic." Some hippopotami form bachelor herds. Dominant males often manage to ingratiate themselves into a maternal group, which may number up to one hundred and fifty. Others, like Dubi and the famous Huberta, seem content to remain alone.

Huberta was born in Natal, South Africa, in the 1920s, and during the course of her short life she wandered, alone, for thousands of miles across the country. She strayed into fields, settlements, and vegetable gardens, where some villagers received her as a good omen, the incarnation of a long-dead chief, while others rued the day she lumbered onto their property. Once, in Durban, she walked calmly down the main street. She nibbled at a fruit stall, then looked in on a local cinema, wherein Charles King trilled, "You Were Meant for Me." She trampled an exclusive golf course and gate-crashed a country club party. Finally in 1931, Huberta met her end; three hunters, unaware of her celebrity, shot her dead in the Keiskamma River. South Africans mourned Huberta, and the killers were hunted down. They were each fined £25 for destroying "royal game" protected by the authorities.

"Isn't he lonely?" asked Suzanne, as Dubi ambled away.

"No. Did you get a good picture?"

"I think so," said Suzanne, "Where to next?"

Suzanne was the first journalist to visit the zoo in six months, and Sami had decided to pull out all the stops to ensure she got what he felt was a good scoop. He had, to her dismay, introduced her to Fateen and offered her the opportunity to stroke Rama's head. He had rattled the bars of the badger's cage so that he woke up and showed his striped nose, and then demonstrated that the wolves regarded him as their alpha male, sending them slinking into corners, tails between their legs.

"The Carnivore Department," he said. Sami led the way, pointing out Wahib the camel, the new Cameroon babies, and Fufu along the route.

Suzanne stopped to talk to the cross-eyed old keeper.

"Hello," she said, "Can you tell me your name?"

"I am Abdel Raouf Joadi," he replied. Unbidden, he continued. "I have worked here for many years and enjoy my job very much. I have a home, two boys and girl, though my past has its sadness. Five years ago, my youngest son Ibrahim was killed by soldiers. He was sixteen, just a boy. He threw a stone, and a soldier shot him. When I got to the hospital, he was already dead. I lost my son for nothing, for a single stone. No one gave me money or offered to help, but one soldier came to my home to say he was sorry. I buried my son with my own hands."

The keeper smiled, shook the journalist's hand, and went back to sweeping.

Next, Sami showed her a baby deer, born just one hour earlier, its umbilical cord still attached. Its tail wiggled with pleasure as it nuzzled its mother for milk. An addax, its shaggy antelope coat still brown for the winter, was limping. "I'll check it tomorrow," said Sami. "It's because of the cold." Suzanne made a note in her spiral-bound book.

At the Carnivore Department building site, work appeared to be progressing nicely. A series of low concrete walls had appeared, marking out the boundaries of the new cages. Clusters of iron struts sprang from them like reeds. A single lilac tree, in early bloom, had been planted in the center of an otherwise barren plot. There were no workers in sight. "These enclosures are for the leopards," said Sami, pointing past the lilac tree. "They will be ten times larger than the cages they have now. And that one over there," he pointed again, "will be for my two groups of bears. Eventually, this will be an international zoo."

"How long will all this take?"

"Two months."

Ruti strolled over and peered over her fence at Sami and his guest. "Do you know the sad story of our giraffes?"

Suzanne shook her head.

With relish, Sami launched into the tale of the death of Brownie. He moved on to the difficulties of obtaining new animals and rattled off a soliloquy on the educational benefits of his new museum. But, though Suzanne responded with the appropriate nodding and raising of eyebrows, she had weightier topics on her mind.

"Is it true," she butted in, "that the new government has banned music in the zoo?"

The question took Sami by surprise. He stopped and stared. "Could you repeat, please?"

"The music," she spoke clearly and slowly. "I was told it had been turned off."

It was true that, until recently, twangy instrumental music had been piped incessantly around the zoo, particularly at weekends and on holidays. It had irritated Dr. Sami, especially when he was trying to think, and probably, he believed, had the same effect on the inhabitants. It was true, too, that the new council had ordered it turned off. Yet somehow, this journalist made it sound terrible.

"Yes," Sami began slowly, "it is true. This is because no international zoos play music. It disturbs the animals."

"So it's not because of religion?"

"No. It is noisy. It was a mistake, and we corrected it."

"And the fountain," she continued, "the one at the entrance?"

"What about it?"

"Why isn't it working?"

"Because it is not complete."

"Not because a fountain is a sort of sculpture, and sculptures are forbidden by the religious authorities?"

"What? No. Not at all."

They walked from the building site, Sami deep in thought, and down onto the main avenue.

"Another thing—"

"Yes?"

"I've heard that you have an employee to separate men and women."

Sami stopped walking and stared at her.

"To keep men and women apart," she repeated.

"Ah," replied Sami, "you mean the kissing man."

Bassam Bogdadi was thirty-four years old. Originally a farmer, he had worked at the zoo for nine months. Most of his land had been taken away to build the Wall, and last winter the small remainder flooded, the Wall preventing drainage of rainwater. He lost his crop of vegetables. "So I came to work here," he told the journalist dourly, "to stop children throwing things at the animals, and to keep people from kissing. I am the couple catcher." He was sallow and unsmiling, with a wandering eye.

"You see," elaborated Sami, "in our culture, we do not show affection in public. Maybe for you, in your country, one man has a girlfriend and he can kiss her in any place. In your country, this is freedom. He can even kiss her in the road, or in a taxi, or in your zoo. But here, we do not wish to see this. This is our freedom." Bassam Bogdadi nodded solemnly.

Sami continued. "So, then, maybe a man and his girlfriend decide to kiss at the zoo anyway. And maybe some other ladies come to sit down and must watch them. And they say 'For shame! They can not do this in the street. Why is this allowed in the zoo?' Then they will report to the municipal council about the terrible things they saw here. And we will bear the consequences. We must stop these things before they start."

"So he doesn't separate men and women entirely?"

"Of course not. Even in a mosque, a man may enter with his wife. There is no separation."

Bassam Bogdadi shifted his weight awkwardly. Two couples strolled past, the men yards ahead, the women, veiled and giggling, following behind. "Not typical," said Sami quickly. "Not enforced. Let's go."

Suzanne took a step forward, but Bassam Bogdadi placed one hand on her arm. She stopped. One eye stared at her intently. "I have only one child," he said. "As a Muslim, I would like to have more, but I do not know what the future will bring."

Suzanne looked baffled. She nodded politely and hurried after Sami, who was keen to impress more indelibly upon her his plans for an international zoo.

◆　　　◆　　　◆

A humane and spacious zoo is generally considered a modern concept. Grasslands mimicking nature, where big cats have the freedom to prowl, aviaries where eagles can spread their broad wings, and desert sands where prairie dogs bob and hide are today the hallmarks of Dr. Sami's international zoo. The public is displeased to see big cats pulling out their hair or polar bears pacing in pits. "Stereotypic" behavior, the bane of zoologists, is no longer tolerated.

The body that certifies institutions worthy of international accolade is the World Association of Zoos and Aquaria, or WAZA, for short. Sami knew it well. Its members must adhere to a strict code of ethics that underlie all the basic tenets on which the zoo is to be run: Conservation. Education. Sustainability and biodiversity. The association was founded in Rotterdam in 1946, and its network extends to some twelve hundred institutions, welcoming more than six hundred million zoo visitors each year. During the 1980s, its influence grew considerably, as more and more Western zoos knocked down their 1960s eyesores, their Bauhaus elephant houses and penguin pools of cool, aesthetic concrete. They evolved. They created teaching programs. They bred endangered species and jumped on the bandwagon of the principled, ethical modern zoo.

It was access to this network that Sami craved. He would be WAZA's first Palestinian member. In the entire Middle East, there were just five members. Three were in Israel; two, a thousand miles away, in Dubai and Abu Dhabi. But Sami's new museum would provide education. He would restart long-abandoned plans for conservation. His Carnivore Department, Crocodile Island, and new, integrated Monkey House would illustrate biodiversity, and his stocks would become sustainable. After the cats, crocodiles, and monkeys, he would start freeing up the birds, the reptiles, and the remaining small animals.

"I will have a large aviary here," Sami told Suzanne, as they passed close to a disused space at the heart of the zoo, "with flamingos, ducks, and parrots. I have many dreams."

Suzanne glanced around. Two little boys were chucking marbles into the lion cage. Bassam Bogdadi was nowhere in sight. She kept her lips pressed firmly shut.

The first zoos to experiment with the illusion of freedom were the ancient collections of the Middle East. Sennacherib, king of Assyria in the seventh century BCE, recreated a vast marsh he particularly admired and populated it with plants and free-ranging animals of its native species. His, some believe, were the Hanging Gardens of Babylon, located not in Babylon itself but at a palace in the city of Nineveh, with terraced ziggurats planted with foliage to resemble vegetation-covered mountains. A century later, the *Paradeisos* pleasure gardens the Persians built in captured Babylon offered spacious grounds for their inhabitants. In the fourth and fifth centuries BCE, captured herbivores grazed in roomy Egyptian paddocks. The sixteenth-century zoos of Akbar the Great, Mogul emperor of India, were established to instill in his subjects a love of animals. Enclosures emulated nature, entrance was free, and each zoo had its own dedicated resident vet.

The man considered the father of the modern zoological garden, however, did not appear until the nineteenth century. His name was Karl Hagenbeck, son of a fishmonger who moved unwittingly into the animal business when a fisherman brought him a gift of two live sea lions. Hagenbeck took quickly to his father's new trade and in just a handful of years became the animal impresario of the age. His Tierpark zoo near Hamburg, established at the turn of the twentieth century, was of its time the finest in the world. Hagenbeck created Europe's first barless cages, and the illusion of infinite freedom for his captives. He landscaped rock faces for his gazelles and a wilderness for his panthers. "I desired, above all things," he said in his 1910 autobiography, "to give the animals the maximum of liberty. I wished to exhibit them not as captives, confined within narrow spaces, and looked at between iron bars, but as free to wander from place to place within as large a limit as possible, and with no bars to obstruct the view and serve as a reminder of captivity."

Hagenbeck was peddling an illusion. The public preferred to see freedom, so freedom was what they saw, though most of those at liberty inside his zoo had started life in the wild. While the luckier lions ended up in his progressive enclosures, others went off to jump flaming hoops and pull chariots at his brother's school for circus animals. And Hagenbeck always expected a 50 percent mortality rate among animals procured for him from the wild; he had his men capture twice the required number, just in case. For one live tiger cub, the whole pride was sometimes slaughtered.

On Suzanne's way out of the zoo, Amjad Daoud, the young ticket clerk, beckoned her into his booth. "I like animals," he enthused as she took down notes and glanced around, "although I have a degree in business studies. My favorite animal here is Dubi." He thought for a moment. "Some people think he must be lonely, in his field all by himself all day long. But me," he smiled at her, "I am in this booth, day after day, all by myself. And I like it very much. I don't feel lonely, although my friends think I must be." He paused and straightened some books of tickets. "I have myself and my thoughts, though perhaps one day I might marry and have a wife. My best friend moved to South Carolina. He telephones often to tell me how much better life is there. Maybe one day, I'll go too."

"You know," considered Sami, as he accompanied Suzanne to a taxi waiting beyond the gates, "maybe if you had read these things in the newspaper, you would shake your head and say, 'Oh, stupid people.' The same as if I read about people in Africa who eat human meat." He chuckled and whistled. "People have a lot of different faces. We all do. I don't talk to my wife the way that I talk to a client or to my friends. The way I discuss something with you is not the way I discuss something with my children. Things are not always what they seem. This is the truth."

◆　　◆　　◆

Suzanne departed that afternoon with a promise to send Dr. Sami a copy of her newspaper story. He returned to his office, exhilarated to have cleared up her misconceptions, and sat down at his desk. A moment later, a knock came at the door.

"Dr. Sami," said Abu Shir, stepping in, "a parcel arrived for you this morning." He handed Sami a brown paper package, tied with string. The postmark was foreign. Abu Shir pulled up a chair and waited.

Sami took his time. First, he set the kettle on to boil. Then he returned to his seat and rearranged some items on his desk. Finally, with Abu Shir hovering over the package, he carefully sliced it open and extracted the contents. He examined the cool cover of a children's picture book, illustrated by a roofscape of red-walled houses, from whose windows huge, ghostly eyes stared down. *La Notte di Q,* The Night of Q, it read. Sami thumbed its glossy pages. A typewritten letter with an embossed letterhead fell out. "We are pleased to enclose a copy of our new book," it read, "and would like to invite you to a book reading, and discussion, on the eighth of May, in Rome." The attached pages, it continued, contained a translation of the book's text. Sami rocked back in his chair.

"What is it?" asked Abu Shir.

"It is a book."

"A book about what?"

"I think," Sami said, frowning, "it is about me."

That night, Sami took the picture book home to his favorite armchair and pulled Hend, his younger daughter, up onto his lap. Uzhdan brought him slippers and a plateful of dinner and settled down beside him.

Sami turned the book over in his hands. Once, long ago, he had dreamed of becoming a writer. For years, as a boy, he had labored secretly over a manuscript, finally sending it off for appraisal to a literary committee in Riyadh.

The results had not been encouraging.

"This story," came the stiff reply, "has been taken from an Egyptian movie. It is not the thinking of one man. The writer needs more experience. He needs to learn about the art of story-telling. This is a man who knows nothing about fiction. This writer should read more books."

Sami had burned the manuscript in a flurry of alphabetical fragments and taken up taxidermy. But he still enjoyed, whenever time permitted, a good book. Uzhdan, since early childhood, had inherited her father's love of literature, and was poised, eagerly waiting for him to begin.

"Some say," he commenced, reading from the translated pages while leafing to the original's corresponding page, "this is the strangest of all strange things ever to happen in the town of Q."

Hend wriggled on his lap. Sami took a bite of spaghetti.

"At a certain hour," he continued,

"on a certain day
of a certain year
(not so many years ago)
the people of Q were ordered into their homes and weren't
*   allowed back out.*
Day in and day out, quiet as mice, still as sunning snakes,
they watched from their windows
and nothing but wind and dust rollicked along the empty
*   streets of Q."*

A key turned in the front door lock. With a rustle of shopping bags, Sami's wife stepped in. She was dressed in a floor-length dull blue coat, a dark headscarf framing her oval face. Quickly, she deposited both on a chair in the corner. Underneath, she wore a tight sweater and stonewashed jeans and emerged into the light as if from a cocoon. She shook her hair, took a tub of olives from a carrier bag, and walked into the living room.

Sami looked up.

"It is about Qalqilya," he told her, "and the zoo."

She perched on the arm of his chair, placed a hand on his shoulder, and looked down at the book. It had been a hard afternoon. After a long illness, her sister's husband had finally died two days before, and the family was in the thick of mourning. Sami had seen his brother-in-law, younger than himself, in his final moments, yellowish and rasping, but had had to leave the room. He found death of that nature far too disturbing. He continued reading.

La Notte di Q told the story of a zoo veterinarian at a time of war. A veterinarian so brave and committed that eventually, in the dead of night and at intense personal risk, he is compelled to break curfew and steal out of his home to provide food for his suffering charges. Ragheb, the youngest son of the courageous hero, follows his father, curious to learn where he might be headed and fearful for his capture.

Sami, spellbound, turned to the last page. The story ended amid the stalls of deer and donkeys.

"I had to come.
I haven't been able to feed them for days.
Enough of them have already died.
From fright and fear
And the gunfire at night.
This horrible curfew, Ragheb."
His voice trailed off and his head dropped.
"I couldn't let them starve."
"I understand," said the boy.

Many of the animals had now reached the light

And were eating the food that Sami,
Veterinarian by trade
And keeper of the zoo
In the city of Q
Had brought them.

Sami finished his spaghetti and scraped the bowl clean. "They want me to go to Italy," he told his wife, "to discuss the book. They think this is the real story. They think I am a hero." He was deeply puzzled. "But I do not have a son named Ragheb. I'm not sure if I ever met these people." He rubbed his eyes and yawned. "I will think about it in the morning."

◆　　◆　　◆

The next morning, Abu Shir was disgruntled. He glowered and pouted, going about his vague business with angry intent. Keepers were cautious as he strode the zoo's avenues, brow furrowed, a piece of paper in hand and a cigarette wedged between his lips. He had learned, from Sami, all about the tale told in the children's picture book. But, he had always maintained, it was he, and not Dr. Sami Khader, who had once saved the zoo.

It was, he stressed whenever the opportunity arose to relate his tale, a time of hardship. The year 2001 was the worst of all. There were twenty-four-hour curfews that went on for weeks. The longest lasted twenty-seven days straight, only broken by a grace period of two hours every four or five days. Then there was a scramble, as people clamored for medical supplies, food, tobacco, bottled water, and candles in case the electricity should fail again.

During these days, neither vet nor keeper could reach the zoo. Abu Shir, alone, stole from his house in the dead of night, flying in the face of the curfew, and entered the zoo through a hidden back door. There he stayed, sleeping in his office for a week, single-handedly tossing food to the animals whenever it was safe to venture outside. He did not, he said, see another human soul.

The markets were closed, so food was in short supply. For the snakes and carnivores, the problem was not so dire, since they only needed food, a great lump of flesh, every few days. The smaller herbivores—the deer, addax, and zebra—could be satisfied by a sack or two of hay or alfalfa. But Dubi, with his enormous hunger for greenstuffs, had an appetite that must be sated. His pool, too, would have to be refilled at regular intervals, since it was midsummer and water evaporated quickly.

At night, Abu Shir crept out to the fields. Crops rotted, and trees hung heavy with fruit. Dubi's diet grew experimental. The zoo manager picked as much as he could carry and curried favors from the only kinds of vehicles still allowed out on the streets: ambulances and the municipality maintenance vehicles sent out to fix the electricity cables and pylons that errant tanks had torn down. He had sacks of vegetables brought to the zoo on stretchers or lugged in with the help of electrical engineers. He left a hose running constantly, burbling inadequately into Dubi's pool, sometimes spilling over to soak with difficulty into cracked, dry mud. He tapped fire hydrants when the pipe ran dry.

Once, during a break between curfews, Abu Shir said he had managed to secure a lorry load of straw for the hippo from Jenin. The lorry arrived at the checkpoint, where the manager was waiting to meet it. A soldier refused to let it pass. Abu Shir spoke, in Hebrew, directly to an officer. "This is not for the people," he said, "it is for a hippo. You will not be helping our people by letting this pass." The soldier nodded, and the lorry passed through. The straw, he recalled, fed Dubi for an entire week.

But Dr. Sami had different memories, and Abu Shir was not among them.

"I am not this man, this hero," he said at breakfast, tapping the picture book that lay gleaming on the dining table. "But I could be. I could go there to that meeting, in that place, and say, 'It's right. This is all true. I saved the zoo.' Why not? It would be very nice. This," he glanced darkly at his wife, "is what some other people would do."

Sami's earliest experience of life amid the intifada had occurred precisely one week before it began. Having recently completed, at Dr. Motke's arrangement, a three-month apprenticeship at a safari park near Tel Aviv, one of Israel's three precious international zoos, he had asked his teachers to visit to discuss plans for the future. They sat in the Friends' Restaurant, sharing a plate of hummus and smoking a narghile, and outlined an idea to open a series of wildlife hospitals across the region. They would conserve indigenous species, track migrating falcons and rare eagles. Sami, they said, would take a specialist course on the subject and head the West Bank clinic. The group was on top of the world, recalled Sami, as they bade each other farewell that afternoon. In his excitement, the safari park's head vet forgot to pick up his briefcase, and Sami took it home to keep it safe. There it would sit, gathering dust in his hallway, for a year and a half.

The first time he came face-to-face with a tank, he was afraid. Sami was a stranger to conflict; his childhood home, though difficult in many ways, had been quiet, and he knew of armed struggle only from the stories of his family. The tank had already been stationed outside the main gate to the zoo for some days, discouraging visitors. The staff had taken to coming in through the hidden back door. Sami was sipping tea with a group of his workers in the picnic garden when the tank shuddered into action and began to roll its way up the avenue toward them. Its gun antenna reeled menacingly. Sami's instinct was to run for cover, but keeper Abdel Raouf Joadi stopped him. "Keep still," he said. "You don't know what they are thinking." The tank stood motionless for several minutes, then swiveled and retreated. Sami raised his teacup with shaking hands.

One morning, Sami woke to the sound of loud voices in the street. The sky was azure, cloudless, and serene. Soldiers had entered early. All men aged between eighteen and forty, barked their announcements, were to leave their houses and be rounded up for inspection. Sami dressed hastily and tripped, bleary-eyed, down the stairs. With one tank in front and another behind, a batch of thirty men, with Sami in their midst, made their way down a quiet hill.

"What will they do with us now?" someone asked Sami.

"Hush," he replied. "Keep on walking."

At the bottom of the hill, they reached a girls' school. The soldiers shooed the men into the playground and ordered them to take off their shirts. The men watched the sun slowly arc overhead as heat rose from the playground floor. Two young soldiers were left behind to guard them, one short and burly, the other tall and thin. Both were pink and sweating beneath the weight of their uniforms. Occasionally, Sami burst into a fit of giggles. "Don't laugh!" cried the thin soldier anxiously.

During the afternoon, a volley of shots erupted somewhere just outside the school gates. The soldiers dropped to the ground and covered their heads with their hands. The crowd chuckled. Later, the men were told to line up with their hands on their heads. "Shut up and show me your identity card," said the burly soldier to Sami, who was first in line. His hands clasped behind his head, he motioned with his eyes to his shirt pocket.

"Do as I say," snapped the soldier.

Sami motioned up to his hands.

"Funny," the soldier allowed with a smile. "Now get the card."

At five o'clock, the men were released, and Sami hurried back to his wife, who was waiting at her brother's apartment. Soldiers had been there, too. One had damaged the front door, though they opened it voluntarily, and put the butt of his rifle through the fish tank. Some of the fish were saved when the children scooped them into a jug of drinking water; others flipped out of reach on the floor.

Although it was dangerous to break curfew, his wife was so concerned for their own home that Sami decided to risk the hundred-yard trip, against dire warnings from his wife's family. When he arrived, he found their apartment untouched.

To signal a break in curfew, the soldiers usually commandeered the town's mosques and made announcements through the minaret's megaphones. Sami would wait anxiously, sometimes for days, for these moments. Then, immediately, he would spring into action, dividing labor between the only two keepers willing to lend a hand, old Abdel Raouf Joadi and reliable Yail Misqawi. Abu Shir, Sami recalled, was nowhere to be seen.

Together, the three men would dash out to feed and inspect the animals. For the herbivores, they stockpiled hay in the barn and rushed to see what could be picked up from the market, which also came to life for those two hours of respite. Some farmers helped the zoo voluntarily, dropping crates of damaged, overripe, or unsold stock at the gates. Others brought dead sheep, goats, or cattle, which were quickly sliced up or fed whole to the big cats. Sometimes the town's electricity supply was cut off. Then they fed the animals in the dark.

Dubi was a special case and caused Sami much anxiety. He left the taps running to keep the hippo afloat, but feared the supply might be severed, the hose spring a leak, or the water run out. He frantically piled rotting fruit, vegetables, and straw into the hippo's shelter but worried the creature might turn it down or eat it all and still want more. What if a hungry hippo broke out of his enclosure in search of food? He might kill the other, smaller herbivores, but he would be no match for a tank. Sami did the best he could and spent the rest of his time worrying, reconstructing skeletons to soothe his ragged nerves.

Often, late at night, Sami sat up in his armchair in the living room, thinking about Dubi. Should he risk breaking the curfew and go out to check on him? Should he sneak away to top up his haystack and his pool? The streets were patrolled by tanks and armored jeeps. Those caught breaking the curfew were shot on sight. What use would he be then to his family and his animals? Would the death of a heroic zookeeper, clutching a bag of apples, help secure them a safe and healthy future?

"This man talks a lot," was Sami's grim response when he heard Abu Shir relating his own tales of bravery. "Perhaps he kept himself so well hidden that even I did not spot him. If I were him, I'd keep my heroic deeds to myself."

Many zookeepers in the world's most troubled zones have shown bravery and forbearance in the face of trouble. The keepers of Jerusalem Zoo, during the War of Independence, faced sniper fire to keep their animals safe. At the Kuwait Zoo, requisitioned by Iraqi forces in 1991, volunteer caretakers collected food and bribed Iraqi soldiers to let them in.

The public, instead of deeming their zoos a needless national burden, has rallied around them in times of trouble. In Budapest during World War II, citizens fought to keep their hippopotami alive despite a dearth of fresh grass. All the straw items in the city—hats, mats, bags, and slippers—were donated, collected, and shredded for the hippos to eat.

Except for three small deer, nothing starved to death at Qalqilya Zoo during even the longest of the curfews. A hose, a haystack, and a supply of overripe vegetables kept Dubi alive. A few weeks after Suzanne's visit, a picture of Dubi's grinning face accompanied a sympathetic story about a struggling Palestinian zoo in a German newspaper.

Dr. Sami would not go to Rome.

Chapter Five
May 2006

A wolf caught a sheep, and when the shep-
herd pursued it, the wolf said, "Who will be
its guard on the day of wild beasts, when
there will be no shepherd for it but me?"
—HADITHS OF AL-BUKHARI, VOLUME 3, BOOK 39

And the wolf shall dwell with the lamb,
and the leopard shall lie down with the kid;
and the calf and the young lion and the fatling together;
and a little child shall lead them.
—ISAIAH 11.6

It was the end of May. Qalqilya's short winter had long since departed, and the building blocks of summer heat were slowly being cemented into place. The fields were thirsty and brushed with thistles. Bougainvillea cascaded violent pink blooms over crumbling garden walls. A prefabricated cabin erected by an Italian charity announced that "Community Based Activities for Youth" and "Psycho Social Counseling" were now available at the entrance to town. The Palestine Photography Studio on the main street was doing a brisk trade. A line of mothers, bored children tugging at their skirts, waited to have stiff photographic portraits taken to accompany enrollment forms for the coming school year. A Druze in a white pillbox hat and flowing robes yelled into his mobile phone and dashed across the street, dodging donkey carts. The mayor had been released from prison.

It was six months since Dr. Motke's visit, four since work on the Carnivore Department had begun, and two months, municipality engineers insisted, until its completion. At the zoo, Dr. Sami was harried and unshaven. It was a busy morning. The night before, one of the last lambs of the season had been born to a Cameroon ewe, who emphatically ignored it. Sami took it home to nurse, plying it with human infant formula from a plastic baby bottle, but it was weak and died quietly in the night. Uzhdan was still crying as she set off for school.

This morning, he had found a second baby lamb abandoned by another dispassionate mother. It seemed stronger than the first, but each time it tottered toward the female to suckle, she kicked it away. With the help of Yail Misqawi, Sami had managed to corner the ewe so that her baby might take at least a few gulps of milk. But the lamb's eager suckling did nothing to induce her maternal instincts, so Sami collected the baby and settled it down into a bed of hay in a cardboard box in his office. Uzhdan would delight in the arrival of a second baby lamb at the Khader household that evening. As usual, her mother would be less impressed.

Sami had arrived early to receive and repair a small silver fox whose back legs had been caught in a hunter's snare. A farmer from a neighboring village had pitied the tiny creature he found whimpering in pain and brought it to the zoo for treatment. It lay sadly in the corner of a dark cage, all eyes and ears. Sami had set its legs in plaster, brought it a portion of fresh minced meat, and tried to tempt it into eating. It sniffed the meal but turned away. Sami feared it would die of shock.

Had this been any normal morning, such events would have provided ample distraction. But the previous afternoon, Dr. Sami had received a telephone call from Motke Levinson. The Berber sheep would finally be arriving, along with a bonus consignment of six spare wolves, in just half an hour's time, and he was required to be at the entrance of town to meet them.

As Sami rushed about his duties on one side of town, another new arrival was taking his place on the other, settling down, and being briefed on the goings-on at Qalqilya Zoo. A secretary clutching two piles of papers hurried about the top floor of the municipality building. She placed the first pile inside Nidal Jaloud's office, where the little international relations officer popped bubble gum and talked on the telephone. He nodded to her and continued his conversation. "I have been on sick *leave*," he said, "but now I am better. Unfortunately," he continued in a different vein, "it is difficult for soldiers to distinguish who might be a Bom-ber. A doctor or an engineer, for example, would not do this. Most Bom-bers are tres jeunes. But the soldiers do not know this. What's that? Oh yes, yes, thank you, I feel much better after my sick *leave*."

Next door, the secretary silently slipped the second pile of papers onto the mayor's wide desk.

Mayor Wajeeh Qawas was a neat man with a fresh-out-of-prison cleanliness. His hair was newly cut and with a sprinkling of gray. His plain gray suit, too, was new. His beard was clipped short and precise, and he wore a plastic digital watch. A serious demeanor masked a young face. He was well educated and had been studying for a master's degree in planning and political development before he was imprisoned.

Despite his ill health, he appeared full of restrained vitality. Yesterday morning, in jail, he had been roused from bed and informed that he was to be released. He had never been brought before a magistrate. An army jeep drove him back to Qalqilya and deposited him at the entrance to town. He had walked home, alone, from there.

Across the desk, Deputy Mayor Hashem al-Masri looked relaxed. He was relieved to be back at the pharmaceutical counter and had come to work with neither a suit nor a tie. His beige shirtsleeves were rolled up, and he leaned back in his chair. He sipped a cup of black coffee and puffed on a cigarette.

For him, the change could not have come at a better time.

The West Bank was in turmoil. Petrol had run out, cash had been cut, and overseas handouts had been suspended. There was no more money in the national coffers, and teachers, doctors, policemen, and soldiers were entering their fourth month without pay. Borders had been tightened and roadblocks increased. In Gaza, according to radio reports and frightened relatives, they were starting to fight each other.

In Qalqilya, the government employee who had not received a check could not pay the rent. The landlord agreed to defer payment until the following month, which left him, too, short of funds. In order to make up the shortfall, he bought his groceries on credit from the baker, the greengrocer, and the butcher. The butcher, baker, and grocer, faced with dozens of people unable to settle their accounts, could not pay their own landlords or their utility bills. Their electricity bills, paid directly to the municipality, went into the red. The municipality, which bought its electricity across the border, struggled to cover the costs of its mounting debt. If it could not, the town's entire electricity supply might be switched off.

But coping with these shortfalls left the municipality strapped on other fronts. Work on the Carnivore Department had been scaled back. The labor was there, idling in the sunshine, but money for raw materials had been diverted temporarily into other channels. Employees of the zoo, who had so far escaped the pinch, were paid direct by the municipality and feared that their pay packets might be the next to go.

"We see in the news rice and flour arriving in Africa, and everyone fighting for it," said Sami to his best friend Mr. Salaa one evening, over a strawberry-scented narghile. Mr. Salaa, his kind, hooded eyes, long lashes, and drooping nose suggesting a sympathetic disposition, nodded and smiled. "It is good for us that we're big strong men."

Abu Shir, meanwhile, complained noisily.

"I have two grown-up sons," he grew fond of relating. "One works as a policeman, and the other is in the army. They have no salaries, so I feed their families, as well as my wife and Mansur, who is still at home. I have a brother who worked in Israel, but he's no longer allowed there, so I support him too. Now, my salary must stretch between four men, their wives, and all their children."

But his beneficence, he said, did not remain solely within the family.

"One man working in the military," he recounted over lunch at a picnic table, "came to the zoo and told me his wife had sent him out to find her something to cook. 'We don't even have bread,' the man told me. So, I gave him one hundred shekels to buy some."

Sami raised an eyebrow and could not resist replying.

"Several days ago, a policeman came to me for medicine for his pigeons. He told me that he couldn't pay, but what could I do? I gave him the medicine and told him to pay me when he can."

A string of red worry beads was laid out in front of the mayor. Nidal Jaloud slipped into the room, bowed courteously, and sat down. The mayor spoke slowly and emphatically. "My main priority," he said, "is to solve these problems, to have all the institutions of a normal town. For women, for childhood, for infrastructure. The electricity, drainage, roads, traffic."

Deputy Mayor Hashem al-Masri nodded.

"It was a double-edged feeling to be elected from a distance," he continued. "On the one hand, it alleviated the pain of prison. On the other, it was a terrible situation, being entrusted with decisions on the part of the people, but being unable to serve them."

The deputy nodded again.

"But," the mayor continued, "there are good signs. Of course, we must be optimistic. It has been said that optimism is life. I look forward to a peaceful, just life."

"I say," Nidal Jaloud interjected, "'Drop the gun, it's time for fun!'"

There was a pause. The mayor looked at his worry beads. The deputy turned his empty coffee cup a quarter turn in its saucer. Nidal Jaloud glanced down at his neatly clipped nails.

"So, the zoo." Hashem al-Masri coughed, breaking the silence. "The renovations have commenced. I am told they will be completed in two months. The vet, Dr. Khader, has a dream to make it an international zoo."

Nidal Jaloud smothered a snigger.

"Currently, of course, you have to put these words in parentheses," the deputy admitted. "Compared to zoos in Europe, in terms of types of animals, size of facility, availability of resources, it is poor."

"It's a dream!" Nidal Jaloud burst out. "A *pipe* dream! Not realistic, never going to succeed!" The mayor glared. "But then," Jaloud continued nervously, "the dreams of yesterday are the facts of today. The dreams of today might be the facts of tomorrow."

"We must be proud, of course, to have it," said the mayor, turning to his deputy, "and we must look forward to developing it. But," he added cautiously, "it is a matter of alleviating the hardships faced by the people before pushing forward with other concerns."

The deputy rose. It was time to get back to the pharmacy. "We are also setting up a Natural History Museum," he said, "which will include the animals that pass away. So nothing, at least, is going to waste."

It was rare that anything went to waste at the zoo. The excess Cameroon sheep were sold for their coats. The innards of animals that Sami stuffed were, where possible, fed to the carnivores. The issue of waste disposal had even caused a conflict among the keepers, who disagreed on the fate of the cage packed with common pigeons.

"What are we to do when there are too many?" asked Abdel Rauf Joadi, who was especially fond of birds.

"We'll kill them, of course," replied Yail Misqawi.

"I could take them home, to my coop."

"This is not allowed."

"Then why not just set them free?"

"Don't be a fool. The crocodiles like them."

Today, however, Qalqilya Zoo was expecting somebody else's leftovers.

The zoo was busy, filled with small boys on a school trip. The municipality had waived the entrance fee in response to the cessation of governmental wages, and schoolteachers were taking advantage of the offer. The cracked, empty swimming pool had been filled to knee height from a single dribbling tap, and dozens of boys in their underwear splashed about. Everywhere, trees were in bloom, sprinkled with tiny mauve flowers. A man was spinning vivid pink candyfloss for a group of girls in pressed blue uniforms and neat gingham pinafores. Sami hurried past to the waiting municipal van.

Abu Shir was already inside. He was in a rare state of happy animation and chatted excitedly. He went over and over the details. *What time had Dr. Motke left this morning? Where had he come*

from? What time would he arrive, and where, exactly, was he now?
Sami ignored him, and the manager's inquiries shifted to the animals. *How many sheep would be coming? And how many wolves? Of which sex, young or old? Dr. Motke told you three? I thought I heard four. Perhaps there'll be four. It would be nice if there were four.* Then, Abu Shir harassed the driver. *Not this way, that way. Turn here. Why don't you hurry past these carts?* The driver pressed his horn and pushed through languid traffic.

At the entrance to town, a flatbed truck had just arrived, hauling a dark green trailer with airholes puncturing the top. To the back of the truck was strapped a large wire cage and two plastic dog carriers. In the driver's seat, an Israeli man, tanned and muscular, sat smoking a cigarette. Dr. Motke pulled over, beside the truck.

Before the municipality van rolled to a halt, Sami jumped out, greeting the new arrivals with enthusiastic handshakes. Abu Shir tarried in the background, trying to calculate the total number of carrying cages. From his vantage point, he could not see the second plastic dog carrier, which was hidden between the wire cage and the rear of the truck cabin.

"They told me four," he mumbled, bitterly disappointed.

Inside the wire cage, one wolf was swaying on its feet, still reeling obliviously in anesthetic. The truck driver, in contrast, looked nervous. He would not venture into Qalqilya itself but would stay behind to guard Motke's car. He had brought with him an ample supply of cigarettes and Coca-Cola and a good strong stick.

It had been virtually impossible, Motke said, to find someone willing to come even this far; few would traverse the checkpoint, let alone the entrance to town.

Qalqilya had not seen so much excitement since the day the lions arrived. Men carving bedposts in a furniture shop stopped to watch as the truck progressed down the main street, with Motke in the driver's seat and Sami perched beside him. Behind them, the municipality van carried Abu Shir, who smoked a cigarette to ease his anxieties. He pulled his mobile phone from his pocket and telephoned Abu Khaled, renovations project engineer, to come to greet the cavalcade.

Back at the zoo cafeteria, the candy floss man was doing a roaring trade in *malabi*, topped with cerise syrup. As the truck pulled in through the gates, little girls spooning the sticky dessert into their mouths turned and stared. Boys clambered out of the swimming pool and ran, half naked, chasing the Nissan pied piper along the overheated avenue.

Abu Shir stepped out of the municipality van into the thick of the throng. "Dr. Motke is a very good man," he confirmed, to nobody in particular.

Suddenly, Yail Misqawi flew by. "Whooo-hooo!" he hooted and lunged at the children, flapping his arms in an attempt to disperse them. They scattered and then reconvened, dripping, behind him. Groups of men started to appear at the fringes of the crowd, swelling its numbers.

Across the way from the Shetland pony enclosure, the truck pulled to a halt. Abdel Raouf Joadi, brandishing his broom, helped Yail Misqawi keep back the masses. The ponies looked on, impervious. One whinnied its disapproval. Abu Shir counted heads, nodding to himself. As Motke unhooked the trailer, he noticed the second, hidden, dog carrier. "It's all right!" the manager cried triumphantly. "They brought five!"

Dr. Motke strode around the truck to investigate the enclosure that Sami had hurriedly made ready for the sheep. Sami caught a small boy banging on the side of the trailer with a stick. He twisted the boy's ear, sending him scuttling away. "Quiet!" he cried to the chattering crowd. "Get back, you boys, and be quiet!

Shall we," he turned to Motke, sweat dripping from his brow, "unload now?"

But Motke was thinking. He stared across the avenue to a larger enclosure containing three ostriches. The male had a pink, featherless rump like that of an enormous oven-ready chicken. Two dowdy females pecked the dust around him.

"Perhaps we should put the sheep in with the ostriches instead," Motke proposed. "The ostrich fence is higher than this one." He signaled to the empty enclosure. "These sheep can jump quite high."

Sami frowned. The cage had been prepared. He had ordered it cleaned, its pond refilled, its sleeping quarters filled with fresh hay. The shaggy, horned Berber sheep of North Africa were experts at jumping, clearing six vertical feet in a single bound if the need arose. But, thought Sami, peering through the trailer's ventilation holes, these sheep looked quite sleepy.

"Here is the problem," he replied. "The keepers will not enter that cage. They are afraid. These ostriches are not friendly." He pointed to the male, who was sizing up a young boy leaning against the fence, with an irritable glint in its eye.

"Hmph," replied Motke.

It was hot, and he hadn't the patience to argue.

Next to the ostriches, the Cameroon flock bleated noisily, its voice like a choir of husky smokers attempting its best impersonation of sheep. Motke unhooked the trailer.

"We were only expecting four sheep," Abu Shir nudged a bystander. "But one of the females delivered, so they threw in the baby. And they brought us five wolves, not the three or four they promised." He smacked the heel of his hand against his forehead. "Too much work!"

Two more wolves were beginning to wake up. Another chased its tail inside its carrying cage.

Clumsily, Yail Misqawi, Abu Shir, and Abdel Raouf Joadi, along with two dozen willing hands from the crowd, lifted the heavy container from the trailer and set it down on the ground. Sami stood in front, issuing elaborate instructions. Ten men gathered on either side, hoisting it onto their shoulders. It proved a mammoth effort to shift it the five yards to the enclosure gate.

Two children thumped on its sides as it passed, and were escorted away by an elderly gentleman with a long beard. In an adjacent enclosure, Wahib the camel lolloped about, upset by the commotion.

Finally, after fifteen solid minutes of shouts, grunts, and gesticulation, the gang of men managed to wedge the container through the narrow gate to the empty enclosure, with Sami straddled on top. "Quiet!" yelled Motke, as boys crowded eagerly around.

With a nod to Motke, Sami leaned down and tugged at an iron rod. The container door swung open. A hush descended. Everyone waited.

Out from the cage, in one skipping rush, came four gray-brown sheep. The crowd surged forward, then, within seconds, thinned and dispersed.

The men moved the container back from the door, and Yail Misqawi set down a smaller pet carrier. He carefully opened the hatch. A baby Berber skittered out. It rushed to find its mother, nuzzled for a moment, then waded into the middle of the small pond and began to drink.

Hot and overwhelmed, Sami locked the enclosure and turned to Dr. Motke. "Now for the wolves."

Sami clambered into the truck's passenger seat as Motke steered the remainder of its cargo across the zoo toward its new home. Sami tutted at the troop of boys that had reassembled, hoping for a second, more exciting delivery.

"I have to send myself to another country," he grumbled. "Really."

Outside the wolves' enclosure, peacocks screeched from perches ranged high along the perimeter wall. Others called back from nearby cages. Purple fruit had fallen from a tree and squelched under the truck's tires. Mushi, the bachelor bear, rocked back on his haunches, watching intently.

Sami and Yail Misqawi manhandled the first of the wolves' cages down from the truck and staggered to the enclosure's entrance at the back of the row of carnivore cages. They passed the leopards, Rama and Chika, and the old hyena, confined to his sleeping quarters. He was suffering from an unsightly skin complaint, huge open sores scattered across his back. Although the condition was not contagious, Sami felt it might repel the public. The hyena's fur was mottled, his back hunched. He had a pug face and a protruding jaw. But his eyes were soft, a pretty hazel flecked with amber. He was timid and seemed lonely.

He took one step forward and watched the wolf go by.

Near their gate, Sami's original wolf pair trotted, agitated, around their perimeter wall. Yail Misqawi unlocked the enclosure door and slid the cage inside. He opened its hatch. Nothing happened. He waited for twenty, thirty seconds, but still no wolf appeared. "Help it," Sami ordered.

Misqawi glanced around and plucked an old rib bone from the floor. Delicately, he inserted it into an airhole and prodded the wolf in the side.

"The scientific method," observed Motke.

Sami wiped his forehead. The bone had the desired effect. The wolf erupted from its cage, made a hasty tour of the enclosure, and dived into the sleeping quarters. With similar encouragement, the next wolf joined it, terrified and cowering.

The third, young and wary, quickly found a corner of the enclosure. It sat down, panting hard, and stared up with interest at a spider on the ceiling. The fourth emerged shivering, its tail tucked between its legs. The last wolf, the only one not to have received an antidote to the anesthetic, swaggered from its traveling cage and promptly lay down, rolling on the sandy ground.

Twenty feet away, Dr. Motke was on his telephone. "They promised me they'd have a new one ready," he hissed. "This one is much too small. But what can I do? They're already here."

Mr. Eesa, the manager's tall, turtlish assistant, sidled up to him. He lit a cigarette and leaned in close.

"Next time, can you tell them to bring us a new giraffe?" he breathed. "We only have one, and he cries all the time since his wife died."

Sami hurried to Motke's side and pulled him away.

"This man," he muttered, "doesn't even know our giraffe is a lady."

Three women walked by, enveloped in white burkas. They giggled behind gauze mouthpieces at the sweaty men packing empty crates onto the back of a truck. Yail Misqawi hastened over to Sami.

"Doctor, I have one question."

"Yes?"

"Is Dr. Motke a real doctor, or is this just his name?"

Sami spun to face him. "My God. How do you ask this question? How do I give you an answer?" He strode away, leaving Yail Misqawi, puzzled, behind.

"Our problem," he said to Dr. Motke as they headed for the cafeteria, "is not with the animals. Rather, with people. From now on, I shall call that man 'Clever Man.' 'Clever, Clever Man.'"

Outside, in a patch of shade, Sami, Abu Shir, and Dr. Motke recovered with fizzy drinks. Abu Shir was busy listing the costs of things, from medicine to builder's cement to car parts. A canteen worker came out of his kitchen and gave each man a chocolate wrapped in shiny gold paper. Sami glared at his and tossed it onto the table.

"So, Abu Shir," said Dr. Motke, "how's the family?"

Sami closed his eyes in anticipation. Abu Shir shook his head.

A few nights earlier, well after midnight, the military had come to the manager's street.

As the household sleepily awoke and news spread, Mansur, Abu Shir's youngest son, felt his chest constricting. He knew they had come for him. Calmly, he packed a sports bag, changed his clothes, and waited.

It was raining, and a sharp wind blew in from the sea. The knock came at the door. The family was ordered out of the house. Abu Shir's old mother-in-law had no time to collect her walking stick; her two eldest grandsons supported her weight. They stood shivering outside in the rain.

A soldier collected a pile of green identity cards from Abu Shir and sifted through them. He consulted a list attached to a clipboard, then looked up.

"Mansur?"

"That's me."

"Stand over there."

Mansur crossed the street. Beneath a street lamp, a second soldier waited. He blindfolded the young man and cuffed his hands behind his back with a plastic ziplock.

A third approached. "Do you know who I am?" he asked.

"No."

"I am a captain with the Israel Defense Forces."

"What do you want?"

"We want to take you with us. Do you know why?"

"No."

"Ask someone to go and fetch whatever you need from your house."

"My grandmother is very old, and she'll be sad. Please let me kiss her goodbye."

The captain paused, then took out a penknife and slit the ziplock. He pulled off the blindfold, watching silently as Mansur kissed his grandmother and embraced his mother. The whole street, barefoot and night-gowned, had come out to see. Mansur walked along the line, shaking hands with each neighbor.

"It's time to go," said the captain. He escorted Mansur to the army jeep, leaving his hands and eyes unbound. The family watched in silence as the jeep drove away.

Abu Shir believed it to be the work of an informer. There were plenty about, willing to provide lists of "suspect" individuals, chosen at random, for a few pitiful banknotes. Sometimes, informers were caught and forced to repent, lying prone and burbling for their lives on the cold mosque floor. If they refused, they were strung up from a street lamp.

The night of his arrest, Mansur had been busy finalizing arrangements for his marriage. He had visited the home of his betrothed, accompanied by his father, to formalize the attachment. They had planned an engagement party, chosen a ring, and discussed a date for the wedding. After the party, Mansur and his young fiancée would finally be able to appear together in public; until now, their meetings had all taken place behind closed doors. Abu Shir went alone to inform the family of Mansur's arrest. The manager and the bride-to-be waited anxiously for news of his son's well-being.

Though he said nothing, Dr. Sami believed there was more to Mansur's arrest. The manager's boy was seventeen and had been working at the zoo for some months as an attendant on the children's electric train ride. He was not, thought Sami, bright, promising, or pleasant. A reliable source had it that Mansur had secretly bought a pistol, on the black market and without a license. One evening, unable to resist showing off, he had brought it to the zoo, wrapped in checked cheesecloth, and fired two live bullets into the air above the playground. His punishment for this stupidity was his name on a blacklist. Who knew what he might have been planning with that gun? Sami slurped the dregs of his Sprite.

"Shall we make a last check of the new animals, Dr. Motke?"

Motke nodded and rose. Abu Shir remained behind.

◆   ◆   ◆

Sheep and wolves together comprise the two species longest domesticated by man. Wolves came first, then sheep, whose earliest fossilized remains were found in Jericho, dating back nine thousand years. Both have, throughout time, suffered from a poor reputation. Poverty is the "wolf at the door"; the wolfish are to be avoided. Legends of werewolves, lycanthropes, and shape shifters swept across medieval Europe, instilling terror when the moon was full. The *Canis lupi* of Palestine, the Indian, Arabian, and Iranian wolves that once ranged its hillsides, were hunted out of existence, considered a pest to humans and a danger to sheep.

To be sheepish is to be meek or dim-witted, a lamb to the slaughter. Though Jesus was both the Good Shepherd and Agnus Dei, the Lamb of God, a "flock" is a term frequently used with contempt.

Often, in literature, the two species have collided. "Beware of false prophets," warns the New Testament, "which come to you in sheep's clothing, but inwardly they are ravening wolves." Aesop, some six centuries earlier, related the tale of a wolf donning a sheepskin to infiltrate the flock. Though enemies, the wolf and the sheep display striking similarities. Both are highly territorial, loathe to venture beyond their well-defined home range. Both can be cunning, able to understand and unlatch a farmer's gate. Domesticated, both will learn to respond to their individual names, and their offspring will gambol happily together in play. The sheepdog faithfully protecting his flock in the remaining fields around Qalqilya is a direct descendent of the timber wolf inside its cages.

At Qalqilya Zoo, sheep and wolves both found succor and favor. But not all were so lucky. Bottom of the heap, lowest of all, was the donkey.

It was a donkey, in ancient Palestine, that carried a burgeoning Mary to a stable in Bethlehem, and another who bore an adult Jesus through the gates of Jerusalem. "Abraham rose early the next morning and saddled his donkey," says the Torah, "and went to the place of which God had told him." Muhammad, according to Shi'ite tradition, rode a talking donkey named 'Ufair, which threw itself down a well after its master's death for fear someone else would attempt to ride it. Another talking donkey, in the Book of Judges, enquired of its master why he beat it. Moses was ordered to remove his shoes of donkey skin before reaching holy soil, and Sunni authorities forbid the consumption of donkey meat. The cross of dark fur across a donkey's spine and shoulders is said to have come from the shadow cast by Christ's crucifixion. White donkeys were for centuries the preferred form of transportation of Christian kings, wealthy Jews, and Muslim prophets. Yet despite their elevated ancient status, the belief persists, stubborn as the fabled ass itself, that donkeys are senseless and feel no pain.

Donkeys remained indispensable in Qalqilya. They carried people and produce, pulled yokes and homemade carts. They were machines with a heartbeat, moving heavy loads with the encouragement of a whip or thorny stick. Many wore harnesses of chain, which cut deep welts into the bone of their noses. Without his donkey, a poor farmer might starve. They were bought for pennies, worked to the ground, and then replaced by a newer, fitter model. The useless were sometimes tortured by children; others were tied to a fencepost and abandoned, or doused in petrol and set alight. The luckier ones were brought to the zoo, where they were stabled until it was time to face the slaughterhouse. Then, their throats were slit and their limbs dished up to the lions.

The first time the Donkey Lady visited, Sami believed she had come with an offer of help. A neat young Englishwoman, she toured the zoo with two colleagues. Tight-lipped, they peered and pointed, then casually enquired what the carnivores ate for dinner. Sami told them. The Donkey Lady shuddered.

After the tour, still uncertain of his visitors' intentions, Sami took them to the cafeteria and plied them with tea and cake. The group lapsed into grim silence and exchanged glances across the table. The Donkey Lady cleared her throat. She had, she said, been alerted to the existence of Qalqilya Zoo in a report published by an international animal welfare organization. It detailed, she continued uncomfortably, the barbaric conditions endured by its inhabitants. Most disturbing of all, to herself and her colleagues, was the shocking news that donkeys were fed regularly to the lions.

"Is it true," she leaned forward, wincing, "that to kill a donkey, you put a sack over its head and hit it with a hammer?"

Sami was stunned. "It is true," he replied, choosing his words carefully, "that we feed donkeys to the big cats here."

There was another painful intake of breath.

"And sometimes we feed them horses or cattle."

This elicited little response.

"But," he continued, "that we kill them with a hammer? What sort of nonsense is this?"

"So," the Donkey Lady whispered, "how *are* they killed?"

Sami smiled soothingly. The donkeys slaughtered at the zoo were strung up, in the usual Halal manner, and their jugulars slit, much as any animal bound for the dinner plate.

"First," he explained, "we inject the donkeys with an anesthetic, and then, when they are completely asleep, we kill them very, very quickly."

She paled but seemed satisfied. Sami was smug. If that were true, the lions and leopards, eating meat laced with heavy doses of anesthetic for every meal, would never rouse from slumber.

"You see," explained the Donkey Lady, "we care very much about donkeys. We would prefer that you don't feed them to your animals at all, but if you must, we want to make sure that you do so in a humane manner."

Sami nodded.

"So we want to find out if there's something we can do to help you to help these donkeys."

Now, Sami felt, he really had heard everything.

The story of the hammer, Sami later discovered, had originated some time earlier as the result of an unfortunate oversight. A journalist, or so she had claimed, had arrived late one day at the zoo to find neither the manager nor Dr. Sami in attendance. Wandering alone, she had taken up with an elderly keeper—"A simple man," said Sami, kindly—and asked him some questions. A small tape recorder blinked red in her palm.

"With what do you feed your lions?"

"Donkeys," he replied.

"And how do you kill the donkeys?"

"I don't know."

"Do you hit them with a hammer?" she asked, encouragingly.

"Yes."

"Until they fall down?"

"That's right," replied the keeper, nodding knowledgably.

"Would you stand over there," she asked, "so that I can take your photograph?"

The keeper walked to the lions' den and smiled broadly. *Click*, went the camera.

A week later, Dr. Sami received an anonymous phone call.

"You are a very bad man," said the voice. "Now, everyone will know." *Click* went the receiver before Sami had the chance to reply.

"So," persisted the Donkey Lady, "do you have any idea how we might be able to help?"

Sami thought. Many of the donkeys he received came to him in terrible health. They had been beaten, used up, and discarded. Some had gaping wounds; others, broken limbs. He stabled them in relative comfort, in the block behind the slaughterhouse, with a handful of hay and a bucket of water. It was warm; it was quiet. They were no longer heaving unbearable loads or being whipped into motion. But most were in pain, and Sami could not afford to treat them. So there they stayed, suffering in silence, until the end finally drew near. Often, he had more donkeys than he required, and they lingered, sometimes for weeks at a time, until they were needed for food.

"There *is* one thing," he said carefully.

"Yes? What? Please, tell us." said the Donkey Lady.

"It would very much help these donkeys if you could provide me with," he paused and looked seriously from one visitor to the other, "a bigger freezer."

There was silence across the table.

"You see," he continued, "this is a very important point. Sometimes I have more donkeys than the lions can eat, and they must suffer while they wait for dinner time. If I had a bigger freezer, I could kill them at once. Then no donkey would have to bear this pain."

The three visitors stared at Dr. Sami and then at each other.

"More tea?" asked Sami.

The Donkey Lady gulped. "How much would a bigger freezer cost?"

"Just a moment," said Sami, springing to his feet. "I will ask our engineer."

At a picnic table outside, Abu Khaled was chatting with a group of friends. Sami strolled over and whispered in his ear. Abu

Khaled grinned in understanding. For once, they saw eye to eye. He pulled a pencil and paper from his pocket and returned to the table with Dr. Sami.

"A moment, please," said Sami. "He will make a calculation."

Abu Khaled scribbled down a series of numbers. He scratched his head with the end of his pencil and tapped figures into a calculator. The group sat in silence.

"Yallah," he finally declared. "Eight thousand dollars."

The Donkey Lady tugged at her necklace. Sami waited with anticipation.

"All right," she conceded weakly. "I will discuss it with our committee. I'll let you know."

"You would be doing a very good thing," Sami assured her, "for these donkeys."

Sami watched as three visitors left the zoo, their shoulders hung low. He was mystified. Surely the zoo's other animals were more important than the donkeys. And Qalqilya's children, who had suffered so much and received so little. Or, at least, those tired old horses also destined for the butcher's knife. What, if not donkeys, should he feed to his leopards and lions? A cow, a sheep? What was the difference?

Sami was unaware of the special place in the English heart reserved for the donkey. He did not know that, far away in a "nation of animal lovers," where A. A. Milne had immortalized Eeyore and where the Society for the Protection of Animals had predated the Metropolitan Police Force by five whole years, sanctuaries dedicated solely to the defense of the lowly creature tallied more than a dozen.

Three weeks later, Dr. Sami received a telephone call from the Donkey Lady.

"I have discussed the matter with my committee," said a small voice, "and I'm afraid we cannot help you."

"I see," said Sami.

"I'm sorry," said the Donkey Lady.

"Then your donkeys will continue to suffer," Sami replied in an uncharacteristic flash of anger, "and you will never set foot here again."

◆   ◆   ◆

All appeared well with the new arrivals. The wolves were still exploring their diminutive territory. The Berber sheep were blasé, nibbling grass. Dr. Motke walked back with Sami toward the green truck.

At the cafeteria, Abu Shir was telling another group of workers of his son's disappearance. "Definitely the work of an informer," he declared.

In ancient Jerusalem, on the annual occasion of Yom Kippur, two billy goats were brought into the Temple courtyard. The high priest drew lots, and the unlucky goat was slaughtered, burned, and offered up to the Lord. The priest then laid his hands on the head of the second creature and transferred to it all the sins of his people. Bearing this burden, the scapegoat was set free to roam forever, sin-laden but intact, in the wilderness.

In slaughterhouses, where mutton is the order of the day, a sheep is trained to lead the others without fuss into the jaws of death. It is kept as a pet and wears a bell around its neck. This sheep is known as the "Judas lamb."

Alone again, Dr. Sami went about his last check of the day. He collected the baby Berber sheep from his office, ready to take it home for its evening bottle on the lap of a delighted daughter. He whistled as he walked to his laboratory, tucked away beside the slaughterhouse, and gathered together the rest of his belongings.

From the adjacent stable, three pairs of forlorn brown eyes watched him draw the door closed and check his pocket for keys.

A dappled horse, a wide-eyed white mule, and a tiny brown donkey, all painfully thin, tired, and malnourished from years of hard labor, were spending their last few nights in the quiet stables at the back of the zoo. For the first time in their lives, they had ample food, water, and plenty of rest. When their time came, they would be led calmly into the white-tiled hangar, to emerge in rubbish bags and wheelbarrows as food for the zoo's inhabitants.

Late afternoon drew on at Qalqilya Zoo. The horse whinnied softly. The baby lamb bleated inside its cardboard box. Dr. Sami headed happily to his clinic.

Chapter Six

June–July 2006

How many a generation have We destroyed
before their time—can you perceive of any of
them, or hear any whisper of them?
—QURAN, SURA MARYAM 98

A figure in fluent robes and close-cropped hair stood motionless outside the lions' den. It was very early, and the zoo's lanes were empty. Rabir, the largest of the three lions, crouched atop a concrete platform in the center of the cage, chewing a bone. Rad and Holi lay inert, eyes shut, a velvet ear occasionally batting away an impertinent fly. The figure mopped its brow and rummaged inside a duffel bag slung twinkling over its shoulder. It pulled out a heavy Nikon camera and removed the lens cap. *Clack,* went the shutter, *clack clack clack.*

"Hello!" called Dr. Sami, hastening breathlessly toward the lions' cage. "Hello there!" The clacking stopped. The figure turned. Sami was surprised to find that it was a woman, a foreigner, in early middle age, her short hair dyed a luminous tangerine. A wobble of red lipstick encircled her mouth; her eyelashes were sticky with blue mascara. She was flushed and, though it was barely eight o'clock, perspiring.

"Hello," Sami arrived and extended a hand, "I am Dr. Sami Khader, head veterinarian of Qalqilya Zoo."

"Nice to meet you," said the woman. "My name is Astrid."

"Hello, Ostrich."

"Astrid," she replied. "I have come to take photographs."

Astrid was, she explained as Dr. Sami led her to his office, a freelance photographer from Berlin, attending a peace conference in Jerusalem. Back home, she had been alerted to the zoo's existence by a small newspaper item involving a hippo and decided to stop in to see the zoo for herself.

She was brusque and direct but secretly rather afraid. It was her first trip across the border, and people had warned her that the West Bank was a dangerous place for a lone Western woman. She had dressed with particular modesty, in layers including a t-shirt, blouse, jacket, and several gauzy scarves. Thick tights clung to her legs beneath a long skirt and stout walking boots. She felt she might faint if the heat grew any worse.

"I hope," she said, "that my pictures will be of interest to a journal of photography."

"Very good," said Sami. "Welcome. We have many things to see here."

The photographer deposited an array of bags beneath the desk. She propped two tripods and a light meter against a plastic chair, then removed one scarf and rearranged a second woolen one, draped heavily around her corduroy jacket.

"I got here early this morning to take pictures at dawn," she said, "because I thought the animals might be more active then. One of your keepers let me in."

Sami was irritated. He preferred to keep a check on alien comings and goings since the unnerving incident of the Donkey Lady.

"I started taking photographs of the lions," she continued. "I thought they would make a good subject for a photo essay. But their cage is so sad. Could you," she took out a notepad, "tell me about them?"

"Certainly," replied Sami, "But first, one question."

"Please."

"How do you take your tea, Ostrich?"

* ◆ ◆

Holi, Rad, and Rabir had previously been Jafir, Jaras, and Nabuko
and had arrived with triumviral ceremony one hot afternoon almost two years earlier. In the zoo's 1980s heyday, there had been
another pair of lions, an endangered Asian strain known as *Panthera leo persicus*, at Qalqilya Zoo. From antiquity to the Middle
Ages, their ancestors roamed, from the Indes, through Palestine,
to the wilds of Byzantine and on into Europe. Aristotle wrote of
the wild lions of the Balkans. But by the late nineteenth century,
Asian lions were down to just a handful, inhabiting a remote
range of northern Indian forest, and were declining fast. The im-
perial government, whose officials had, until then, gladly blasted
the beasts into rugs and trophies, saw fit to issue a mandate for
their protection. Thirteen breeding pairs survived and multiplied.
Though they remain severely endangered, today they number
several hundred, all descended from those the British bureaucrats
decided to spare.

Both Qalqilya's Asian lions, already middle-aged by the time
they were bequeathed, died without progeny, leaving the zoo
without the King of the Beasts that had once roamed its own forest floor.

Then, to Sami's astonishment, a call had come in August 2004
from Dr. Motke.

"Sami," he said, "I have good news for you."

Good news took the form of three adolescent male lions,
African ones this time, all urgently requiring new homes. They
had been bred, explained Motke, at the roomy safari park near Tel
Aviv but were ousted by the pride. All attempts at integration

were met with violence. The park had been forced to keep them in isolation: The only suitably secure enclosure was a tiny, windowless cage into which no natural light could penetrate. There, the lions languished.

The safari park's management was now in a tight spot. The lions could not be released into the grounds for fear of injury, or worse, at the tooth and claw of the highly territorial, well-established pride. Likewise, they could not live out their lives in such abject misery. Word had spread throughout the area, but it soon became clear that no one was interested in a surfeit of adolescent *Panthera*. All three lions were castrated and thus useless for breeding. Sterilization had deprived them of their luxuriant manes, so they failed equally to serve any decorative purpose. Though healthy, young, and vital, they were, said Motke, surplus stock. Unless a new home could be found at short notice, it was likely the solution would be final.

Motke had managed to persuade the safari park's management that, though Qalqilya could not offer conditions equivalent to those of its own pride, the move would be better for the lions than an early grave.

"Well, Sami?" he concluded, "Do you want them?"

The lions had arrived in a procession that slung half a mile along Qalqilya's main road. The parade was led by the animal wagons, followed by several officials from the safari park. Then came the press and photographers, mostly local, though a few from the international wires had sniffed out the story. Dr. Sami rode up front with the lions. He was joined, along the way, by a ragtag assortment of locals, on foot and bicycle. An interested donkey cart brought up the rear. The day was declared a public holiday, and children jostled for position as the animals were hauled, slumbering, into their new cage. Sami assured the safari park's curator that a new enclosure would be built forthwith and that the lions' conditions would quickly improve. No sooner had wagons rolled back toward the border than he ceremonially renamed the recommissioned trio.

Rad, Rabir, and Holi settled in and consumed their first meal gladly.

Though their cage was small, not one of the lions had, in nearly two years at Qalqilya, begun to display the stereotypic behavior of an unhappy captive animal. They were not pacing their cages, or endlessly licking the walls, or worrying at their skin until it bled. Mostly, they slept. They ate well and did not seem particularly susceptible to coughs, colds, or other trivial complaints. They had space to stretch and roll. Their cage possessed neither range nor vista, but it was, at least, open to the elements. Finally, they could feel the sunlight, the wind, and the rain.

◆   ◆   ◆

The lions' move had worked out well for everyone. The safari park had avoided the unpleasant necessity of three quiet bullets and benefited from positive publicity. The press thrilled to the "bridging of a Middle East divide" and "the generosity of the bequest." Sami could barely contain his excitement. "Lions are the king of any zoo," he told reporters. "When you have no king, you have a problem."

The park's staff departed for home from Qalqilya that night, heartened by the knowledge that they had improved the lives of the children of Qalqilya and that the lions, too, had profited modestly from the move. Dr. Sami, Abu Shir, and the old Municipal Council could not have been more delighted. The lions' victorious arrival was feted as a triumph over adversity in the local press and brought flocks of summer visitors to cushion the zoo's coffers.

Though still eclipsed in popularity by a captivating giraffe, the King of Beasts, the Beast of Kings, had finally returned to Palestine.

Since the first menageries of Ur and Mesopotamia, the lion has almost always commanded a zoo's center stage. Three thousand years ago, a lion stood guard at Egyptian pharaoh Ramses II's tent by night and escorted him into battle during the day. Nebuchadnezzar II, king of Babylonia, was an expert at leonine husbandry, as was the ruthless Emperor Nero. Scimitar, third-century emperor Marcus Aurelius Caracalla's favorite pet lion, ate beside his master, while his other felines were frequently released for fun into the darkened bedrooms of drunken houseguests. In the eighth century, Charlemagne kept a pet lion sent by the pope. By the thirteenth century, almost every nobleman and potentate worth his salt had his own, as a symbol of his passion, courage, or ferocity—and his dominance over even the strongest forces of nature. A medieval belief held that cubs were born dead and their mothers breathed life into them after birth. Francis I, the Renaissance "Father and Restorer of Letters," slept with a lion next to his bed. Wild lions, in the Middle Ages, still ran free in the hills of Palestine. They formed the symbols of the Mamluk sultan Baibars, "Lion of Egypt"; of the Jewish tribe of Juda; and of Richard, Coeur de Lion. Jerusalem, the medieval "navel of the world," today bears a lion on its crest.

In Rome, a period of bloodlust accompanied the arrival of the lion. In 186 BCE, lions were first killed in staged hunts, simulated in the city's amphitheaters. Later, they were plied with intoxicants and pitted, in great quantities, against prisoners of war, Christians, gladiators, or each other. Pompey killed six hundred in one sitting. Trajan slaughtered thousands to celebrate his military success. Only Cicero protested. "What pleasure," he asked, "can a cultivated man find in seeing a noble beast run through with a hunting spear?" The spectacles continued, unabated, for centuries.

By the eighteenth century, public shows where blood flowed ankle-deep had swung out of vogue. The excesses of Rome and the Middle Ages had led to a paucity of lions in North Africa and the Levant, and lions turned from symbol of domination to one of prestige. They formed a permanent fixture at the Tower of London, where they were believed to have the power to discern a virgin in a crowd. In 1716, a lion was the very first exotic animal to set foot in America. Exhibited in Boston at the home of Captain Arthur Savage, it moved, in 1720, to the home of one Martha Adams, where a hand-painted sign declared, "The Lion King of Beasts is to be seen here."

In the nineteenth century, the training and display of captive lions was revolutionized by Karl Hagenbeck, the German animal dealer, who decreed that animals "react to meanness with meanness, and to friendship with friendship," and so did away with "old, cruel methods of training animals." The result was four trained lions who pulled a Roman triumphal chariot and rode horseback at the 1893 Chicago World's Fair. "I have," Hagenbeck concluded in his autobiography, "had lions, tigers and panthers who were great friends to me. . . . I was able to behave with them exactly as I would with a domestic dog, and with as much confidence."

The importance of lions to an animal collection did not diminish in the twentieth century. In 1951, Reuben David, an Indian wrestler-turned-veterinarian, stopped in Ahmedabad and established a zoo with the remnants of a traveling show that a penniless showman had been forced to leave behind. Though the elders of the city refused, with a lofty regard for their religious principles, to invest money in flesh-eating creatures, David resolved that lions were critical to the zoo's success. He purchased lions for his Hill Garden Zoo himself, then managed to convince the governors that they were simply a generous, anonymous bequest. Though good Hindus all, they could not look gift lions in the mouth.

Reuben David proved a sound guardian to his zoo, though much of what he accomplished was through trial and error. He established a Natural History Museum aimed especially at children. He paid close attention to every one of his charges and made time for each. Yet he had a few wayward passions that sometimes dominated his sensibilities. He was fascinated by albinos and by "nature's mistakes," by Siamese twins, strange crossbreeds, and lambs with two heads.

Dr. Sami, likewise, was excessively proud of his bottled oddities and of the two-headed lamb that graced a shelf of his own Natural History Museum.

◆　　◆　　◆

Sami had not developed as personal a bond with each of his lions as Hagenbeck had with his charioteers, but he still felt a tremendous amount of affection for each of them. It was their claustrophobic quarters that pained him the most and that he was most anxious to improve. At quiet times during a busy day, he would slip away to check on them, bending down close and whispering through the bars. He was happy that they were alert and healthy, and keen that everyone should know his plans for their improvement. It made him sorry that this Ostrich had photographed them in their current, unacceptable state. "Soon," Sami pointed out to the photographer, who was fanning herself with her notebook, "my lions will be moving to the new Carnivore Department, where they will be very happy. Like Nature. I will also find a new pair, for breeding. Perhaps then you will come back to take more photographs."

He sipped tea and glanced out of the window. A faint heat haze shimmered over Ruti's enclosure. An extra stretch of fencing had been erected around the top of its perimeter in an attempt to stop Ruti's snacking before she entirely destroyed the trees fringing her borders. The overhanging branch had been cut back and the leaves pruned vigorously. Workers sat beneath a tree, eyes closed in the shade.

Outside the zoo, tempers were soaring with the mercury, as money troubles continued. In Ramallah, government workers stormed the parliament to demand their wages. In Gaza, there had been shootings. In Qalqilya, arsonists had set upon the YMCA, and someone had tried to burn down the Italians' Psycho Social Counseling cabin at the entrance to town. At Sami's museum, electrical wiring had been stripped down by thieves in the night. "These wires cost two thousand shekels," Sami sighed, "but they will probably sell the copper for just one hundred. Thievery," he added, "has increased because of this pressure."

Still, compared to the chaos outside, the zoo was an oasis, and Sami felt safe. So far, he had even managed to keep the workers busy, despite the unbearable weather. Within the new enclosures' low walls, he had overseen the erection of a dozen compact sets of sleeping quarters. Each had already been painted white, and the walls tiled to shoulder height for easy cleaning. Men covered in whitewash and grout wandered about the Carnivore Department, red faced and panting. Progress was finally tangible.

Astrid adjusted a camera lens and glanced around impatiently. With a brief knock, Abu Shir appeared, clutching a scruffy black folder full of scraps of paper. He nodded a greeting to Dr. Sami and then turned to the guest, who was carefully wiping her lens with the corner of a shirt cuff.

"This," said Dr. Sami, "is our zoo manager, Abu Shir. Abu Shir, this is Ostrich."

"Astrid." She looked up.

Abu Shir gazed down at the photographer, with her layer upon layer of sensual, radiant clothing and makeup slowly sliding down her cheeks. He graciously extended one hand, while with the other he handed Sami a receipt for a sack of cucumbers. The manager smiled, puffed up his chest, and was smitten.

"Last night," he announced, shaking himself back to business, still surreptitiously eyeing Astrid, "Deputy Hashem al-Masri and Mayor Wajeeh Qawas were both arrested."

It had happened at two in the morning, unannounced, as part of an army sweep that had bagged sixty-four Hamas members in the West Bank and Gaza. Most thought it a response to the kidnapping of a young Israeli conscript, which had occurred on the Gaza border three days earlier and for which a Hamas-affiliated group had claimed responsibility.

The mayor—just a month out of prison—and his deputy, along with a clutch of other men, had been taken to a detention center in Israel, and nothing further had been heard of them. The mayor's wife fretted that he had not taken his heart medicine with him.

The municipality, said Abu Shir, was in shambles, as it scrambled to come to terms with the unscheduled leaves of absence of both mayor and deputy. No one had any idea how long they would be away.

His own son, Mansur, Abu Shir explained sorrowfully to Astrid, was in the same predicament. Sami yawned and sat back in his chair. Luckily, the boy had been able to make contact with the family through a mobile telephone smuggled into prison inside a sandwich.

"I am well," Mansur had told his parents, as his mother wept into the telephone receiver. "They are treating me fine. When I asked why I was here, they said my file was 'Top Secret.' But things aren't so bad. I have a lot of friends here. We have time to talk, to make plans and play cards."

"I recall," said Sami, interrupting the manager's monologue, "that your wife is visiting the prison for the first time today."

Abu Shir scowled. "She spent the whole night cooking his favorite foods and left at four this morning. But they will probably not even allow the food in. They will throw it out, just like that. Still, she wanted to do it. She is stupid."

"A sandwich got in, though, didn't it?" remarked Astrid.

Abu Shir looked bashful. "It did," he said gently.

She slung a camera strap around her neck.

"May I photograph the animals now?"

"Of course," said Sami. "Anything you want, you can say. Anything you can say, you can do. But first, come with me."

Inside the Natural History Museum, Astrid eyed a shelf of pale, bottled specimens with mistrust.

"This," announced Sami, "is the Biological Hall." Beneath the stoppered jars sat the crop of spent shells and grenades Sami had gathered from his enclosures.

"They don't look very biological," she remarked.

Sami pretended not to hear.

A large velvet-covered Visitors Book had been placed on a lectern. Inside were hand-drawn columns:

"Name."

"Signature."

"Impression."

"Concentrate, please," said Sami, leading her into the next room. "All that you see here is my own creation."

"What does that say?" She pointed to an Arabic phrase carved into a concrete lintel.

"'Allah Created All,'" he replied. "'Praise him.'"

Passing the hyena tableau, Sami reached into a fuse box, hidden behind a twiggy bit of wall, and flipped a switch. With a whirr, the desk fan started up. A red lightbulb glowed behind billowing strips of fabric. "Oh, fantastic," said Astrid. "A campfire."

Sami drew to a halt around the next corner. "I'll tell you something." He lowered his voice. "These people are very simple. Sometimes they come here and ask"—he pointed to the massive spider, poised ominously in its web—"'Is this real, doctor?'"

Astrid laughed, but Sami shook his head gravely.

"Soon," he said, "I will have to go to Africa and live in a hut. Now, please come this way. I would like your help with the snakes."

"What's this?" Astrid asked, as they stepped over massive plaster-of-Paris vertebrae protruding from the floor.

Sami was disappointed. "You should not come to a museum and ask, 'What is this?' Things should speak for themselves."

"Is it a centipede," Astrid pressed, "or a fish?"

"Neither," said Sami. "It is a backbone. Now, please listen. This is a very important point. I have discussed the light here in the Snake Hall with many people, and I believe it is not good. You are a photographer," he assured her. "You will know."

Astrid peered into the gloom at an array of serpents draped between tree stumps, over dried ferns, and across the immense, coiling metal python. She did not wish to appear rude. "For photos," she conceded, "it's quite dark."

"I knew it! This Mr. La'aba is a very stupid man. Now, please. It is important to me to increase the lights. I am glad you are here."

Astrid walked obligingly around for several minutes, squinting at stuffed snakes.

"It's atmospheric, like this," she said eventually.

"But it is not good."

"It *is* a bit spooky."

"Exactly! 'This is not a Fear House,' I told Mr. La'aba, the engineer. 'This is a Scientific Museum.' This is a very important point."

"You could," Astrid suggested, "put spotlights in the darkest corners."

Behind Dr. Sami, Abu Shir materialized. He flashed Astrid a wide, incongruous smile. "Dr. Sami, we have another visitor. Mr. Hagi Ilan has come to see us." He glanced, again, in the photographer's direction.

"Hagi?" Sami's eyebrows shot up in disbelief. "This is a very important man," he told Astrid, "one of the head inspectors of the Nature Reserves Authority in Israel. He is an old friend of the zoo. I have not seen him here for years. Abu Shir," he said, turning to the manager, "I must show him the Carnivore Department. Please stay here." He motioned toward Astrid. "Ostrich is going to show you the dark corners."

◆　　◆　　◆

Hurrying from the bewitched manager and his vexed charge, Dr. Sami made for the ticket booth, where a tall, thin man with a mop of curly black hair was waiting patiently.

"Dr. Sami!" he cried. "How are you?"

Hagi Ilan had first visited Qalqilya when the zoo was still a twinkle in a former mayor's ambitious eye. He had become involved on an advisory level until the second intifada became too dangerous for him to travel to the town. Now, years later, he had heard from Motke Levinson that new animals had been delivered and had decided to risk dropping in.

"I remember it all like it was yesterday!" He clapped Sami on the back. "Come on, show me what you've got."

As they toured the zoo, Hagi nodded his approval. "I have to admit," he said, "it's not as bad as I expected, given your circumstances. What about those new cages?"

Dr. Sami led him to the Carnivore Department.

At the far end, Abu Khaled, renovations project engineer, was inspecting a huge new palm tree that had been installed and was supported by an iron strut.

"Is this for the lions?" asked Hagi, pointing to the first in the series of cages.

Sami nodded.

"You know, don't you, that you must make the cages four hundred and eighty centimeters high," said Hagi, "in order to meet the standards of the association?"

"I know," replied Sami, making a mental note.

"And have you considered glass walls instead of bars? It's much more modern."

"Isn't that dangerous?"

"No, just expensive. And if the animals enjoy jumping up at it, it'll get muddy. You also have to be careful how you position it, otherwise at certain times of day, you'll only see your own reflection."

"We will use the bars, I think," Sami considered.

"All right. Let's have a look inside."

Inside the lions' new night quarters, a pyramid of paint tins occupied one corner. "International Paint Corporation," announced the labels, "Main Road. Nablus." A smiling Abu Khaled clambered in to join them.

Sami immediately seized the opportunity.

"In your expert opinion, Hagi," he began nonchalantly, "what must the floors be made from?"

"Something tough and easily cleanable," Hagi replied. "Like the floor of a garage."

"Epoxy," said Abu Khaled.

"Precisely," agreed Hagi.

Abu Khaled laughed and shook his head. "This is much too expensive."

Hagi turned squarely to face the engineer. "You must understand, sir, that if you do these things wrong, you won't have any animals at all."

Dr Sami shot Abu Khaled a haughty glance.

"I understand," said the engineer, his smile fading.

"When do you think it will all be ready?" inquired Hagi.

"Two months," said Abu Khaled.

"So, September?"

"In my professional opinion," replied the engineer cautiously, "all the materials are available. Tarmac. Gravel. Cement. Sand. Concrete. Tiles. Fencing."

Sami looked up and spotted Astrid striding purposefully across the zoo toward them. Abu Shir staggered along behind her, laden with cameras and equipment.

"Glass. Wood. Fencing," Abu Khaled continued. "Paint. Mortar. And," he cleared his throat, "epoxy."

"Very good," said Hagi. "Now, is anyone around here going to offer me a drink?"

As they turned toward the cafe, Astrid and Abu Shir finally puffed up.

"I have explained where the spotlights should go." The photographer was disgruntled and had not shot a single frame since the lions.

"Then please come to the cafeteria, for refreshments."

"Refreshments," cooed a perspiring Abu Shir and rearranged a tripod.

Dr. Sami and Hagi Ilan walked ahead.

"You need to get some more animals soon," said Hagi. "These ones," he glanced at the hyena, "won't last forever. Have you approached any of the zoos in Israel lately?"

Sami shook his head. "This municipality is not an easy one. But," he confided, "I do have a plan."

"Oh yes?"

"Giza Zoo," he whispered reverently, "in Cairo. It is world famous. I once read all about it in its Centenary Publication."

"Really?" asked Hagi doubtfully.

"Yes. I will go there, this summer. Without any . . ." Sami lowered his voice further and glanced behind them, "obstructions."

"Are you sure it's still a good zoo?"

"The best."

"And you're sure they will help you?"

"I know it."

Hagi was skeptical. "How?"

"They have a great history. They rose up to become international."

"But a long time ago, I think."

"Yes."

"Well," Hagi allowed, "if you say so."

"They are good people. They will understand our problem. They will give us new, breeding animals. A new giraffe. A polar bear. Or a pair of tigers, for the Carnivore Department."

Sami's confidence had been buoyed by recent successes. The Carnivore Department was finally coming together, and Hagi seemed impressed. His Natural History Museum, too, was on the brink of completion, and he was pleased with his own hard work. The new animals, the wolves and the sheep, were thriving. He felt sure his newest scheme would be the icing on the cake.

Hagi smiled faintly and said nothing. They passed the crocodile cage.

"This will be knocked down," Sami quickly apologized, "and replaced by Crocodile Island."

"Very good," Hagi peered in and sniffed. "The smell is rather bad."

"We change the water every two days."

"I don't believe you."

"Every three days."

Hagi glanced at the top of the cage, upon which an array of old bottles, cans, and plastic bags lay strewn. "You could put those in your Natural History Museum," he said, pointing. "They look ancient."

Behind them Abu Shir struggled on, Astrid's obliging porter. She paused beside the playground for a second to catch her breath and noticed a signpost. "Safe Playground Project," it read. "A gift from the Bill and Melinda Gates Foundation." Astrid turned to Abu Shir.

"What's this?"

"It is just a man who gave us some money."

"You do know that he's one of the richest men in the world?"

"It must be a different man. It was only very little money."

In honor of Hagi's arrival, a canteen worker at the picnic ground was quickly loading a table with drinks, cakes, and hummus with minced meat. They sat down to eat. Astrid perched uncomfortably at the far end of the table. Abu Shir pressed himself close beside her.

"Mr. Hagi," said Abu Shir, carefully slicing a thin morsel of vivid pink sponge cake and offering it to the photographer, "I know that the mayor would have liked to have shaken your hand. You have helped us very much in the past with the zoo. But, unfortunately, today he has gone to prison."

Hagi nodded. Abu Shir turned to Astrid.

"I am sure he would have liked to shake your hand also. Although," he considered, "he is a religious man, so he could not."

Sami changed the subject. "What," he asked Hagi, "is your belief about the new lion cages?"

"Very good," said Hagi. "Better than I had imagined."

"And better than their former home in Israel?"

"That's right." Hagi nodded thoughtfully and scooped a forkful of hummus neatly into an open pita.

After lunch Hagi departed, with tentative words of encouragement for Sami's new plan. Having waved him good-bye, Sami discovered that Astrid had given both himself and the manager the slip.

"Where is Ostrich?" Sami asked Abu Shir.

"I don't know," he sulked, and lit a cigarette.

Sami found the photographer back at the lions' cage, staring down at a dead rat that lay, feet to the heavens, in the middle of the pavement. She reached for her camera. Sami was just in time.

"Why are you looking at this?" he enquired, close enough to her right ear to make her start with fright. "Come. Now I will take you to see live animals. Better than dead."

They left the rat behind and embarked on a circuit of the zoo. Sami paused to show off the obliging Dubi and stopped in at the giraffe enclosure, where Ruti's long, curious tongue hunted raisins in Sami's pocket.

"Please take snaps," he commanded. The photographer, usually so assertive, felt compelled to obey.

Sami posed for one picture standing next to Ruti, another stroking Rama's nose, and a third pointing into the wolf enclosure. Half an hour later, they had toured full circle. He beamed at the photographer.

"So, do you have everything you need?"

"I—" replied Astrid.

"Very good, because it is now time for me to go to my clinic. My car became very ill, so I sold it for scrap. Nowadays, I walk to work, but you should not come with me. Shall I," he inquired, "telephone a taxi?"

She nodded limply.

"It is very important," he concluded, "that you send me copies of the pictures. I think they will make a very nice brochure."

Dr. Sami saw Astrid out of the zoo and waved a final farewell as the yellow taxi whisked her away.

"Goodbye, Ostrich," he called.

Behind him, Abu Shir slipped into his office and bolted the door. The telephone rang. It was his wife, calling to say that she had been allowed to take in Mansur's stuffed cabbages. He seemed healthy and well fed. Things in prison, she told him, were not as bad as she had feared.

After the taxi deposited her at the mouth of town, the heavily laden photographer walked the final half mile back to the checkpoint and crossed on foot. With no public transportation in sight and the afternoon heat bearing down, she decided to hitchhike.

An old man stopped to offer her a ride, in a truck loaded with sloshing bucketfuls of halloumi cheese. At a traffic light, he slipped his hand onto her knee, and she jumped out. She walked for a while, then waited for more than an hour at a deserted bus stop, peeling off layers of defunct protective clothing, until a bus arrived to carry her back to her conference and Jerusalem.

Several days later, spotlights were purchased, and the Snake Hall was adjusted according to Astrid's recommendations. The same afternoon, as Sami stepped back to admire his handiwork, a municipal secretary telephoned to inform him that the official opening of his Natural History Museum had been scheduled for the following Monday.

Sami spent the remainder of the week smoothing ruffled feathers and straightening stray limbs. Outside the museum, the elaborate courtyard fountain had been completed for the occasion. The flick of a switch produced a loud whooshing noise and water cascading in a complicated fashion from three corners of the terrace. It ran, through a deep channel, to encircle the central island, turfed a ferocious green. Once it gained momentum, the noise was deafening, like the roar at the base of a waterfall after snowmelt. Butterflies and dragonflies were undeterred and flitted cheerfully about the fountain's gushing channels. They alighted on pinpricks of flowers, planted in municipal colors atop the grassy island mound.

On Monday the ninth of July, there was a buzz in the air outside Sami's Museum of Natural History. A small crowd had gathered in anticipation. The press was slowly trickling in. A local television station had sent a cameraman, who adjusted his settings while an enthusiastic young reporter tested a microphone. Secretly, Sami was annoyed. He had enjoyed keeping his project under lock and key and felt little compulsion to share it with the general public. Nevertheless, the minister of planning, whisked all the way from his smart office in Ramallah especially for the occasion, would be snipping the green ribbon at 3 PM sharp.

At a quarter to three, Sami stole away to his clinic and busied himself in the preparation of a narghile. He turned on the ancient portable television in the corner and sat back to watch his creation become part of Palestinian public property.

"And now, the ribbon is cut by the honorable minister!" yelled the television reporter above the fountain's roar.

The minister turned and flashed a toothy smile to the crowds. His short and dignified declaration was lost beneath the din of rushing water.

"And Qalqilya is treated to its first sight of the very first Natural History Museum in the natural history of Palestine!" exclaimed the reporter.

Sami lit his narghile and turned off the television.

Three nights later, the same young reporter reappeared on Qalqilyan television screens with an update.

"Five thousand people," he enthused, "have passed through the museum's doors in the last few days! Several of those this reporter talked to said that they are most impressed by the museum's exhibits and will return once again for closer inspection! The demand has been so great," he concluded, "that a time limit has been imposed on visitors. Those wishing to read the information posters thoroughly must buy another ticket and take their place once again at the end of the queue."

Sami reclined in his armchair and kicked off his slippers. "People can't believe it," he said to his daughter. "I am very proud to have done something for my country." The next sensation, he thought, would be the Carnivore Department and new stocks to fill it from Egypt.

Sami yawned and peeled a cucumber. Only two dark smudges blotted an otherwise satisfactory horizon. The first was the baby Berber sheep, now nibbling at his woolen sock. Bold and inquisitive, a far cry from the quaking creature he had brought home, it was playing havoc with the soft furnishings and his wife's ragged nerves.

The second, more discomfiting, source of anxiety was the looming summer holiday. Though it held the promise of Giza Zoo, long imagined by Sami as a place alive with fauna, foliage, and a thousand exotic birds, the trip to Egypt came with a heavy price—a long-anticipated, and long-avoided, visit to his mother.

Chapter Seven
August 2006

God loveth the steadfast.
—QURAN, SURA AL-IMRAN 146

B efore Sami left home for the first time in seven years, he considered the alternatives for his temporary replacement. The choices were not illustrious. Of the four vets in Qalqilya, only he had experience with anything more exotic than an expensive heifer. The bill of fare for his rivals, at their clinics in wealthier parts of town, was purely of the field and farmyard, along with the odd rheumatoid dog, coughing songbird, or fancy pigeon. No one, not even the imprisoned deputy's brother, could manage an ailing ostrich, or worse.

The decision was taken out of Sami's hands. The cogs of the municipality turned, made their selection, and sent the unwilling locum over to Dr. Sami to receive his training. Passing over the busy surgery vets, with their smart practices in town, the council settled on their alternative: the Qalqilya municipal slaughterhouse veterinarian. Though trained, long ago, in the usual gamut of veterinary concerns, his duties nowadays were limited to the approving and stamping of slaughtered meat as it made its way from abattoir to market. He was paunchy, puffed up, and complacent. His wife, a coiffeuse on the high street, made more money than he did. He was not excited by the appointment.

"You came here," queried Sami, the first time the vet arrived at the door to his office, "to do what?"

"Nothing. I will just walk around and observe the zoo."

Sami was frosty. "There is an eye doctor," he said, "for eyes. There is a tooth doctor for teeth, and more kinds besides. There is also a vet for poultry. If you bring him a horse, he cannot do a thing. A zoo is something else, quite apart from these concerns."

The visitor stared but said nothing.

"What do you want from me," asked Sami, "before I leave?"

"I must be taught what to do. How to administer to these animals."

"What do you want me to teach you? Medicine? You and I are the same. What I studied, you studied also. The examinations I took at university, you took them too. What you really need to know is something different, something about yourself. If a lion gets sick and you must give him medicine inside his cage, will you be afraid?"

"I will not."

"Very nice. Then come with me."

Sami and the slaughterhouse vet walked in silence across the zoo to the wolf enclosure.

"One wolf is lame. He is limping. You see?" Sami pointed.

"Yes."

"So what will you do?"

The slaughterhouse vet shrugged.

"First, you will enter the cage. And to enter the cage, you must not be afraid. This is a very important point."

"I am not afraid."

"Good." Sami scrutinized the vet's face. "Now comes your most important training."

The slaughterhouse vet hesitated. "Can I take a stick?"

"A stick?" Sami chuckled and shook his head.

The vet swallowed. He climbed the barrier dividing the cage from the pavement and glanced back at Dr. Sami.

"Go on."

The pudgy man tiptoed cautiously, along the rear line of carnivore cages, to the enclosure door.

"If they feel you are afraid," Sami called, "they will bite you. You must be fearless for them to believe that you are their leader. If you cannot enter, you can do nothing."

The visitor looked into the cage. He hesitated, trembling, then froze. Sami grinned.

"Watch," he said. "I will show you how it is done." He nudged aside the vet's quivering paunch and stepped in, empty-handed. The wolves scattered and took to the corners. They cringed, eyeing him suspiciously. Sami thrust back his shoulders and strutted to the center of the cage. The alpha male stood his ground, panting slightly. Sami glared down at him. Slowly, the wolf's tail slipped between his legs. He slunk off. "You see? Now I will examine this limping wolf. It is easy work, if you are the right man for the job. This," he said, "is a very important point."

Abu Shir was displeased at the choice of replacement.

"It is not right," he told Sami. "It is a terrible mistake."

The slaughterhouse vet had just departed, having already complained about the strength of the coffee at the Friends' Restaurant and the dearth of an adequate filing system. Abu Shir feared the worst.

"You and I," he continued, "understand each other. We work well together. We have the same ideas."

Sami smiled.

"But this man will interfere. He will ask questions and make suggestions. Perhaps," Abu Shir's voice dropped to a hoarse whisper, "he will try to *change* something."

Amelia Thomas

"I know the manager's mind," Sami confided gleefully to his wife that night, watching as she folded his shirts and piled them into a large suitcase. "It will not be easy for him while I am away."

Sara nodded. "Sit here, please," she said, gesturing to the suitcase, from which the contents threatened to spill. "I think we are ready to go."

◆　　◆　　◆

Securing fistfuls of permits and tickets had taken months. Stamps, visas, and perforated papers had all had to be arranged for Sami, Sara, Uzhdan, and Hend, and for Sami's sister-in-law, still freshly widowed and in need of a change. For Qalqilyan men aged between eighteen and fifty, permits to leave town were elusive. With time and persistence, Sami succeeded.

The common white stork, migrating high on the wing above Qalqilya each summer, sails to Cairo in three hundred serene and uneventful miles. The Khaders would take a more circuitous, terrestrial course.

From Qalqilya, through checkpoints and border crossings, they would take a succession of buses east to Amman, capital of Jordan, where they would stay until granted an Egyptian visa. Then, they would head south to the seaside playground of Aqaba and board an aging ferry west across the Gulf, to the moon landscapes of Egypt's Sinai Peninsula.

From there, an ultra-deluxe bus would carry them along fourteen hours of barren desert highway, through military roadblocks and passport inspections, to deposit them, unceremoniously, at the Ahmed Helmi Bus Terminal in the rumble of downtown Cairo.

Sami blanched at the thought. His visit to Giza Zoo was the one and only reason to suffer such unpleasantness. He had read, a decade ago, in a dog-eared copy of the zoo's Centenary Souvenir

Brochure, of the late and legendary Mr. Stanley Flower. Now he wished to see Mr. Flower's spectacular zoological results and learn from them himself.

But he could not escape his family.

Stubbornly ignoring how difficult such a visit was to arrange, they had, for years, been haranguing him to come to call. He was a younger son and, as such, was expected to fulfill his filial duties by visiting his mother and bringing presents. He would inevitably be greeted with a host of relatives transplanted from Palestine and Saudi Arabia, all demanding to know why it had taken so long for him to finally turn up.

Sami's father, at least, would be absent, along with his second wife and their new children who remained, year-round, in Saudi Arabia. But his mother, proud of her Egyptian ancestry, would be there, holding court over the ranks of her family. There would be sisters, refugee aunts and uncles, great-aunts and great-uncles, cousins, second cousins, and third cousins, once and twice removed. It was a horrible prospect.

◆　　◆　　◆

The voyage went surprisingly well.

After just six days, the Khader family arrived, bus-jangled, on a stifling Wednesday afternoon, to spend three weeks in the bosom of the city long known as *Misr um al-dunya*, the Mother of the World. Sami's shirt collar was gray and crumpled. He was dusty, disheveled, and filled with trepidation. For him, this seething cauldron of sixteen million souls was the opposite of all that was sedate, orderly, manageable. For his daughter Uzhdan, it signaled a thrilling release.

Save for their annual visit to an old aunt in Nablus, Uzhdan rarely escaped her Qalqilyan home. She stared, open-mouthed, from the window of the grimy taxi, watching the bright casino boats that lined the sluggish Nile, the glittering needlepoint of the Cairo Tower, the grand colonial relics capped with neon billboards. Here, where many spent their lives in appalling poverty, the desiccated outskirts of the city crumbled into space and infinity to rejoin the embrace of the Sahara. The sights, the sands, the possibilities of the big city overwhelmed her.

The family spent its first night at the home of Muhammad Badar, Sami's oldest friend. They had grown up on the same street, attended the same school, kicked a football on the same summer tarmac. Muhammad had gone south when Sami went east, to run a factory that chugged out frozen chickens. His wife was a doctor, specializing in diseases of the lungs. They lived with their three young daughters in a modern apartment, on the eleventh floor in the leafy suburb of Daulat al-Nasser. The welcome was warm. Muhammad reached for his narghile, and the women made a fuss over the new arrivals.

The view from the Badars' expansive living room windows, stretching out across the city, was dazzling. There were fresh flowers in vases, and the apartment was sleek and streamlined. Muhammad's daughters wore shorts and tight tank tops. Sami's wife and her sister, perched like sparrows on the sofa, seemed dowdy and gray beside the doctor's embroidered headscarf and dramatic eye makeup. Sami unpacked his portable water pipe from its travel box and carefully assembled it. The men spent the evening talking of the old days in the chicken industry, their smoke whisked away by an efficient air conditioning system. The women chatted politely and played with the girls.

Sami's appointment at Giza Zoo was scheduled for the morning of the twenty sixth of August, a full two weeks away. The family reunion, however, could not be held off for more than a day or two.

As Sami expected, it was strained. His mother's home was in a barren new district littered with cheap, utilitarian apartment buildings erected by the government. The apartment across the hall was windowless, its ill-fitting door crooked on its hinges. Mrs. Khader's house was neat and new, but its appliances incongruously old, as if transported from another space and time.

"You are fatter than before," said one sister, kissing Sami coldly on the cheek.

"And you have more gray hair," said another.

Sami's mother embraced him stiffly. She was small and silent, with green catlike eyes. Bracelets jangled at her wrists. She gave off a faint whiff of disappointment.

"You don't care about us?" asked an uncle, clapping Sami too hard on the shoulder.

"It is life," responded Sami, "life that has kept us apart. It is not easy for us. The situation has been very hard. We can not travel at the drop of a hat."

After coffee, Sami brought out gifts. A dress for his mother and two gold rings. Sweets and linens for the aunts, sisters, and uncles; fresh, fragrant olive oil and *zaatar*, crushed thyme with sesame and hyssop, for the cousins. The children were thrust toys and ushered off to play, as the adults sat back stiffly to examine their goods.

Above them, solemnly encased in a heavy black frame, presided the portrait of a young boy, smiling in a school uniform. The last acceptable photograph of Omar, Sami's younger brother.

One winter evening when Omar was six, a Filipino servant, on his way to a lover's tryst, had borrowed his employer's car. The engine purred as he turned it over, leaving the headlights off to avoid attracting attention. He reversed. Omar, playing on the curb behind the car, was struck full force in the side of the head. He hit the ground, bleeding profusely. Hearing the screech of brakes, the

Khader women rushed to the window. They saw the little boy lying in the dust and a car speeding away into the night.

But this was not Cairo or Qalqilya. It was Saudi Arabia, where many women would not venture out, unchaperoned by a male relative, for fear of retribution at the hands of the *Mutawwa*, the religious police. Sami's mother watched from the window as the night sky closed in overhead and waited for one of the men of the household to return home.

By the time they finally reached a hospital, the damage had been done. Doctors cut away a third of the child's skull and warned that his understanding of the world would likely always remain that of a small child. Omar was confined to a wheelchair, unable to fend for himself. Sami's mother undertook his sole care, taking him along with her on her frequent trips to Egypt. She purchased an apartment with an elevator, so that they could more easily move about. She adapted her home and her life to his needs.

"Hello, habibi," he was fond of saying to visitors. "You are my friend. Give me a kiss." He liked to listen to his mother and sisters gossiping and was, they said, a very good boy.

Finally, at the age of twenty-six, Omar succumbed to his injuries. He was buried nearby, and his mother was finally free of two decades of burden. The Qalqilyan Khaders did not receive permits to travel in time to attend the funeral.

◆   ◆   ◆

To pass the time until his visit to the zoo, Sami tried to make the most of the vast city. He showed his wife and daughters the Mosque of Ibn Tulun and took them shopping through the dazzling alleyways of the Khan Al-Khalili bazaar. He climbed the Cairo Tower to admire the view and ate steaming tubs of *kushari*, its hot rice and lentils mingling irresistibly with crisp fried onion and fiery tomato sauce, and strawberry ice cream from street-side stalls. Twice, he went to the Egyptian Museum to look at the mummies. He studied papyri depicting the grizzly death ministrations of the ancients and picked up a few tips.

One afternoon, while the girls wandered the riverside gardens with their cousins, Sami watched anglers' floats bob and dither on the murky Nile. Sitting on a bench, dreaming of landing a bass or a perch, he was surprised to find Uzhdan at his side.

"Daddy," she said, "my school report came today."

As usual, Uzhdan's performance had been exceptional; she had excelled in literature and the natural sciences. Sami was pleased. Next year would be her final year of compulsory education, and the one that determined her future. If she kept it up, she could continue on to university to carve out a solid career.

But she was a teenage girl, becoming, he feared, more interested by the day in fashion and pop music. She would need to apply herself, putting her books before her other, worldly, desires, if she was to succeed.

"This year is the most important of your life," said Sami, glancing through the glowing report. "It will show you the way. Maybe you will become a doctor or an engineer. Or, if you don't concentrate on your studies, you will have to sit at home and do nothing."

"Daddy, you know I want to be a vet. Like you."

"I have already told you. This is forbidden."

They had been through the same old argument many times before, since Uzhdan was a very little girl.

In another world, she might have made the perfect apprentice. She loved animals and cared tirelessly for the feeble newborns he often brought home. She adored the zoo and was constantly badgering him to allow her to attend his clinics, though he always declined. She sorrowed at the death of an animal yet took an active interest in how the corpse was to be preserved. She was caring but usually unsentimental.

He recalled, however, how upset she had once been at the fate of a pet chicken, raised faithfully from a hatchling, which had lived on his balcony.

One evening, his wife and daughters off visiting in Nablus, an aunt, fat and overbearing, had come to visit. She was appalled to see a plump chicken living like a queen out on the balcony.

"What is that chicken doing there, nephew?" she asked Sami.

"It is Uzhdan's chicken. Her pet."

"But chickens are not for petting. They are for eating."

"But auntie. . . "

"Aren't they?"

"But. . . "

"*Aren't* they?"

"Yes, auntie."

The aunt licked her lips.

"Come, Sami. It's time for supper."

Uzhdan had not talked to her father for a full fortnight after coming home to find her pet had been roasted in olive oil and served with couscous to a nasty old lady.

But Sami had more important concerns for his daughter's prospects as a veterinarian. The majority of work for a Palestinian vet, himself excepted, revolved around the goat and the cow, the sheep, the horse, the farmyard fowl. Farming was a male profession, and invariably for the poor and uneducated. Life in the West Bank was different from life in Cairo, where rich ladies carried Pekingese and Pomeranians around in their handbags. His daughter would stay in Qalqilya, and a vet in Qalqilya must be able to win clients. Those clients would not wish to see a lady with her hand up the rear of their prize bull.

Better, he thought, to choose a safer profession. Just look at Suha, the doctor of lungs and diseases: there was a career woman, successful and respected in her field. Uzhdan listened quietly and went back to strolling with her cousins in the garden.

◆   ◆   ◆

On the long-awaited morning of the twenty-sixth of August, Sami rose early and donned his jacket and tie. He shaved, combed his hair, and boarded a spluttering bus to the southern district of Giza. He watched with distaste as the churning city went by and tried to recollect all he had once read about the famous Giza Zoo.

Giza Zoo, now 115 years old, was originally the luxuriant harem garden of Ismail Ali Pasha, khedive of Egypt and grandson of Muhammad Ali Pasha, who had once sent giraffes to Charles X and George IV. The ruler commissioned miles of sugared-almond pathways through verdant undergrowth, installed coral grottos beside contemplative ponds, and erected a wrought-iron suspension bridge designed by Alexandre-Gustave Eiffel.

Then, on the first of March, 1891, in a gesture of benevolence, Khedive Ismail Ali cooped a handful of his menagerie animals into small iron cages and opened his gardens to the public. In the first year alone, twenty-four-thousand visitors came to savor delights hitherto open only to a flock of Circassian concubines.

By 1897, the heavy footfall of peasantry had taken its toll, and the zoo was shabby and floundering, its animals miserable.

In 1898, its savior arrived. Stanley Flower was English and of sound zoological stock. His father had been president of London's illustrious Zoological Society and director of its Natural History Museum. Before arriving in Egypt, he had traveled with his young bride through Malaya and Siam, reporting on its natural sciences to his government, and had penned the much-admired *A List of Zoological Gardens of the World*. He was a man of action and, with only the most basic ingredients at his disposal, set about transforming Giza Zoo with imagination and finesse.

First, he tackled the cages, replacing iron bars with open spaces. He erected fences along the gazelle enclosure to prevent them from drowning, as they frequently did, in an adjacent canal. He laid out grand plans for the elephant enclosure to allow them to explore a wide open space and created new diversions for the zoo's big cats. Creatures, he said, could be kept in captivity quite happily, if only they were entertained. He was a good fifty years ahead of his time.

"The free animal does not live in freedom," Zurich Zoo curator Heini Hediger would famously state in 1950, in his seminal manual on the principles of zookeeping, "neither in space nor as regards its behavior towards other animals." Cages, Hediger would argue, could prove satisfactory living spaces so long as certain needs, including mental stimulation, were met. Thus, he said, "The surroundings of the captive animal lose their significance as a place to escape from at all costs, but gain on the contrary the significance of an individual living space, to be defended against all and only forsaken under compulsion." Zookeepers still abide by Hediger's principles today.

At Giza, Flower's methods worked. Breeding rates shot up as cage bars were torn down and entertainments for the animals introduced. The lemur and monkey exhibits were the best of the age, and Flower's giraffe enclosure, completed in 1910, was the largest on the planet. His endangered egrets, bred from just two colonies left in the wild, were so content at the zoo that once set free, they did not wish to leave. A zebra that jumped in a fit of high spirits out of its paddock waited patiently at the gate to be let back in. By 1906, annual visitors exceeded two hundred thousand. Giza, like Hagenbeck's Tierpark in Germany, was the talk of the zoological world.

◆   ◆   ◆

After a meandering, belching bus journey, Sami arrived at the wrought gates of Giza Zoo with just moments to spare. He was ushered by a ticket clerk—who, he noted, kept a very orderly booth—through a side door and into a waiting room. There, a secretary handed him a booklet on Egyptian plovers. The waiting room, he thought, was rather shabby.

He tried to concentrate on Qalqilya and on the zoo, mentally preparing his speech. How pleasant, he thought, to return fresh and triumphant, with the promise of new animals and allegiances. He allowed himself to wonder whether, at home, the Carnivore Department might almost be complete.

"The manager will see you now, sir," said the secretary. Sami tucked the booklet into his jacket pocket and went inside.

The well-fed manager of Giza Zoo sat stolidly behind his desk. His office furnishings were faded and old-fashioned.

Sami was anxious to impress upon the manager the urgency of his mission. The manager settled back into a thick, padded chair, and Sami began.

The manager listened with declining concentration to the explanations, elaborations, and descriptions provided by his earnest visitor. He was informed of the geographical location and social situation of Qalqilya. He was told of the renovations and of the new museum. He heard a complete, annotated list of animal casualties and another of the specimens they required. He learned of Sami's intentions to transform Qalqilya into an international zoo and the efforts involved in such a proposition. He nodded and frowned, at appropriate intervals. He smoked a cigarette. He flicked through a pile of correspondence. He drank a cup of mint tea.

Eventually, Sami ground to an exhausted halt. The story, so far, of Qalqilya Zoo seemed complete. The manager looked up.

"I would be pleased," he said, "to help you."

Sami's heart missed a beat.

"But," the manager continued, "I am afraid this will not be possible."

Sami swallowed.

"No. You see, there are plans. Plans to expand. Plans for another seven zoos throughout the country. In Aswan, you see. In Luxor. Alexandria. And we are committed," he picked a mint leaf from between his front teeth, "to stocking them."

"I see." Sami's voice faltered. He had been so sure. Where, now, would he turn?

"Not even," he croaked, "one or two animals? Small ones?"

The manager shook his head. "But perhaps," he considered gently, "your mayor could send us an official letter, requesting future spare animals. We could put it in our files."

"Files," repeated Sami. "Yes. Thank you."

The manager regarded Sami intently.

"Life is difficult for you, is it not?"

"It is."

"It is not easy for us, these days, either." The manager contrived an air of sorrow. "Life is hard for the modern zoo." He looked at his watch. "Now, if you'll excuse me, I have a lunch appointment."

Sami nodded and rose weakly to his feet.

"Still, we must press on," said the manager, extending a hand from the comfort of his office chair. "We must not give up. Our heart," he concluded, "is with the Palestinian people."

On Sami's way out of the office, the manager's secretary furnished him with several further booklets. One depicted an array of stuffed animals being examined by an amputee. She smiled sympathetically, handed him a complimentary ticket to the zoo and a poster describing the migratory routes of North African birds, and showed him the door.

Sami's spirit drooped as he left the waiting room. Just twenty minutes had passed since the beginning of the meeting, a meeting he had been planning for months.

The trouble and obligation of a visit to his family, he thought dourly, all for a few, admittedly attractive, booklets.

He unfurled the poster. It would look very nice, he considered, on his office wall. He scrutinized the pictures of the stuffed animals and the interested amputee. These were very nice booklets indeed. He stopped for a moment. Perhaps, he considered, he would create something similar with the photographs sent by Ostrich.

◆   ◆   ◆

Though hot, disappointed, and faintly grimy, Sami felt it a shame to waste his complimentary ticket to Giza Zoo. After all, the manager had promised future spare animals, if only Qalqilya's mayor would pen a good, beseeching letter. It made sense, then, to take stock of the zoo's inventory.

He strolled along the main avenue and took a turn toward the large animal quarters.

What Sami saw, as he wandered, filled him with surprise. The hippo enclosure, though larger than Dubi's, was scattered with rubbish, its pond scummy and shallower than his own hippo's modest bath. The elephants, though still housed in Flower's wide open space, were shackled to the ground. They swung their trunks listlessly, their eyes clouded and faraway. Swarthy keepers hovered with mean-looking elephant hooks.

Sami approached the giraffe compound. Suddenly, with a sharp pang, he missed Ruti. He had, he thought, a toffee somewhere for her distant cousin. He unwrapped the sticky sweet and offered it up to the long, welcoming tongue of a pretty female giraffe. Immediately, an unshaven keeper in dirty beige overalls appeared. "Twenty piasters," he hissed, "Baksheesh. You feed animal, you give me."

Sami was scandalized.

As he progressed further through the zoo, what Sami saw was much of the same. He felt his spirits lifting. Cages were, contrary to his imagination's blissful vistas, thick with filth and iron bars.

The baboons were all mad, madder even than Fateen. Many of the other animals were old, moth-eaten, or unhappy. And everywhere he turned, rude and unruly keepers were demanding tips. One jabbed a pitchfork at a leopard. Another took money from a small child in exchange for a snapshot with a delirious lion.

The pride of Egypt's capital until the 1950s, Giza Zoo, it transpired, had suffered during the chaos of the revolution. Since then, it had slowly settled into neglect. Its museum, once Flower's temple of learning, seemed to hold more ragged specimens than its cages. The zoo was a place favored by picnickers rather than those seeking a window into the animal kingdom.

So this, thought Sami, stopping to observe a ragged pelican, was the fruit of old Mr. Flower's efforts. He could, he believed, do better.

◆　　◆　　◆

Sami was impatient to get back to Qalqilya, to his animals, and on with the new plans he had been developing, during long family evenings, for an Agricultural Museum. He was tired of being a visitor. He was tired of his family, and he was heartily tired of Egypt.

"These people don't live as well as we do," he grumbled to his wife. "You try to eat their bread, and you can't eat it. Also, their rice is very bad."

The evening before the family's departure, Sami's wife and daughters packed their bags, fingering silken scarves and folding fashionable new clothes. Uzhdan, in particular, did not wish to return home. A new term would be starting, and though she intended to study hard, her future did not seem as bright and exhilarating as that of her new Cairene girlfriends.

"Why don't you come to visit us, mother?" Sami's wife asked her mother-in-law dutifully.

"I am afraid of that place," Sami's mother replied. "Life will get worse. You should stay here."

Sami could not suppress a snort, and both women glared at him icily.

That night he escaped to the home of Muhammad Badar.

"Qalqilya is quiet," he told his friend. "I like quiet places. This city is too big. Here, too many people are running. I sold my car, and now I walk to work."

Muhammad nodded, but said nothing.

"Here, you do not feel like a person, an individual. When I had the chance to go back to Palestine, I thought about it only for one night. Saudi Arabia is not my home. Egypt is not my home. Palestine is my home. I had to go back."

"But how can you call that place your home," asked Muhammad, "when you are trapped inside it, like a cage?"

"The meaning of home," Sami replied, "is the place where you have everything you need. In Qalqilya, for me," he drew deeply on his narghile, "I believe this is so."

Chapter Eight
September 2006

Beware the barrenness
of a busy life.
—SOCRATES

The slaughterhouse vet was waiting for Sami at the zoo's front gate on the morning of his return. A red bloom appeared on the bridge of his nose and progressed across his mealy cheeks. "While you were away," he began, "the male leopard became ill. He was sick and lazy, and only ate half his food. I went to your office to find vitamins, but it is such a mess. I could not find anything."

Sami smiled. He was happy to be home. He had eaten a good meal, seen friends, and had his hair smartly cut by his local barber.

From the window seat of a long-distance Egyptian bus, he had thought carefully on his meeting with the manager of Giza Zoo and decided, in retrospect, it had been a success. Of course there must be formalities. Of course there must be a letter from the mayor. This, he now was certain, would be the key to the "future spare animals" Giza's manager had all but guaranteed.

"You left the zoo," griped the slaughterhouse vet, "and you forgot to teach me. Now the leopard is very sick."

"Then I will cure him. Please excuse me." Sami strode away, swinging his briefcase. Inside he carried plans for his new Agricultural Museum, and he was keen to set the wheels in motion.

The vet glared after him.

Rama the leopard had lived at the zoo for more than ten years. His mate, Chika, was smaller and more beautiful, with a narrow face and bright eyes. She lived next door. In the wild, leopards are unsociable creatures, creeping off into the branches of trees to savor their kill. Encounters with the opposite sex are brief and perfunctory. Although, in captivity, female leopards have been known to produce healthy young at the age of nineteen, most reach the end of their reproductive lives at roughly eight and a half. Chika, like Rama, was more than a decade old, but the pair had never managed to breed and now were past hope of producing a litter. They lived solitary lives, side by side, in empty quarters.

Rama was frequently ill. Sami, Motke, and even the deputy mayor's brother had offered various theories, from renal and chest infections to a lack of Vitamin A as an infant. In the wild, Rama's advanced age would be cause enough for ill health, but captive leopards easily double their natural life expectancy. Still, he often picked up coughs and sneezes in winter, which Sami believed to be the fault of drafty quarters and regularly treated with generous doses of antibiotics.

Leopards, in the wild, are the hardiest of all the big cats, capable of sustaining life in any terrain, from rainforest to desert floor. But the last time Rama fell ill, Sami almost lost him altogether.

It had happened in the winter of 2004, one particularly miserable, rainy day. Yail Misqawi had completed his usual feeding rounds and alerted Dr. Sami to the fact that the leopard seemed uninterested in his breakfast. When Sami went to investigate, he found the sleek, handsome animal lying on his side, the shallow rise and fall of his chest the only indication he was still alive.

Without hesitation, Sami entered the cage.

Rama raised his head and regarded him. Satisfied that the doctor's presence bore no threat, he let his head thud back to the ground. The big cat whined softly and closed his eyes. Sami crouched, placed one ear on Rama's flank, and listened. He extended a front leg and felt the outstretched tendons. He raised a lip, exposing killer fangs, and opened one eye, whose white was tinged with yellow. Pneumonia.

Sami rose and went for his gun.

The zoo was empty, except for two ladies in long black coats and white headscarves. Sami hastened past them, clutching his rifle in one hand, a fishing rod and tackle box in the other. The ladies conferred as he passed. They lingered for a few moments and then followed with curiosity.

Sami stopped outside Rama's cage and knelt down. He opened the fishing box. It was filled with an assortment of glass bottles and syringes of different sizes. The two ladies arrived. A pair of men munching sunflower seeds joined them. A young woman in a long red coat, gripping the chubby hand of a toddler, appeared. Sami selected a bottle and syringe and filled one from the other.

"Don't worry, I'm not going to kill him," said Sami, as he loaded the homemade syringe, with its flight of tufty hen feathers, into the end of the gun. He had created all his own medicine delivering darts, which could be retrieved and reused several times, to save the zoo the considerable expense of disposable syringes. "He knows what I am going to do."

Rama raised his head and hissed. With an immense effort, the leopard rose to his feet and crawled to a platform at the back of the cage. He struggled to hoist himself up onto it and then lay down, resting his head heavily on his paws. Next door, Chika watched discreetly from behind her water bowl.

The Syrian bears looked on with interest. Rama growled softly as Dr. Sami lifted his gun and took aim. The lady in the red overcoat let out a little gasp. The child huddled into the folds of her robe. Everyone held their breath. Chika froze.

Dr. Sami shifted his position slightly and fired.

With a thwack, the syringe hit Rama squarely in the middle of his left flank. The leopard roared with anger. The noise was fearsome; the onlookers shrank back despite the metal bars protecting them. Sami cast a line with his rod and extracted the syringe, dragging it back through the bars.

Rama swiped at the pole and growled again, with the deep dawdle of a slowly revving engine. The anesthetic was beginning to take effect. His paw lolled, then dropped to the floor.

Sami turned to his appreciative audience. "In a few moments, this animal will be fast asleep. Would the little girl like a photograph with a leopard?"

As the leopard slept, Sami dispensed an antibiotic drip and prepared a follow-up course to be administered for the rest of the week. The next morning, Rama still found it hard to stand, but his eyes were clearer and his breathing less shallow. On the second day he was back on his feet, and by the third his appetite had returned. After seven days of mortal illness, Rama was fully recovered and as taciturn as ever.

Now, eighteen months later and in midsummer, it was with trepidation that Sami approached the leopard cage. What, he sighed, could be wrong this time?

The first thing he noticed about the zoo, however, was the litter. A curious fortnight-long commercial fair had risen up amid the wasteland at the center of the zoo, Sami's future international aviary, turning it into a hot, cramped exhibition ground. Allowing himself the distraction, Sami swerved off into the narrow ranks of stalls, whose lights were extinguished and cash registers unmanned. There was an overabundance of food. Al-Jebrini Dairy and Food Industries proudly displayed their cheeses and yogurts, while boxes of Chipsy Land chips were imaginatively stacked into cityscapes at the Chipsy Land stall. Wasps buzzed greedily at a confectionary stand. Sami, struck by the mess and unbearable heat, helped himself to a Club Lemon soda from a refrigerator and plucked a barber's shop drinking straw from a cardboard box.

Further on, the produce gave way to an astonishing array of merchandise. There were washing machines, fridge freezers, wedding dresses, and water pumps. Nablus Paints offered a matte, gloss, or silk finish in a variety of shades; Qosmar Brothers displayed computers. There were schoolbooks and satchels, pipes, seeds, marble tiles, and cleaning products. A whole stall was devoted to Sinoria Beef Luncheon Meat; another sold lounge chairs in the shape of stiletto shoes. There were tents and hammocks, teeming tanks of goldfish, prayer mats bearing Yasser Arafat's grinning face, and t-shirts—for both adults and children—depicting masked men with Kalashnikovs emerging fiercely from a ditch.

Judging from the debris, the enterprise had been a great success for several successive nights. The aftermath was sticky and stifling, buzzing with bluebottles and flying ants. The close smell of crowd still hung in the air. The floor was littered with brightly colored tickets. A handful of stall guards lazed in makeshift shade. A sweeper went about his task without enthusiasm. Sami heard the strains of a song from a nearby classroom. "We are living," a class chanted cheerfully, "but we have no life." Sami could only imagine the noise each night, as crowds thronged through, disturbing the animals.

He steered back onto the avenue, toward Rama's house. One hog deer, he noticed, had lost a dramatic amount of weight, and its ribs pronged its sides. Sami pulled a pencil from his pocket and made a note on a scrap of paper. He paused at the ostriches. A female's wing hung low, flapping uselessly. It might be broken, but only an anesthetic, and a good investigation, would tell him for sure. Passing the Shetland ponies, Sami noticed a length of pipe and some wooden planks lying among them. He looked up to see Yail Misqawi striding briskly past, a kettle and two teacups tucked under one arm.

"Yail, hello!" Sami called. "I have a job for you. The ponies."

Misqawi looked back over his shoulder but did not slacken his pace. He shook his head.

"No time, Doctor," he replied, "I am busy."

Sami watched as the keeper stopped at a wooden pergola, sat down next to a young lady, and poured two glasses of tea. Sami slowly shook his head. "What kind of people are these?" he said to himself, and took a sip of Club Lemon soda.

Though alarmed at the chaos reigning over the zoo, Sami was also a little pleased that all had not gone entirely smoothly without him. Rama seemed glad to see him when the vet arrived at his cage, and rubbed against his hand. Sami regarded the leopard closely. Rama was not faring too badly. It could be an infection or internal parasites. He decided on a course of antibiotics, just to be sure. The fool, he thought, to think that vitamins would do the trick.

Heading to his office, to collect his dart gun and medicines, he stopped to greet Fufu and then Ruti. Both were well and appreciative of his attentions. He veered left and stepped through the Carnivore Department's gate.

His eyes widened.

Save for one solitary worker, drinking coffee in the shade of what was to be a bear's bedroom, no one was there. Nothing, not one wall, one fence, or one lick of paint, appeared to have changed.

"Two months," he laughed gloomily, looking about at half-built structures, at doorless white-washed buildings with their sand-colored, fenceless dividers.

"Hey, you!" he called to the workman. "Where are the others?"

"At the amusement park," he replied, tapping a cigarette from its package, "putting up the Ferris wheel."

◆　　◆　　◆

The amusement park had erupted quickly and quietly in Sami's absence. It stood on a wedge of land just south of the ticket office, land that the municipality seemed to have appropriated from a willing seller overnight. Swift meetings had been held and a decision unanimously reached: The best use of space, by far, would be a collection of fairground rides to inject new interest and revenue into municipality pockets. Unlike the commercial fair currently occupying the zoo's center, the amusement park was to be permanent.

Soon, bright fairground rides had arrived at the zoo gates, in tight polythene bearing mysterious Chinese symbols. There was a dodgem ride: Twenty shiny new cars upholstered in faux leather, sprayed shades of metallic red, green, and blue. A roundabout, where toddlers could sit on enormous ladybirds chugging over a colorful fiberglass track. And the pièce de resistance, a Ferris wheel, with twelve powder-pink gondolas, each topped with a white plastic umbrella. Sami arrived and gazed up at its skeleton with a mixture of awe and dismay, as his Carnivore Department workers busied themselves with bolts, screws, and pinions.

Silently, he turned on his heel and headed for the comfort of his office.

On the way, Dr. Sami thrilled to discover a small sign that not all progress had entirely ceased in his absence. Tall tubular barriers of chicken wire and wooden stakes had sprung up to protect the trees surrounding the giraffe enclosure. Ruti, it transpired, had not been the sole culprit responsible for the trees' destruction. Teenage boys were frequently spotted balanced precariously on each other's shoulders, snapping off branches to poke through the bars to the grateful animal.

It had to be stopped, Abu Shir had declared. New trees would be expensive.

Sami gladly retreated into his office. He found it mercifully untouched, save for one unexpected addition. In the far corner, where a birdcage had formerly stood, was a brand new computer. He smiled, surprised. Perhaps things were not as bad as he suspected. He set the kettle on to boil and walked over to admire his new equipment.

Instantly, the office door opened, and Abu Shir appeared. He slumped down opposite Sami's desk.

"You have returned."

"Yes, thank you."

"Things are terrible."

"I see."

"Terrible. Are you making tea?"

◆　　◆　　◆

The worst of it, related Abu Shir as he sipped hot tea, was that responsibility for the zoo had changed hands. He could no longer call himself, he grumbled, zoo manager. In Sami's absence, the municipality had seen fit to transfer the zoo, until now an autonomous department, to the jurisdiction of the engineering department. Abu Shir's duties remained unchanged. But he had been demoted. He was now, he choked, "branch manager, Engineering Department."

Further, he had been informed by a petulant official who called himself "the municipal job inspector," that he was now answerable, on a daily basis, to Qalqilya's chief engineer, the elegant Nabil Baron. Forthwith, he was charged with the responsibility of a report, to be submitted in writing to the municipality at the end of each working day.

"So," concluded Abu Shir, "I shall be expecting yours on my desk by lunchtime."

Though ancient zoos were sometimes known to keep accounts of significant events and acquisitions, the first modern daily zoological report was not penned until the twenty-fifth of February, 1828, with the opening of London Zoo. First, the report focused on building works. "The boundary wall for supporting the bank next to the Bear Pit began," it noted. Then, it moved on to noteworthy happenings. An emu had laid an egg. An otter had died, "in consequence of a diseased tail." Setting the standard for later zoos, its "Transactions" book was delineated clearly with "IN" and "OUT" pages. There, new arrivals were recorded on their procession "in," and causes of death for those outgoing were valiantly described. Other zoos soon followed suit. Amongst the Tower of London's animals, an alligator died of "exhaustion"; a jackal of "decline." Two birds died "from fright," and the Angora cat was "killed by the dingo." Later, at Giza, Stanley Flower took up the mantle of thorough record keeping, filing reports on every aspect of zoological life, from the acquisition of foodstuffs to those animals disposed of as "spare," "fierce," or "undesirable."

Sami was unimpressed. He would now have to write a daily report, which the manager, it seemed, would pass off as his own and send on to the chief engineer. From this, the chief engineer would type another and pass it on to the mayor. And from there? Who would read all these neat, detailed, daily reports? Allah himself? Now he understood why higher powers had seen fit to furnish him with a computer.

"The beginning of the end," griped Abu Shir. "Like the Soviet Union."

Sami stared at the branch manager, Engineering Department, in intense irritation.

"Abu Shir," he said, "on my holiday, I did some reading. There is something I would like to discuss."

All the way back from Egypt, Sami had been bothered by what he witnessed at Giza Zoo. Though his animals did not bite the bars of their cages or bang their heads against the floor, he had seen the misery imposed by boredom and experienced it first-hand, with nothing around to skin, stuff, or examine for several long weeks. He had read, in a paperback work on zoo animals, of "environmental enrichment," and was intrigued.

Captive monkeys, he had learned, fared better with something practical to occupy their time. In the wild, the majority of their day was spent foraging, and monkeys' moods could easily be improved by a simple addition to their den. Fill several inches of cage floor, Sami had read, with wood chips or shavings. Then, at each mealtime—a time to be varied from day to day—sprinkle food among the sawdust, turning it over underfoot to hide the treats and tidbits. The group would happily spend the afternoon sifting through the chippings, extracting their dinner bit by bit. Social interactions, he read, would improve in this manner. Health and fertility would follow.

He read, too, that leopards, fond in the wild of an arboreal home, fared better when a "vertical dimension" was added to their exhibit. This, a study explained, could take the form of a branch, a series of tree branches, or even a simple concrete ledge.

Thinking over his leopards' housing arrangements, Sami was satisfied. For now their cages might be small, void of the luxury of space or foliage, but they did, at least, have a concrete ledge.

"These ideas," coaxed Sami, "are very inexpensive, and will be good for the animals."

Abu Shir scowled. Over the past month, he had had his fill of people coming to him with their good ideas. First, there had been Dr. Sami's replacement. A complainer and a troublemaker, poking his nose where it was not wanted, making all sorts of suggestions for things he knew nothing about. Not once had he offered the manager one of his wife's fancy imported cigarettes or stopped to chat over a cup of tea. Next, the shake-up within the ranks and the prospect of mountains of paperwork, each report requiring his full and detailed daily attention. And then, just as he felt things could get no worse, the municipality had turned up on his doorstep with their designs for fancy rides that whizzed and screamed. The new amusement park was merely steps from his office, and the test runs had given him a throbbing headache. He simply wished to be left alone.

"It is," he replied, shaking his head and draining his tea, "not for now."

"What do you mean?"

"Too messy. Too much work for the keepers."

"But it will be worthwhile."

"Too much work," repeated Abu Shir and hastily rose to his feet. "People are busy enough." He stopped at the doorway. "Perhaps in the Carnivore Department," he permitted, and vanished.

Sami stretched and rose to refill his teacup. Abdel Raouf Joadi arrived, eyes wheeling giddily, a bucket in hand. Without a word, he offered it to Sami.

"Thank you," he said, taking the handle.

The keeper departed. If only all the staff here, Sami thought, could be so obliging. He glanced into the bucket. Thirty eggs of different shapes and colors. Pigeon, chicken, quail, and owl. All fresh and ready for his super deluxe turbo incubator.

The super deluxe turbo incubator was another of Sami's homespun inventions. It stood in one corner of his kitchen cubby, a black metal box with a small glass door. It had a knob to control the temperature and another to set the timer. When he flicked the "On" switch, it issued a low hum, and a green light glowed. Sami placed the eggs carefully, nestled in cotton, on the shelves within. In its former life, his incubator had been a dishwasher.

Hala qadd lhaafak midd rijleik, thought Sami. *Stretch your legs as far as your quilt will cover.*

Sami had fashioned forceps for treating snakes. He had made tongue depressors from lollipop sticks and old wooden spoons and learned to cast a broken limb with strips of an old shirt. There were the feeding bottles for the orphaned animals, the woven nests to encourage the birds to breed, and the artificial mother, though she had not been used for a while.

Sami peered in through the window at the ranks of eggs. If only a few would hatch, he could rear the fledglings to maturity. He poured more tea. One last cup, he decided, and he would wander down to the museum. He glanced at the clutter on his desk. A white envelope stared blankly up at him. "Dr. Sami Khader," it read, "Qalqilya Zoo." It bore the stamp of the municipality. Sami took a surgical knife and slit open the envelope.

The document announced itself as an "Official Job Description." Each municipal employee, outlined the preamble, had been furnished with a similar brief, tailored to the extent of his or her duties. This description, it continued, would form the basis for future discussions on status, authority, and salary. It provided a comprehensive overview of every element of the employee's working life, drawn from detailed study, and made clear the tasks expected of him or her. Below was a simple chart, divided into two columns. "Duty," said one; "Description," said the other. Beneath "Duty," the solitary word lurched out from the page. "VET." The second column's message was equally succinct. "Treat sick zoo animals," it said. "Make them better."

Sami stormed from his office. Why, he fumed, heading down the steps, had he toiled over his Natural History Museum for these ungrateful people? He'd received no vote of thanks, no praise, no bonus; just this letter, stating that, as far as the authorities were concerned, he was nothing more than a common VET. They had not noticed his efforts at all. "For the people," he comforted himself beneath his breath, as he stalked to the museum gate, "I built it for the people."

Inside, the lights were off, and the air was clammy. Sami closed his eyes and inhaled deeply. The guest book stood open on its lectern. Sami thumbed the stiff leaves. It was filled with comments.

"All the city writes here!" he brightened.

He noticed a neat paragraph of praise from Aziz Dwik, a prominent Hamas politician, and noted the date. Lucky, he thought. The politician had been arrested and carted off to prison the following day. He thumbed on. The next page was filled with scribbled comments and obscene suggestions. A quickly penned baboon, performing something unmentionable on a crocodile. He flipped further. The next page, the same.

"Africa, here I come," he growled.

Sami tucked the book under one arm and continued his inspection. One of his stuffed snakes, he noticed, had been trodden on, and was squashed, like a length of hose pipe, in the middle. An empty space in the middle of a display cabinet betrayed the theft of an ostrich egg. Cigarette ends littered the floor. He continued to the final room. The head of Sami's prize African python drooped sadly. Several of its ribs were missing. Sami stopped to inspect the damage, secreting the guest book behind the snake's pedestal.

The African python, once shiny, lithe, and living, had fallen victim to one of Sami's previous disastrous leaves of absence. It was winter 2002, and he had taken a week's holiday at home, closing up his clinic to concentrate on the things he liked best. He rested; he met friends, pottered, and stuffed animals. His wife provided hearty lunches every day. He napped throughout the afternoon and helped Uzhdan and Hend with their homework each evening.

Upon his return to work, he found that his biggest snake, sleek and handsome, had perished.

It appeared that on one of the iciest nights, the snake's heating system, an antiquated radiator of the type commonly found in old schoolrooms and hospitals, had not been turned on. In the nineteenth century, Mr. Cops, warden of the Tower of London menagerie, wrapped his reptiles in blankets and warmed them gently over a stove to help them survive the harsh English winters. At Qalqilya, no one had considered even the electrical options. The snake had frozen to death.

◆ ◆ ◆

The slaughterhouse vet caught up with Dr. Sami as he was administering Rama's second antibiotic dose of the day. Sami knelt beside the leopard, filling a syringe and softly cooing into the big cat's ear.

"You have isolated the problem?" asked the slaughterhouse vet.

"Yes."

"Are you are giving him vitamins?"

"No. That would be a stupid thing."

The slaughterhouse vet glared. "If you wished me to do this job better," he sniffed, "you should have provided training."

"I should have taught you which medicine to use? You were trained, the same as me. I should have taught you how to use the anesthetic gun? You might have hit a passerby. You don't know the weight, the type of animal, or how to calculate the right amount to use. You need to hit a special place in the animal's body. If you give him too much, he will die. Too little, and he will wake up. You will kill him, or he will kill you."

The slaughterhouse vet looked away.

"A leopard does not change its spots," said Sami, glancing at Rama. "This is an important point. Dead is dead."

The vet took a deep breath. "You are quite right, and this brings me to my important point."

Sami raised an eyebrow.

"Now that you have returned, *my* holiday can begin. You will be my replacement at the slaughterhouse. Be there at four o'clock sharp each morning; your duty lasts until nine. You must also perform a meat check at the market in the afternoon; I imagine you will make time between the zoo and your clinic. I will be away for one month exactly. I am not leaving town, but will be resting and recovering, at home. The municipality requires that you write two slaughterhouse reports per day and turn them over to me. I trust," he turned to leave, "you require no training."

Chapter Nine
October 2006

Sabaa saniyeh, wellbacht daayeh.
Seven trades, and luck is lost.
—PALESTINIAN PROVERB

he word "Ramadan" is derived from the Arabic *ramida*, an intense scorching. It had come early this year, in the last shriveling week of September. The wind was hot, and Sami felt sucked dry by the crude world of slaughter.

For several weeks Sami had risen before dawn to play the part of municipal meat inspector. With no time even for tea, he left the house at half past three, making his way on foot to the slaughterhouse. It opened early, as the first strains of the muezzin sang hoarsely out, and the first sheep and oxen were herded in. It was a miserable job. The smell was unpleasant; the atmosphere one of subdued terror. The floors streamed scarlet, and the workers were coarse. One Saturday night, for the first time in many months, Israeli troops streamed into town in military jeeps, and a curfew was declared until morning. No one at the municipality seemed to know why. The slaughterhouse could not open, and man and beast experienced a brief reprieve. Sami slept in, oblivious to the shouts and gunfire outside his bedroom window.

At work, he decided to follow in the footsteps of his predecessor. He installed himself behind a desk in the back office and engaged in a mixture of thumb twiddling and paper pushing. All he was obliged to do, at the end of each shift, was poke a head around the door to the freezer room and sign a paper to confirm all was in order. Later, he trawled the butchers' shops at the market. His visits were swift and superficial.

At the zoo, there could be no such slacking.

◆　　◆　　◆

On the first of October, well after nine in the evening, Sami, weary from another long day, was examining a dairy cow on the pavement outside his clinic. Sami's friend, Mr. Salaa, had stopped by for tea and answered the telephone when it rang.

"He is," said Mr. Salaa.

He paused and listened. A small, rattling voice shrieked from the receiver.

"Abu Shir," Mr. Salaa mouthed to Sami.

Sami rolled his eyes. Mr. Salaa listened for a few seconds, then hung up.

"You are needed urgently," he reported. "I do not know what he wants."

"This man will be the death of me," grumbled Sami. "Would you like to come?"

Sami packed his briefcase, dispensed the cow and its worried owner, and locked up the clinic.

Outside, the night was airless and still.

"What could it be?" asked Mr. Salaa, hailing a passing taxi.

"Allah only knows," replied Sami, "but I hope it is important."

At the zoo gates, they were greeted by an animated Abu Shir, who was able to compose himself just long enough to gabble the facts.

Yail Misqawi, on performing his last, moonlit, round of the night, had heard strange squeaks coming from the monkey cages.

"Abu Shir!" he had called, dashing to the manager's office. Abu Shir was sitting outside, entertaining several members of his extended family with warm drinks and cakes from the canteen. With the arrival of Ramadan, afternoon tea was being taken in the middle of the night.

"There is a rat with the monkeys!" cried Yail Misqawi. "A rat!"

Stubbing out a cigarette and reaching for his flashlight, Abu Shir had set out to investigate. In the first three cages, Fateen, the harem, and Nora and Nira were free from intruders. The baboons screamed and huddled as his beam illuminated them. Abu Shir tutted. *Misqawi's imagination*, he thought, and proceeded to the fourth cage. Inside, a tiny furless creature trembled and gripped the cage bars.

Abu Shir pulled out his telephone and called Dr. Sami.

Sami listened with foreboding. His youngest pair had never yet produced young, and he was loath to watch another hysterical mother smashing her baby to pieces. If, this time, the female was intent on rejecting her baby, he would have to be swift.

"Come," he ordered, "Abu Shir, Mr. Salaa. Follow me."

The monkeys were dim silhouettes when the group arrived. Sami took the manager's flashlight and made a prompt assessment of the situation. He had little time.

"Abu Shir, take this torch," he ordered. "Point it directly into the lady monkey's eyes, and do not move." This, he thought, should hold her fast, at least for a little while.

"Now, Mr. Salaa," he pointed up the avenue, "fetch a hose pipe. Hurry."

Mr. Salaa rushed off and returned with a length of garden hose. Sami attached it to a hydrant beside the enclosure.

"All right," said Sami.

Inside the cage, the female was transfixed by the torch's beam. Her mate chattered and bared his teeth. Intermittently, his voice rose to a violent scream. There was no time, Sami knew, to go for anesthetic.

"Mr. Salaa," Sami was deadly calm, "take your hose pipe, and point it at the floor, between the male monkey and the cage door. Do you understand?"

Mr. Salaa nodded and turned on the hydrant.

Sami's monkeys detested water. The plume from the hose, he calculated, would be enough to discourage the male from lunging at him as he extracted the baby.

"Stay close to the bars, Mr. Salaa," instructed Sami. "And you, Abu Shir, keep the light pointed into that lady's eyes."

Nervously, they obeyed. Sami unlocked the door. "Steady, now," he said, and stepped into the cage.

Opposite, the male baboon hopped and screeched, held back by a bow of icy water. Sami advanced.

The female, though paralyzed by the flashlight, growled throatily. The baby shuddered. The male shrieked and threw himself at Mr. Salaa.

"Help!" cried Mr. Salaa, losing control of his hose. It snaked wildly into the air, soaking both Sami and the monkey, and breaking the steady beam of the torch.

"Stupid!" yelled Sami. He made a grab for the baby monkey. It shivered violently and clung tight to the bars. He tugged.

Mr. Salaa struggled to regain control of the thrashing hose, but it was too late. The female broke from her trance and bowled toward Sami. Her mate let out one great ear-piercing whoop, and leaped from his perch. Sami, baby dangling from one hand, took a neat backward step, cleared the cage, and slammed the door shut.

Two incensed baboons collided at full steam, teeth bared and baying for blood.

"In this work," Sami inspected the tiny, quaking baby beneath the faint beam of a street lamp, "I like the happy ending." Water dripped from the end of his nose. "I will name him"—he considered for a moment—"Rambo."

As Abu Shir and Mr. Salaa recovered from their ordeal, with the help of strong coffee from the cafeteria, Sami tucked Rambo snugly inside his jumper and headed to his office. The monkey clung to his chest with tight little fists. A good sign, thought Sami. He is strong. He rooted out a cardboard box and filled it with hay. It was late, and he was expected home. Sara would not be pleased.

◆　　◆　　◆

Sami reached his front door just before midnight, hoping for the helpful cover of darkness. A low play of light on the corridor wall suggested that, to the contrary, someone was awake and watching television. Sami peered timidly around the door frame.

His wife was curled up on the sofa, watching an old Egyptian romance, the volume turned down low.

"Hello," she yawned, stretching and rising. She padded softly over to take his jacket. Immediately, she spotted the cardboard box placed carefully in the darkest part of the corridor. "What is this?"

"Just an animal," Sami mumbled. "Is there any dinner left for me?"

He tried to bustle his way toward the kitchen, but was blocked by a firm hand.

"What *kind* of animal?" Her voice brimmed with suspicion.

"An orphaned animal," he replied, casually. "Now, what about my dinner?"

"A monkey," Sara hissed. "You've brought home a monkey."

"Actually, a baboon," Sami could not help himself, "but only a very little one."

She drew a deep breath and raised her hands to her hips. "You, and your very little friend. Out!"

Sami unleashed, on the orphan's behalf, a battery of compliments and promises. He cajoled. He appealed to his wife's maternal instincts. And, as a last resort, he reminded her that Ramadan was a month of charity.

"I will allow it," she finally relented, "but I am not happy."

Sami would be the animal's guardian, its sole provider, she conditioned. It would remain in its cage at all times, and Sami would not leave it in the house, unsupervised, when he went out to work.

Sami triumphantly moved the cardboard box to the corner of the kitchen as Sara, satisfied by her own leniency, heated the saucepans to serve him supper.

Sami labored through the night, faithfully feeding Rambo on the hour with baby milk from a cracked plastic teat. By first light, the baby baboon was comfortably installed in a modified plastic pet carrier, his neck adorned with a thin chain bearing a charm against the Evil Eye and a small tinkling bell, and the artificial mother had been retrieved from the cupboard.

Sami's artificial mother comprised a foot-high wooden stand that could be tilted at various gradients to allow the monkey to cling to it. Motherly fur had been added, in the form of an old piece of Cameroon sheepskin, padded out and fastened tight around the angled wooden platform. To either side, Sami had attached crudely sewn sausages of lint-stuffed fabric, threaded through with wire, to resemble arms. The baby could thus be tricked into feeling he was held fast by nurturing hands. To the top of the stand Sami had affixed a black plastic ring, on a hinge, angled downward. It held a baby bottle, filled with infant formula, allowing Rambo to suckle as if from his own mother's breast.

Sami had discovered the artificial mother in a dog-eared text-book, *Reproduction in Mammals,* published two decades before by Short and Austin. The device had been invented by Dr. Harry F. Harlow, who, throughout the 1950s, had performed experiments on Rhesus monkeys, separating babies from their mothers at birth and offering them a choice of two artificial replacements, one made of terry cloth stretched over a wooden frame and the other of wire mesh.

Though only the wire-mesh mother was outfitted with a bottle for suckling and an electric lamp for heat, the babies rarely stayed longer with her than was necessary for sustenance, preferring to snuggle up to the soft cloth version. Harlow, fascinated by what he called the "science of love," concluded that food and physical warmth alone were not enough to govern a baby monkey's desires.

It would take several months of constant care before Sami could go about his daily routine, traveling from home to zoo, zoo to clinic, and clinic to home again, without his simian companion. Meanwhile, Rambo thrived. During early mornings, while Sami idled at the slaughterhouse, the monkey slept. At the zoo, he played like any curious baby, exploring Sami's office. He trampled across the desk, knocking over pots of pencils and paper clips. He chattered to himself and took refuge inside an old sandal. He explored cupboards, chased ping-pong balls, and tried tenaciously to scale mountains of files and folders. At the clinic, he sat quietly, watching goldfish glide by.

Within a fortnight, three personalities dominated Rambo's world: The first, a silent, benevolent sheepskin-coated stand. The second, a large creature in climbable nylon trousers and warm tweed jackets. And the third, a white toy elephant, on which the little baboon rested his oversized head every night.

The monkey, thought Sami, would spend his life inhabiting neither one world nor the other. He would never fit in with other monkeys. He was wary of people he didn't know. He squealed with alarm and bared his blunt teeth if anyone attempted to prize him from his adopted father, his white elephant brother, or his moth-eaten, pungent, and much-loved artificial mother.

◆　　◆　　◆

During the third week of fasting, Sami dragged himself to the slaughterhouse for the last time. If this slaughterhouse work, he thought, was a leisurely profession, he was glad to be industrious.

Yet recent events at the zoo had left a taste in his mouth, bitter as a Ramadan morning.

A fortnight earlier, Mayor Wajeeh Qawas had been released once again from administrative detention. He had been hospitalized in Israel on account of his heart condition. As soon as he stabilized, he was hastily set free.

Sami wasted no time in penning the mayor several frank missives.

First, he sent a long letter welcoming the mayor home, outlining his several recent accomplishments, and explaining, in some detail, his enterprising visit to Giza Zoo. He emphasized the necessity of an official, heartfelt plea to its manager which, he felt sure, would proffer future spare animals.

A week later, he had not heard back. Irritated, he sent a second note, in a different vein.

Dear Mayor Wajeeh Qawas,
This is Dr. Sami Khader again, of Qalqilya Zoo.
I do everything here, from letter A to letter Z.

*I have created a Natural History Museum and am
planning another, of Agriculture. You are welcome to visit,
free of charge.*

*I have, however, only three letters in my title. The letters
V, E, and T are not enough.*

Please send somebody to discuss, urgently.

Still, he heard nothing.

"These," he complained to Abu Shir one evening, "are stupid
people."

◆   ◆   ◆

Sami swung Rambo back and forth inside his carrying case as the
slaughterhouse became a glad speck in the distance. Sparrows
chattered in a break of pine trees. A road sweeper turned lazy arcs
with a sparse-bristled broom.

It felt strange, uncharacteristic, to be so upset by such set-
backs. Sami was realistic. He knew that things took time. But it
was almost a year since his meeting with Dr. Motke and the
deputy mayor, and his international zoo seemed no closer to
fruition. The Carnivore Department was unfinished, a ferocious
Ramadan torpor had descended, and no one else seemed to care.

Though the Natural History Museum was still pulling in a tidy
profit and Rambo was flourishing, he felt he could not keep this
up, without help, reward, or recognition forever. He was tired. He
sensed his spirits flagging and, for the first time, worried that he
could not lift them himself.

A solitary man rode by on an improvised horse and cart.
Shade from the morning heat was provided by an old beach umbrella bolted to its back, declaring "Coke Is It." Sami considered
thumbing a lift, but refrained. The walk was good for his stubborn waistline, and he did not feel like explaining the monkey.

At the zoo, the atmosphere was soporific. Workers reclined around empty picnic tables. Three snoozed in the front seats of a van. The keepers lumbered about like two-toed sloths. A solitary gardener had set down his hoe and prayed, nose pressed deep into the turf, beneath a tree. Around him fell fat figs, like juicy temptations from God.

In honor of the holiday, the fountain at the entrance had finally been fixed and finished. "Allah Akhbar," it announced, in pebbles. "God is Great."

"Good morning. Where is Abu Shir?" Sami asked ticket clerk Amjad Daoud, who was wearing a large pair of wraparound sunglasses.

"I don't know," Amjad replied miserably. "His office is locked."

The ticket clerk was nursing a nasty eye infection. He would not treat it by day, lest eye drops should trickle mistakenly down his throat and break his Ramadan fast.

"He is still in bed," carped Sami, "because he is the only person fasting this Ramadan. If you see him, tell him I am awaiting a very important visit. Do you understand?"

Amjad took off his sunglasses and nodded.

Today, Chief Engineer Nabil Baron was expected to stop by to put bureaucratic pen to paper, granting official permission for work to commence on Sami's Agricultural Museum. After that, Sami hoped to spend the whole day working, undisturbed, on his project. Even that prospect did not entirely cheer him up.

"Do you understand?" Sami repeated.

"Yes," replied Amjad, distractedly examining his swollen eye in a pocket mirror and then replacing his sunglasses. "A very important visit."

Behind them, a po-faced man in a smart suit was regarding the fountain.

The man turned. "Dr. Sami Khader?"

"Yes?"

"I have come from the municipality. I am the municipal job inspector."

"Hello! Such a surprise!" Sami broke into a broad, welcoming smile. "I am very happy to meet you. And so," he held up his pet carrier, "is Rambo." The job inspector looked queasy as he shook Sami's hand.

He was here, he explained, to investigate a complaint received by the municipality. A complaint, he said, was something for which he did not care.

"I will follow you, today, for this one day of your activities," he concluded. "And from this, I will make my judgment."

"You are welcome," replied Sami and sprang into action.

First, he took Rambo to his office, feeding the monkey a carefully warmed bottle and scattering a few toys about, to keep him from looting the cupboards. The inspector took shallow breaths, shielding his nose discreetly, as Sami cleaned the carrying case of droppings and wiped the monkey with a wet tissue. He was hungry, and the smell was turning his empty stomach.

Behind the inspector stood an emu, recently deceased and newly stuffed with pink shredded paper. Sami checked the glue holding two marbles in place until genuine glass eyes could be sourced and adjusted the metal rod fixing a broken femur.

Next, they embarked on a round of the cages. Sami made elaborate notes at each halt in a brand-new notebook. "This is very important. It is the basis of my daily report to the manager," he explained.

The inspector seemed indifferent but kept pace.

At Ruti's enclosure, Sami pulled two small cakes from his pocket. "Ruti," he joked, "is not a Muslim. Would you like to feed her?"

"No, thank you," said the inspector, regarding the cakes with pain.

All seemed well with Sami's myriad inmates, though plastic sheeting had appeared, for no apparent reason, in the tortoise cage. "This must be removed," Sami pointed. "It is dangerous. I will instruct a keeper."

With the inspector close at his side, he walked through the zoo to locate Yail Misqawi. He found him seated at a bench, ogling a lady whose small daughter played on a swing. "Remember this expression," Sami advised, "'In Ramadan, do not chase your tail.' Now, go and mend the tortoises." He leaned forward until his lips almost touched Yail's ear. "If you do not," he whispered, "the job inspector will get you." Yail jumped to his feet and scurried off. Sami turned back to the inspector.

"Please," he said graciously, "come this way."

They went to the laboratory. Sami tampered with several creatures in various stages of de- and re-composition. "For the museum," he explained, holding an ostrich leg aloft. The inspector gazed in troubled wonder at the implements and remains on display.

They picked their way back through the zoo's slaughterhouse to the stables behind, where Sami looked in on two lambs, thoroughly checking their eyes, mouths, and behinds. The job inspector watched as they suckled their mothers.

Then they headed back across the zoo.

"Still with me?" Sami asked.

"I am here," said the inspector.

The Carnivore Department was deserted. Remarkably, the outer walls had been completed, painted beige, and stippled with a faint safari motif. Sami spent time inspecting the area, prodding and poking at each budding enclosure.

"Ha!" he exclaimed suddenly, from somewhere deep inside the lion's sleeping quarters. "I knew it!"

The inspector reluctantly stepped inside. Sami pointed up at the ceiling, where light bulbs had been newly installed and were covered by translucent glass shades. They would, explained Sami, prove easy prey for a lion who, with one idle bat, could lacerate a paw, or worse.

"Clever work," Sami snorted. "It would have been very difficult, I suppose, to consult me first. It will have to be changed."

By the time they reached the Natural History Museum, the inspector was tired. His feet had swollen in the heat. He was thirsty, a problem he would not be able to solve for eight long hours. It was time to depart. Back to his nice, air-conditioned office, leaving this strange veterinarian and his foul-smelling creatures behind.

"Would you like to see some embryos?" Sami inquired.

"No," replied the inspector.

"What about the new glass case for the python skeleton?"

"No. Please just go about your work. As normal."

"As you wish. Now, come and see my Agricultural Museum."

The museum was to be housed in the vacant building next door. At present, it was empty except for piles of rubbish, building materials, and a makeshift desk made of an old door balanced on a stack of upturned crates. On top sat a fat pile of schoolbooks, a mug filled with felt-tipped pens, and a block of drawing paper. Pages of technicolor designs were taped to the wall. Sami tapped at his drawings and explained the plan so far.

Visitors would enter the first of the museum's three domed chambers between two ten-foot toadstools—one poisonous, the other benign. On either side would range representations of agricultural equipment throughout the ages. The first room would house a display of plastic floral cross-sections, already delivered from Messrs. Shiv and Patel of Ambala, India, and lying dormant in a stack of cardboard boxes. With the help of his new office computer, Sami planned to label all parts, in English and Arabic.

Next, in the center of the second chamber, would be a squat replica of a wishing well, cordoned off with a hefty length of iron chain. The chain would be supported by concrete tree trunks, and from it would hang plywood approximations of a scribe's parchment scrolls.

"Each scroll," Sami told the job inspector, "will give information on one aspect of Palestine's water situation. Water used for irrigation. Water wells, old and new. Water stolen by Israel." Mr. Salaa worked for the water board and had been a wellspring of useful information.

"At first I thought it should be a real wishing well, with real water," Sami added, "but this might cause a problem with the museum's humidity. Or with small children."

In the final room, Sami was planning an exhibition on Palestinian honey. It would offer information on home cures and herbal healing, utilizing ingredients the average Qalqilyan might have at home in the kitchen cupboard. In the middle of the room would be a vast honey bee stand.

"This honey bee stand," said Sami, "will answer many important questions. What are honey bees? What is the benefit of honey? How long do honey bees live? What is their life cycle? What other products are made from honey?" He looked expectantly at the inspector.

"I do not know."

"Of course you don't. This is why I am creating the exhibition. For your education."

The inspector checked his watch.

The information would be presented by means of a giant honeycomb, each hexagonal cell as big as a window, and at its center a large model queen bee.

"In my spare time," Sami emphasized, "I am busy finding equipment for this display. An old Palestinian bee hive. A bee-keeper's outfit, with smoke bellows. I will stuff some bees. This will be very interesting for the children."

Sami had compiled the information for these new displays, as he had done for his Natural History Museum, with the help of curricula provided by the Education Ministry. He had ensured that the topics he covered touched on issues dealt with in every grade of school, from six to sixteen. "Education," he reminded the inspector, "is very important to the international zoo."

As they climbed over debris back toward the door, Sami pointed out a tall, dusty pile of slowly desiccating brown paper folders. "Here," he said, "is the final touch."

Between each page was a skeletal leaf, a spindly stem, a dried, fuzzy seedpod, dotted about like an outburst of punctuation. Together, they represented the entire botanical distribution of Palestine, a sample of every single species of tree, shrub, grass, and cactus flower. Sami had collected them himself and intended to display them along the walls of his new museum, in a series of red-, yellow-, and violet-painted frames.

"When will work begin?" asked the job inspector, flicking idly at a *Hyssopus officinalis*.

"Chief Engineer Nabil Baron," replied Sami, "is coming today to put his signature to the project. In fact," Sami frowned, "he was supposed to be here before lunchtime." The inspector flinched at the mention of lunch.

"Let us go and see."

They returned to the ticket office.

"Well?" Sami asked Amjad Daoud.

The young man was watching a chicken, slowly roasting on a spit, on an ancient black-and-white television.

"Yes, doctor. Your important visit came."

"What do you mean?"

"I told him I would call you, but he said he had no time. He said that if you were not ready and waiting for him, he could not stay. He said he is a very busy man."

The job inspector nodded in sympathy. He normally inspected secretaries, accountants, or clerks in comfortable offices and was happy that way. It was not his lot to be out on his feet, in the heat and the dirt and the appalling smells.

"But why did you not come to find me? Why did you not make him stay? It is very important that I see him."

Amjad shrugged.

"Then he must come back."

Sami picked up the telephone and punched numbers furiously.

"Hello, Mr. Nabil Baron? This is Dr. Sami Khader. It is very important that I see you today." He listened for several seconds. His face fell.

"I see. Yes, I understand. Thank you." He replaced the receiver with a bang.

"He says he is a very busy man," Sami told Amjad and the inspector. "The museum, he says, will have to wait." Sami turned away. "But we will see."

Finally, Sami took the inspector back up to his office. He tossed a prayer mat from a plastic chair in the corner and offered his visitor a seat.

"I am sorry," he said crossly, "that I cannot offer you tea."

The inspector nodded. There were bluebottles buzzing about, and he wished to leave this stuffy office, redolent of must and monkey.

"So," Sami continued, "what is your belief?"

Rambo skittered up to the inspector, screeched impertinently, and then dashed away.

"My belief?"

"This man, who wrote this paper, he wrote that I am only a V-E-T. But without me, who would fix these dead animals? Who would build a museum? I look after the orphaned animals." He pointed to Rambo, who was trying to climb the inspector's trouser leg. "I am building new enclosures. Education programs. Seeking new stocks. The man who wrote my job description, what does he know of what I do? He has never been here. It is a stupid mistake."

"I wrote the job description," said the job inspector stonily.

"Ah."

He stood, dusting down his jacket. "And with consideration this morning"—the inspector's stomach rumbled noisily—"I believe you are"—he smirked—"a vet."

◆　　◆　　◆

Through the final searing days of Ramadan, as most lazed, Rambo went from strength to strength. Sami enjoyed the nighttime feeds, since he, too, could snack along with the little monkey. On Laylat al-Qadr, the Night of Power, a time of mystical revelations and wishes granted, Sami looked up to the starry skies and made a wish.

But the next day, he remained downcast.

"In some parts of the world," he complained to Mr. Salaa, "the vet is at the top of the food chain. Here, he is below everything else. Perhaps I should start tearing tickets. Maybe that way, I'll end up manager."

On the eve of the Eid ul-Fitr feast, Sami was finally granted an audience with the mayor. He arrived, between shifts at the zoo and clinic, disheveled and thirsty. Rambo chattered quietly to himself in the carrying cage placed carefully on the mayor's neat carpet. The mayor looked pale, older than before.

First, Sami inquired about Giza Zoo and his request for future spare animals.

"We must not beg," replied the mayor, "for help. We must wait for help to come to us. Now," he said firmly, "was there anything else?"

With as much enthusiasm as he could muster, Sami made his case. He ran thoroughly through recent achievements, detailing the revenue derived from the Natural History Museum and the money saved by his inventions and initiatives: "Anesthetic guns," he listed, "snake forceps, wolf forceps, crocodile restraints, syringes, hatcheries, and orphaned baby care." Sami paused for breath. "Do you remember Dr. Motke?"

"Yes."

"He is a very old man. And even he can't do all the things I can do. He cannot, for example, stuff a dead animal."

"I see."

Sami looked into the mayor's distant eyes.

"If I decide to leave, to work abroad, who will replace me? I will tell you. If I leave this zoo, you will have no replacement."

"I see."

"All I require is some sort of recognition of my efforts."

Sami paused and looked at the mayor, who stood, adjusted his tie, and offered his hand.

"You will have an answer," he said.

"How long will this take?"

The mayor picked up a cardboard desk calendar and examined it closely. "You will have an answer," he repeated, "by the end of December." From inside the carrying case came an indignant squeak. Two stalks of straw were deposited onto the carpet.

"In two months."

He showed man and monkey the door.

Chapter Ten
November 2006

He created the earth for all creatures. . .
which of your Lord's marvels do you deny?
—QURAN, SURA AL-RAHMAAN 10, 13

It was the middle of the Eid ul-Fitr holiday, and Sami was busy outside, shaking snakes from plastic bottles. They were pencil-thin and shiny green, found in Qalqilya's back gardens, wardrobes, or wellingtons, and either pounded with a garden spade or brought to the zoo in hopes of a reward. They rarely lasted longer than a few weeks. Sami believed it was down to the food he had to offer. Grass snakes could be choosy, and though he tried valiantly, collecting ants and crickets from the town's verges, the snakes were, generally, displeased.

Two teenage boys with oiled hair and tight t-shirts watched as Sami attempted to shift a glossy, coiling creature from its bottle into an empty fish tank sprinkled with stones. The snake was alert, its tongue twitching. Sami sighed. This was not the fare of the international zoo.

"I caught it with my glove," said one of the boys. "It might have bitten me. Is it poisonous?" He glanced at his friend and grinned. "Is it deadly?"

"No," said Sami, "it is very common. There are many, many snakes like this."

Sami considered the native fauna, brought in by locals seeking profit, to be his least impressive specimens. His usual tack was to

215

offer to take the animal off its captor's hands for the greater good of the Qalqilyan people. In this manner he had amassed a good range of exhibits, at no cost, with which to fill empty cages.

There were his five tawny owls, raised from orphan chicks, as hollow-eyed as his workers on a long Ramadan morning. A single badger rescued from the kitchen of a hysterical housewife. There was the little snared fox with the broken legs, if not thriving, at least alive. The porcupine saved from the clutches of poachers and hustled in, with great injury to its rescuers, in a burlap sack. Spiders from bathroom corners, lizards extracted from drinking wells, and a dozen or so tortoises, plucked while crossing roads or browsing contentedly in Qalqilyans' vegetable gardens.

The boy was crestfallen. "How do you know it's not poisonous?"

"Look," snapped Sami, "do you see its eyes?" He gave the bottle one forceful shake. The snake straightened and slithered out into his hand.

"Yes."

"What shape are the pupils?"

"They're round," the boys agreed.

"Poisonous snakes do not have round pupils. Theirs are oval. Is that all?"

The boys dallied, disappointed but unconvinced, as Sami went back to shaking snakes. When they were sure there was no reimbursement or deadly snakebite imminent, they disappeared.

Six snakes later, Sami's tanks were once again well stocked. Except for the arrival of four unpleasant ostriches from Tulkarem the week before, it was his biggest intake of stock since the wolves and the Berber sheep in May.

"If not for the mayor," Sami muttered, "we could be expecting a giraffe, and tigers too."

In the absence of all other progress, Sami had decided to pour his energies into his Agricultural Museum. He had yet to receive chief engineer Nabil Baron's blessing, but he nevertheless forged ahead. He had worked hard through the last of the Ramadan lull, the doors locked and shutters fastened to deter unwelcome guests. In just a fortnight of sawing, sculpting, mixing, fixing, plastering, and mounting, it had come together. It was, he felt, a useful channel for his frustrations and a means by which to illustrate his disapproval of other people and their tardy affairs.

The grand opening was scheduled for tomorrow, the last day of the holiday. A government minister was coming all the way from Ramallah. In the distance the sound of brassy pop music, accompanied by bangs and squeals, announced that workmen were testing the amusement park.

As Sami slid the final snake into its new home, Abdel Raouf Joadi appeared across the way, clutching a cardboard box of Action Stations Chocolate Wafers. He began to feed them, one by one, to the bears.

A group of mothers with their little girls gathered to watch.

"They like sweets," Sami noted, "too much."

"Can we feed the bear, sir?" asked one little girl, stepping forward.

"No," said Sami. "It is too dangerous. But here is a toffee, for a monkey."

◆　　◆　　◆

Feeding time at the zoo has always been a popular affair, with visitors flocking to watch the gluttonous frenzies of penguins and seals and elephants shelling peanuts with their trunks. Until the 1980s, chimpanzees' tea parties, with chintz, scones, and flowery frocks worthy of the Women's Institute, were a special favorite. In the nineteenth century, feeding the zoo animals was actively encouraged as a means of controlling costs. Several centuries earlier, the Tower of London offered free admission to anyone bringing along a pet dog or cat as food for its famous lions. The first feeding bans, in Manchester and Dresden, were met with fierce public opposition.

Zoos, until recently, have varied considerably in their opinions on appropriate foodstuffs. Elephants drank beer and port wine well into the twentieth century. Throughout the nineteenth, an extensive range of caged species were fed on bread and milk mixed with rice. In Europe, fruit was deemed unsuitable for apes, who regularly dined instead on roast beef and hot puddings. One elephant at the Jardin des Plantes existed happily for many years on a daily dose of bread, wine, and gruel. During the 1930s, a chimp in Geneva ate three square meals of oatmeal and chocolate a day. Happy Jerry, a well-known mandrill at Polito's Menagerie on London's Strand, dined on venison with King George IV at Windsor and enjoyed a nip of gin.

Others fared less well. "I'll make thee," wrote Shakespeare in *Henry VI*, "eat iron like an ostrich." An old French bestiary had proposed that ostriches had the power to digest nails, and it took a number of painful and unproductive experiments to finally prove it a fallacy. A moose in Geneva was fed an apple peppered with nails by an old lady who believed it the Devil incarnate. A rash of poisonings accompanied the opening of London Zoo to the general public. Fruit was spiked with razor blades, buns with arsenic or phosphorous. Animals were killed off, regularly and inexplicably, by the people who paid to see them.

As the bears settled down to their stale chocolate treats and the snakes into their new homes, Sami was anxious to put the finishing touches to the Agricultural Museum.

Outside, workers were busy sprucing things up. Rusty fences had been painted in bright stripes of turquoise and candy pink, and the sharp, pearish smell of fresh paint glinted in the air.

Turgid water was being drained from the courtyard's ornamental channels. Avenues were being swept, and a man was airing the cafeteria.

Abu Shir stood beside the museum gates. In one hand he held an electric drill, without power cable or battery pack. He intercepted Sami as the vet hastened to the door.

"Here, Doctor." Abu Shir fumbled in his pocket and produced a small brown paper packet. "Annual bonus. From the president."

Sami tore open the package. One hundred and seventeen shekels, in change. Twenty dollars. He tucked it into his jacket pocket.

"Mansur telephoned last night," Abu Shir offered, hoping for an invitation into the museum. "He still does not know how long he will be gone. He wished me happy holidays."

"Very nice, Abu Shir. Very nice," said Sami and vanished inside.

The manager heard a key turning in the lock. He glanced down at his drill, then again at the door, and wandered away.

◆　　◆　　◆

Inside the Agricultural Museum, Dr. Sami held a yellow tin sign in one hand, a hammer in the other, and a long nail between his clenched teeth. "No Smoking" read the sign. He banged it into a concrete pillar, fashioned to resemble a tree trunk. No one would take any notice. He stippled spots onto a giant mushroom and arranged a display of plastic fruit in a nook.

Sami went to a shelf in the corner and picked up a plastic container. Inside, a dead tarantula rocked on her back, her legs curled tight into a furry thorax. Across her scuttled her offspring, dozens of tiny baby spiders barely bigger than grains of sand. Sami watched as the babies sucked their mother's body dry. He sat down on an upturned crate. Had he, he wondered, occasioned an end in his harried attempts at pressing forward?

The journalist had come at the end of October, from Israel. Sami had attempted to interest him in Rambo, who was growing, teething, and behaving these days like a willful toddler.

"When my own children were babies, my wife did everything," Sami joked. "But now I have become the mother."

A photographer snapped away at the baby monkey, who held tight to his grubby toy elephant and glared into the camera lens. But the journalist was more interested in Ruti.

"Isn't she beautiful?" He stroked her nose. She nudged his shoulder, then licked his palm. "Can you tell me her story?"

Sami could not remember exactly what he told the journalist, for he had related the tale of Qalqilya's giraffes a hundred times or more. He knew he had stressed that Ruti was in need of a friend. He knew he had emphasized his hope that someone, somewhere, reading the story might be able to help. He knew that the journalist's visit had been during Ramadan, and he had been hungry and thirsty, hot and tired.

But when, on the second of November, the story was released, it caused a small commotion.

"Qalqilya Singleton Seeks Israeli Stud" read the headline. "An Israeli Safari Park is full of eager candidates but due to administrative squabbling, poor Ruti is still waiting."

Sami did not think he had said exactly that, nor what followed.

"I called the Safari and they said, 'Sure, no problem, send Ruti here for a few months. Our males will know what to do. But their condition was that they weren't to be held responsible if she became ill, so we asked them to bring one of their giraffes here. They said no.'"

It was not long before Sami received word from the safari park's elderly curator.

"We have given you lions; we have given you zebras to replace those that died of gas," she scolded. "Before your time, we gave you wolves, and caracals, and many other things. Over the years, we have offered you training, and given you advice. And this is what we receive in return."

It was not true, she said, that they had refused to donate a giraffe. Indeed, they had no giraffe of the same type to donate and had, in the past, always been generous with their bequests. It so happened, she went on, that they had been considering a gift of two giant Sudanese tortoises, commanding weights of over two hundred pounds, to swell Sami's inventory.

"But the damage has been done, and will be difficult to undo. I only hope," she concluded pithily, "that the public has a short memory."

No matter how he tried, Sami could not recall what had really been said.

He gave the spider pot a shake, watching the babies slide and scuttle around their mother's corpse.

With ends, he thought, come new beginnings.

The journalist's lonely hearts tale had reached another zoo, this one in Jerusalem, whose giraffe population had recently exploded and was now closely controlled by contraceptive means. A young zoologist, intrigued by the notion of this mysterious little zoo on the opposite side of the Wall, had taken a tentative interest in Ruti's plight. He might, he considered, be able to find her a friend. Sami was overjoyed.

But, the zoologist had carefully conditioned by telephone, there were many things to consider. What was life like for the creatures of Qalqilya? What would the zoo do with its young, were Ruti to prove as fertile as the females in his own collection? How well were the giraffe keepers trained to do their job? They would need to know, of course, about management issues, about feeding strategies and maintenance. And what sort of health precautions did the zoo take? Were there facilities for x-rays and treatments, analyses and operations? Jerusalem's giraffes enjoyed acres of free range across imitation grassland, with a large watering hole that they shared with zebra and white rhino. What were the size and condition of Qalqilya's giraffe exhibit?

Abu Shir entered Sami's office and sat down, listening closely.

"Ruti is very healthy," Sami replied quietly into the receiver. "Please come and see."

But the zoologist was not finished. Most crucial of all, he emphasized, was the question of money. Giraffes, notoriously difficult to tranquilize, were better shipped awake. A crate would have to be specially built and a keeper engaged to accustom the animal to its traveling quarters. That would take time, and no inconsiderable expense: perhaps twenty thousand dollars or more.

Sami swallowed. "Please, come to visit," he repeated. "You are welcome. You can see; she is very happy. We will discuss."

"My wife won't like that. It's dangerous," replied the zoologist. "I'll try."

Abu Shir frowned, and rose. "This matter is my responsibility," he grumbled. "Next time, this man must talk to me."

"We should not," said Aristotle, "childishly neglect the study of the meaner animals, because there is something wonderful in all of Nature." Of the thirty million species in the world, 95 percent are small enough to contain in the palm of a hand. The Jerusalem zoologist had left Sami with a parting suggestion. Qalqilya Zoo, he had heard, was small and cramped. Why not, then, use Qalqilya's limited space for some of the smaller and more unusual of God's creations?

The zoo would be following a well-trodden path. In 1893, Lily, the three-foot pygmy elephant, proved the star performer in Karl Hagenbeck's offering to the Chicago World's Fair. Numerous bands of trained cats talked, strummed, and serenaded their way around the salons of London and Paris for several centuries. In the early nineteenth century, a tiny white poodle named Munito toured Europe, dazzling the public with skills including mathematics, palmistry, and winning at dominoes.

Smallest of all were the flea circuses. The *Pulex irritans*, or human flea, was collared with silk thread or fine gold wire, harnessed to a chariot, and taught to walk a tightrope or kick a ball. Fleas were dressed up as historical figures, in costumes so small they could fit through the eye of a needle. With a life cycle of just four weeks, maintaining a flea circus required a keeper with a deep commitment and an exceptionally steady hand.

Other diminutive exhibits had appeared more recently: The wide-eyed mouse lemur of Madagascar, the smallest of humanity's close relatives, which communicates in frequencies too high for the human ear and can cling to a finger nail. The Caribbean gecko, barely half an inch long; the *Hippocampus denise*, a tiny seahorse named after Dionysus for its carefree nature.

There are stout miniature cattle and tiny hogs whose litters can be contained in one hand. The minuscule bumblebee bat of East Asia; the zumzúm, or Cuban bee hummingbird; the dwarf hippopotamus. And the *Onychomys leucogaster*, the North American grasshopper mouse; a beastly, fanged carnivore that stalks its prey, kills with a bite to the neck, and rears up to bay at the moon.

One nineteenth-century Indian zoo, recorded Giza's Stanley Flower on his travels, even equipped itself with a parasite room, wherein a man would be strapped to a bed to allow tiny parasites to feed on his blood. Feeding time proved a hit with visitors.

But Sami knew his audience. They were not excited by creatures, fierce or otherwise, that were anything less than statuesque. Ruti was their favorite, then Dubi, the lions, and the bears. Though

Fufu was affectionate, the badger cuddly, and the peacocks exquisitely plumed, they were usually lost in the fray.

Some people, he thought, might be happy peering at dormice and beetles, but most of those could also seek access to the real zoological stars: the lions, tigers, polar bears, and rhinoceroses. For the Palestinian people, there was no such option. Qalqilya Zoo was the only place they could see wild animals in the flesh, the huge and the commanding. Sami did not want to disappoint them. The natives—the grass snakes and the porcupines—did not make the grade.

Sami replaced the dead spider and her ravenous offspring on the shelf and looked around the museum. It was ready.

◆　　◆　　◆

The next morning, on the fifth of November, the zoo swarmed with visitors. Sami affixed a ribbon to the doorframe of the Agricultural Museum and brought a pair of sharp scissors from his office. He sat down on a plastic chair, positioned outside the front door to the new museum, and awaited the minister from Ramallah. Rambo played beside him in the dust. The monkey, Sami feared, would wreak havoc if left alone in his office for long.

The first official to appear was Renovations Project Engineer Abu Khaled.

Sami prepared himself for an affray.

"As-salaam al-lekum, Dr. Sami. Abu Shir said you wished to see me."

"Yes, Abu Khaled. It is about the Carnivore Department."

"Two months," Abu Khaled said, smiling blithely.

"No," Sami took a deep breath to steady his welling temper, "I want to talk about the bears."

The bears' enclosures had, at first, progressed well. Struts to support the fencing were all in place; the outdoor area had been landscaped and raised several feet above floor level. But most important of all to his bears, Sami knew, was water. On hot days, they would wallow and splash in their footbath of a pond for hours. In the dead of winter, they would break the ice to take a bracing dip. With that in mind, Sami had carefully designed his two new bear enclosures to range around a single expansive pool, deep and broad enough for them immerse themselves entirely and swim.

What had transpired was quite contrary to his written, spoken, and diagrammatical wishes.

Two separate bear pools had hastily been constructed, one at either corner of the two cages, against the fence separating bear from visitor. They were semicircular plunge pools with steep, narrow steps, difficult for a bear to negotiate. Sami was horrified.

"These pools, Abu Khaled, are too small and in the wrong place. Bears love water. They love to swim. What will they do with this kind of pool? This is stupid work."

Abu Khaled tried to disguise his irritation with a smile.

"They are built now. We cannot change them."

"But they're not at all as I specified."

"You should have told me before they were built."

"I *did* tell you."

"If you had told me correctly," Abu Khaled spoke slowly and clearly, "I am sure I would not have built them any other way."

Sami fumed. "I will go to the mayor."

"Do as you see fit," said Abu Khaled haughtily. "Good morning."

Sami returned to his plastic chair. He would, of course, pursue the matter, but was quite certain it would come to nothing. He checked the time and watched as a throng of young, shouting children disappeared into his Natural History Museum. From around the corner, a billow of cigarette smoke appeared and behind it, Abu Shir. He was grinning maniacally.

"Dr Sami, hello!"

"Have you heard anything from the minister, Abu Shir?" Sami was finding the morning increasingly taxing.

"Good news."

"Oh?"

"Mansur was released this morning!"

"Ah," Sami said, "I see. Very nice. You must be very happy."

"He was taken to Nablus by police car and borrowed a telephone from a man on the street. He did not know until this morning. I must leave at once to meet him!"

"Good news."

"Good news!"

"Very nice."

"Very nice!"

Abu Shir prodded Sami excitedly in the ribs.

"And have you heard anything from the minister?" asked Sami patiently.

"Who?"

◆　　◆　　◆

Sami and Rambo sat waiting together outside the museum until six o'clock. The crowds thinned out as citizens went home for supper. Mr. Sherif, the Natural History Museum's squabby, gap-toothed attendant, emerged from next door. He had once been a falafel vendor and sometimes stood in as manager when both Abu Shir and his assistant, Mr. Eesa, were away on leave.

"It's hot in there," he said, wiping sweat from behind his ears, "and crowded."

Sami picked up Rambo and took his jacket from the back of his chair.

"Are you leaving?" the museum attendant asked.

Sami glanced at the uncut ribbon. "Good evening, Mr. Sherif."

On his way home, as dusk washed in over distant hills, Sami received a telephone call from Abu Shir. "The minister from Ramallah called," he said. "He said that the climate was not good to come to Qalqilya today. What do you think this means? The weather?"

Sami switched off his telephone and tucked it back in his jacket pocket.

◆　◆　◆

"If you've touched that monkey, don't touch me," Sara called from the kitchen, as Sami crept wearily in through the front door. He set down Rambo's cage.

"I will wash."

His wife was short-tempered after a long day stewing meat, grinding spices, and kneading dough for pastries.

"How did the opening go?" she called.

"It did not." replied Sami.

Sara emerged from the kitchen.

"And your new animal area," she asked. "Almost finished?"

"Carnivore Department," Sami corrected. "Two months."

"And your salary, from the mayor?" Her voice was high and strained.

"Two months," Sami sighed.

She untied her apron strings and rubbed her doughy hands together. "Sami." She stepped toward him. "You are not paid extra for these things. They don't even thank you." Her tone grew tender. "You could give it up; work only at the clinic. All the other vets here are rich. We could have a bigger house. A new car. Good money."

Inside the carrying case, Rambo shrieked. Sara recoiled.

"And do other doctors bring their patients home?" she demanded. Without waiting for an answer, she flounced back into the clammy kitchen, a puff of flour tumbling behind her.

Sami placed his briefcase carefully by the front door in the hall. Perhaps, one day, he would have dozens of animals too big to bring home to look after. Perhaps the Safari's lady curator would calm down after a while and reconsider those Sudanese tortoises. And then there was Jerusalem and the slim hope of company for Ruti. One day, he thought, though the thought was an effort, he would have tigers, too. Rambo chuckled. Sami kicked off his shoes. He tickled the monkey beneath the chin and sought solace in a tutti-frutti narghile until dinner was served.

Chapter Eleven
December 2006

*There is not an animal that lives on the
Earth, nor a being that flies on its wings, but
forms part of a community like you . . . they
shall all be gathered to their Lord in the end.*
—QURAN, SURA AL-AN'AM 38

Rambo, thought Sami, was lonely. The little monkey was two
months old, stronger and more adventurous than ever,
but with his newfound agility he became less and less
portable. It was December, wet and windy, and Sami performed
his daily rounds in solitude. There were no workers at the quag-
mired Carnivore Department. Keepers shuffled in and out of the
gloom, wraiths beneath fur-lined hoods. Abu Shir and Mr. Eesa
rarely emerged from the manager's office, which was cosily lit and
fitted out with an electrical heater.

As Sami had feared, the manager had done nothing more to
enlist the help of the zoologist from Jerusalem.

"Why not telephone?" coaxed Sami, "Or else, I could."

"I am manager here," Abu Shir took a sip of steaming coffee. "I
will do it when I have time."

Opposite the manager's office, Amjad Daoud huddled in his
ticket booth and gazed at crumpled postcards of America.

Sami's toes and fingers froze as he examined a zebra's stiff
ankles. His mind wandered. It settled on a picture of a warm

surgery, with an orderly queue of patients waiting outside the door. An X-ray machine. A secretary to fetch tea. He flinched as the zebra kicked, freckling his trouser leg with mud.

Ruti was always pleased to see him on his rain-sodden inspections. Fufu, Dubi, Rama, and the lions perked up when he approached. Sami was glad of the unqualified affection.

Meanwhile, Rambo was shut up in the office alone, too young to brave the elements alongside his foster father. He clambered, chewed holes, and tried diligently to extract the stuffing from the seat of a chair. He simply could not keep his sharp nose out of trouble. The time had come, Sami decided, to find Rambo a friend.

The trouble was to find one that was suitable. Sami would not attempt integration with any other of his monkeys for fear that a dominant male would rip the youngster to shreds. Nor did Rambo belong to the human domain, where he was prone to all manner of hazards and where he would no longer be welcome when he achieved the gross proportions of an adult Hamadryas baboon.

On the tenth of December, Sami had an idea. He had spotted a friendly stray kitten, a little calico female with thick fur and pretty green eyes. Though shy, she would not hiss or wail when approached. Her face was gentle where her brothers' and sisters' were wily and hard. By placing a bowl of tinned salmon on the floor beneath a bench for three successive days, Sami had managed to entice her down from a low branch. On the fourth day, she allowed him to stroke her head with one finger; on the fifth, she purred slightly and rubbed against his leg. Finally, after a week, as she licked her fishy bowl clean, Sami bundled the little cat into a bag and took her up to his office.

"What have you done this time?" Sami asked the monkey, shaking rainwater from his overcoat. "You know I don't like surprises." The contents of the waste paper basket were strewn across the floor, and the room smelled terrible. A string of meaningless phrases had been tapped out onto the computer screen. "Come here and see what I have for you."

Sami crouched on the floor and gently opened the bag. Nothing happened. He waited several seconds. Rambo approached warily, sniffing the air. Suddenly, in a streak of fur and whiskers, a figure shot out and hurtled toward the cabinet in the corner.

"Meow," came a plaintive cry from beneath the cabinet. "Meow."

Immediately, Rambo went to investigate.

Sami watched with anticipation as Rambo first peered, then crawled, beneath the cabinet. He knelt down on all fours, his face pressed close to the floor, to see Rambo reach the kitten and grab tufts of her fur, on either side of her face, with both hands. He shook, vigorously, then turned his attention to the kitten's tail, nibbling, scratching, and pulling. He screamed in her face and pushed her hard. The cat, a little larger than the monkey, did nothing. Even when Rambo grabbed her by the scruff of her neck and hauled her out from beneath the cabinet, she offered no gesture of self-defense. Instead, she stared at him. Then, she started to purr. Mystified, Rambo sat down opposite the little creature, who sat looking back. For a full five minutes, Sami thrilled to see their unbroken stare, Rambo alert and tense, the little cat relaxed and purring. Finally, the monkey turned, nonchalantly, to groom one leg. The cat curled up tight and closed her eyes.

"Very good," said Sami. "She will be your babysitter."

Over the next week, a calico kitten was carefully introduced to the Khader home. Now everywhere, along with Rambo, came Bussi-Cat—Bussi, for short. Soon the pair was inseparable. Sami was amazed to see that Bussi did not hiss when Rambo sniffed at her precious salmon dinner. She refused to play games with Sami, shunning the piece of string, the catnip mouse, or tinkling ball, and would gambol and chase only with the monkey. The little white elephant now lay forsaken in a corner of the carrying cage. Rambo preferred his furry, purring companion, clinging tightly to her when frightened and refusing to let go. Bussi did not mind heaving him slowly around the room on her back, her belly pressed close to the ground under the strain. They liked to nap together on Sami's prayer mat. "Monkey or cat?" said Sami to visitors, "cat or monkey? Which do you think they think they are?"

◆　　◆　　◆

Qalqilya Zoo had fostered several unlikely friendships. Dubi the hippopotamus had lived happily for many years with successive generations of peacocks, strutting and squawking beneath his feet. The ibex and hog deer lived in harmony, as did the zebras and goats. But the strangest companions Sami had ever seen were his ancient hyena and the zoo's band of stray cats.

Cats infested the zoo. They knew the feeding times of the animals and hung about the slaughterhouse when the kill was fresh. Their nightly din overwhelmed the sounds of the lions and the monkeys. Scruffy kittens clung to tree trunks and became scratching, spitting cyclones when cornered. They served a useful purpose, hunting down unfortunate rodents, keeping the zoo free from cockroaches and other unpleasant vermin. So they stayed unmolested and had, over the years, made friends with the spotted hyena.

Hyenas are known, in the wild, as much for their gross and ruthless habits as for their ugliness. Their faces are pug, their backs hunched, their fur patchy, and their heads too big for their bodies. They mark their territory with greasy, pungent, anal secretions. Victorian apothecaries mixed hyenas' powdery white feces, known as *album graecum,* with honey to soothe sore throats. The hyena is able to crunch and digest the pieces that other carnivores leave behind—the teeth, bones, and viscera—providing it with an overabundance of calcium. Females can thus tenderly nurse their pups for well over a year.

Spotted hyenas prefer to hunt or scavenge in packs, and their bands are the biggest of any carnivorous mammal. They greet their kin with a lick of the penis, with which both males and females are identically equipped. To others, they are far less affable. The hyena kills its prey by disemboweling, slowly eating it alive from the inside out. It fearlessly confronts lions and has been spotted chasing leopards and cheetahs from fresh kills, afterward claiming them as its own. There is almost no living creature, given the opportunity, that it will not try to devour.

Sami's hyena was an exception. He was old and tired and could eat only soft, mashed food, though he still enjoyed gnawing gummily on a slice of ribcage or hip bone. He seemed unaware of his breed's reputation for ferocity. Each morning and evening, faithful as clockwork, he could be observed sharing his food with the family of stray cats. During the day, they lay together in the sunshine. One mother allowed her kittens to clamber on him while he snoozed. The cats slept, at night, inside a concrete tube on the hyena's small patch of grass.

The territories of wild animals, living in the forest, brush, or desert plain, overlap like pieces of a patchwork quilt. A hawk, a fox, a boa constrictor, a family of roe deer, and another of shrews will claim tenure to the same home and its varied resources. Cohabitants are tolerated or ignored. A wild cat, wrote Heini Hediger, will refrain from killing the prey that lives within its immediate domain. The marten, he said, will "spare the dovecots and hen runs closest to its home."

Beyond neighborly relations is symbiosis. The most famous are the mutualists. The Egyptian plover is accorded safety in exchange for feeding on the unpleasant parasites of the Nile crocodile. The clownfish resides between the stinging tentacles of the sea anemone, chasing away anemone-munching fish to pay for its fortified home. The blind shrimp shares with the goby fish its tidy burrow, dug from the soft sand of the seabed. When a predator approaches, the goby warns its companion of danger with a tap to the tail, and both retreat to safety.

The black piapiac bird is a commensalist. It rides the backs of wild giraffes, pecking at flying insects from the comfort of an elevated perch, without harm to its host. Herds of others, too—wildebeest, ostrich, and zebra—graze close to the sentinel giraffe, using its superior vantage point as an alarm system for impending danger.

The flea on the belly of the dog, the tapeworm lodged stubbornly in the intestine, and the tickbird pecking blood from the oozing sores of the African black rhinoceros are parasites. Likewise the common cuckoo and the South American cowbird, whose females mimic the appearance of another bird's egg in order to infiltrate its nest.

Helotists are the least common symbionts. "The worst degree of slavery is when it is real and personal, as that of the Helotes among the Lacedaemonians," wrote Charles de Secondat, Baron de Montesquieu, who coined the phrase in 1752. The *Formica sanguinea* ant enslaves the *Formica fusca,* contriving raids on the others' burrows to carry off its larvae. The slave ants are then raised to carry out the others' digging, food gathering, and feeding. Another twenty species of ants employ slave labor, so dependent upon their captives that they will die without their travails.

"It fills me with shame, you human beings," said Claudius Aelianus in his *De Natura Animalium*, "to think of the friendly relations that subsist between animals, not only those that feed together nor even those of the same species, but between those that have no connection through a common origin." Infant otters will sometimes share their playtime with beaver cubs. Mongooses frequently attempt to engage other animals, from lizards to squirrels, in their games. Stories of animals rearing or protecting abandoned human children pepper literature, from Romulus and Remus, suckled by a she-wolf in antique legend, to the feral children, raised by monkeys or defended by wild dogs, of modern India, Russia, and Pakistan.

At the 1459 reception of Pope Pius II in Florence, animals including a bull, boar, lion, and giraffe were pitted against each other in the Piazza della Signoria. The lion lay down and refused to fight. An eighteenth-century guidebook to the Tower of London recorded, "A spaniel dog being once thrown into a former lion's den at the Tower. . . instead of hurting it, the lion cherished it, and contracted such a fondness for it, that he would never suffer it to be taken out again, but fed it at his table till he died, which was not till several years after." According to the Tower's records, a similar friendship had been struck up between a lion and a lamb two centuries before. At the Jardin des Plantes, following its decimation during the French Revolution, just six of its original animals remained. There was a quagga, a hartebeest, a pygmy hippo, a crested pigeon, a lion, and his best friend, a small dog.

◆　　◆　　◆

On the twenty-fifth of December, as Christians caroled in Bethlehem, Sami found a letter on his desk from the mayor.

It referred to his complaint regarding the new bear enclosures, apologizing that nothing could be done about the state of their pools, since they had already been built. "Financials," it said, "will not allow it."

Sami was angry and telephoned the mayor directly.

"Next time, before anybody does this sort of work," he said, "they must check with me. If they make it wrong, it comes back to me; it is my fault. If they do not know how the lion or bear lives in nature, the whole effect will be wrong. We need healthy buildings, international standards, for happy animals." Sami paused for breath. There was silence at the end of the line. "Finally, these bear pools are too close to the public. There will be a bad smell."

"I see," came the answer. "As-salaam al-lekum, Doctor." The line buzzed dead before Sami could inquire about his pay rise.

Not long after the telephone call, Abu Khaled appeared at Sami's office door.

"Would you like to meet my monkey?" Sami asked, as the engineer strode in. Abu Khaled's habitual smile was conspicuously absent.

"No."

"Then perhaps some tea?"

"No."

"A seat?"

"No, Dr. Sami. I am very angry. I am angry that you went twice to the mayor with your complaints."

Sami bristled. "You know only about buildings. What do you know about animals?"

"What do *you* know about engineering?"

Sami snatched up his old Berlin Zoo brochure and flapped it at the engineer. It opened on a page depicting penguins splashing in a figure-of-eight pool. "I know," he thundered, "that *this* is international. *This* is nature. And that what you have made for these bears is a"—he struggled for a second—"a Jacuzzi!"

Abu Khaled took a deep, belligerent breath. Rambo appeared from beneath a cupboard and dashed across the room. A sheepish knock came at the door and a hunched workman entered.

"Dr. Sami," he mumbled, "there is an emergency. A flood, in the building next door."

Sami replaced his brochure. The building next door, currently vacant, stood beside the Natural History and Agricultural Museums, and was the setting for Sami's newest scheme. The germ of an idea sprang forth in his mind. "Thank you," he said. "I will be there soon."

The workman nodded and scuttled away down the steps.

"Actually, Abu Khaled," Sami collected himself, "I am glad you are here." He issued his most convincing smile. "There is something else I want to discuss with you."

"Really." Abu Khaled raised a suspicious eyebrow.

The Agricultural Museum had finally opened two days late, with no minister from Ramallah to cut the ribbon. Despite the driving rain, it was proving as popular as the first, entertaining daily groups of schoolchildren and turning a healthy profit.

Sami, paralyzed by winter and the apathy of others, had decided to turn his attention to a third and final museum. This, he believed, would be the most ambitious and very best of them all.

"I am dangerous, sometimes," he had confided, several weeks ago, to Abu Shir. "Even when I am unhappy, I can not stop these ideas from coming."

It would be, he envisaged, a Museum of Everything.

"Everything?" asked Abu Shir, frowning in confusion.

"Everything," affirmed Sami. "Outer space, the universe. Everything."

"What do you mean?"

"There will be," Sami began, "a solar system hanging under the roof. The planets and the stars, illuminated, big and small. There will be one large volcano, with colored lights, smoke, and eruption of lava. There will be a big moon, with a crater detail. A scale replica of a spaceship, the *Discovery*. And the whole world, from the bottom, upward. From ocean stratum, to the beach, to the fields, to the very tip of the mountains."

He pointed to an old, faded poster on the wall. "World Resource at Risk" read the headline, below which was an illustrated, annotated cross-section of rainforest strata. "Like this," he said.

Abu Shir nodded. "Very good. I like our idea."

To attempt to raise his spirits, Sami had already set to work, going about his creative process in the usual way.

First, he stood in the empty space.

"What are you doing?" asked Mr. Sherif, the museum attendant, popping his chubby head around the door.

"Imagining. Asking myself questions. Go away."

Then he spent several sleepless nights mulling over the possibilities, leaping suddenly from beneath the covers to make a note or a sketch on a drawing pad on the dining table.

Next he chalked out areas, dividing the empty building into various sections: "Sea," "Mountain," "Sky," and "Further."

This, Sami believed, would be a bigger job than the last. What he needed now was a modest budget to be released and some helpers allotted.

"So you see, Abu Khaled," he concluded, "if you will provide this small permission, I will be able to begin."

The engineer threw him a level stare.

"Is this the same permission you needed for the Agricultural Museum?"

"That is right."

"The one you did not wait to obtain?"

"The chief engineer was too busy. It was Ramadan. He did not come, and I could not wait."

The engineer sat back in his chair and stretched. "You know," he said, "I think I might have that tea after all."

Downstairs, inside the third, empty museum, ten surly men in wellington boots stood knee-high in rainwater, which poured in through a hole in the wall. The farthest from the door held a leather bucket covered in stiffened sackcloth.

Beneath an umbrella, Mr. Eesa watched blankly from a distance.

"Bad weather," he observed to Yail Misqawi, who was struggling by with an armful of equipment. The bucket moved down the human chain, the last of the ten men emptying it with a splash onto the path outside.

Back upstairs, Abu Khaled leaned back and drained his teacup. "You see," he yawned, "I myself am also interested in developing a museum. I have thought about it and have some very good ideas." He glanced at the drawings on Sami's desk. "Quite similar to yours. Perhaps we should work on this, let's see, this 'Museum of Life.' Yes, that's nice," he paused and looked Sami in the eye, "together."

Sami blinked. "I'm afraid, Abu Khaled," he said, rising, "I must go now. I have my report to write, and there is an emergency in progress." The engineer smiled and departed with a nod.

Alone, Sami sank back down into his chair. The engineer had made notes, looked thoroughly over all his hard-wrought plans. Now Abu Khaled would request involvement in this most ambitious of the three museums, leaving Sami to do all the work, and then take the credit for himself. Sami wearily pulled out a piece of paper and wrote the day's date at the top. "Visit of Abu Khaled, Renovations Project Engineer." He chewed his pencil, then added, "Big disaster at the new museum."

He stood up, fastened his raincoat, and tucked the report into his pocket.

Outside, Sami was surprised to find that Yail Misqawi had brought the flood under control. A pump motor spluttered, connected to a fat, laid-out length of nylon hose. Sami nodded in approval and continued on his rounds.

The animals all seemed to be withstanding the cold and damp. The four new ostriches were still laying and preening, though their allotted keeper, Abdel Raouf Joadi, was frightened of them and refused to clean out their enclosure. Except for the zebras, who appeared to enjoy the stormy weather, most others had taken to their beds. Sami inspected the birds, whose cage fronts had been covered with plastic sheeting. "Birds wrapped up for the winter," he wrote in his report, walking on. "Tortoises also."

He stopped at Ruti's enclosure, unlocked the gate, and offered her an apple. Though the new fences prevented Ruti from destroying the trees, they also deprived her of tidbits from what dribble of visitors braved the weather. It cheered Sami up to step inside the cage and offer treats to his gentle giant.

Next, he went to the ibex enclosure. "Come Fufu," he called, as he opened the door. She skittered behind him, slipping occasionally on the wet tarmac.

Sami and Fufu headed together up to the Carnivore Department and surveyed the miserable, muddy scene. Stretches of bars were now in place, and a stack of heavy iron cage doors had been delivered. Sami wandered into the lion house, out of the rain. "Dangerous light fittings removed," he noted.

Back outside, along the perimeter line of the new cages, a row of feeble, waterlogged saplings had been planted.

He looked down at his sodden report. The rain was making the ink run.

"There's word from the municipality," hissed a grim voice, suddenly, in his ear.

Sami started. Abu Shir, a plastic anorak hood pulled up tight over his head, stood glumly behind him in a puddle.

"What word?" asked Sami.

"An ultimatum. The Carnivore Department must be finished soon, or I will be in trouble. They say it is my responsibility." Abu Shir looked helplessly around at the mess.

Fufu nuzzled Sami's leg, and the vet put one hand, reassuringly, on her forehead. She rubbed against it. Abu Shir took out a cigarette and struck up a lighter. The rain immediately extinguished the flame.

"What do you think they will do," he sorrowed, "if it is not finished in time?"

Sami could not help himself. "Perhaps you will lose your job. Perhaps they will make Mr. Eesa the manager."

Abu Shir looked aghast.

"So you had better hurry."

Abu Shir attempted the lighter a second time. It scraped a blue spark, then puttered out. "I will help you," Sami relented, "don't worry."

Abu Shir nodded and looked down at his boots, into which puddle water was slowly seeping.

"How long," asked Sami, "have they given you?"

"Two months," said Abu Shir dourly, and squelched away.

Sami glanced at his wristwatch. His shift was over. He headed down through the zoo, past the empty cage that had housed his little broken fox. It had not survived. Unusually overwhelmed by the loss, he had been too sad to stuff it and had buried it beneath a hedge. When they were older, thought Sami, Rambo and Bussi would live there, in its place.

◆   ◆   ◆

Sami held high hopes for his cat and his monkey. In just the past fortnight, the excitement generated by the indivisible pair each evening at his clinic had been considerable. Clients were beginning to arrive clutching animals with ailments they would usually have overlooked, to get a glimpse of the monkey and kitten bounding gleefully together across the floor.

Late on the thirty-first of December, Sami was operating on a goat. Mr. Salaa had dropped in at the clinic to join him, keen to share his thoughts on the current climate. Life was getting worse, he prophesied. Salaries had still to be paid; military incursions once again occurred almost nightly. Gaza was restive; the camps of the West Bank, too. The number of women about town in full *hijab,* students at the Islamic University, and adherents to the extremist end of the Hamas regime was on the up. Signs, he said, did not bode well.

"We're talking about neighbors," said Mr. Salaa. "It is like a ship on the sea. If the people living at the bottom start to drill a hole, we'll all sink. I'll bring coffee," he added. "Back soon."

Mr. Salaa left the room by the back door. A few seconds later, Sami put down his scalpel and allowed his arm a rest. He looked up to see a small, rapt crowd gathered beneath a canopy of umbrellas at the window. On the opposite side of the room, Rambo and Bussi were seated on the floor, in front of the fish tank. They watched, their heads swiveling in unison, as the largest of the goldfish swam by. Rambo's right arm was draped casually around Bussi's shoulder, his head inclined toward hers. Outside, children shrieked with delight.

"Perhaps," Sami said to Rambo and Bussi, "we should all run away together to Africa."

Neither the cat nor the monkey seemed to be listening.

Chapter Twelve
January 2007

Kal mustajeer minar ramadaa binnar.
Out of the frying pan, into the fire.
——ARABIC PROVERB

⟨T⟩he twin bears were born on a bitter January night, in circumstances startlingly similar to the birth exactly a year
before. The firstborn, blind and hairless, cried out for its
mother. As Sami watched, helpless, she took its tiny head between her jaws, and the crying ceased.

Sami was not expecting another cub but observed that Marla,
his she-bear, was restless, and waited, with his gun this time, just
in case. Sure enough, half an hour later, another baby bear was
born. Immediately, he anaesthetized the mother and took the
baby from her cage. He plied the sleeping mother bear for
colostrum, but not a drop would come.

For three days, Dr. Sami stayed at home to nurse the infant.
Every two hours, this time without fail, he fed it milk from a tiny
plastic teat. He fussed over the temperature of the incubator. He
constantly checked its breathing, monitoring its every flailing
move. He dreamed of a clumsy, happy-go-lucky teddy bear cub,
affectionate as a puppy, joining playtime alongside a baboon and
a calico cat. Third time lucky, he hoped.

On the fourth morning, despite his very best efforts, the baby
died.

"It couldn't be helped," he replied despondently to anyone who asked.

Cold January rain lashed the West Bank. It created fast-flowing eddies in the wadis, turning the fields to paddies and flooding Qalqilya's souk. The streets were deserted, whole families warming themselves beside oil-fueled radiators and kitchen fires. Despite grand inaugural promises from both local and national governments, it seemed that little had changed for the people one year since the election that brought Hamas to power.

Sami sat in his office, still awaiting word on his salary from the mayor. He took bones from a box and arranged them in neat piles on his desk.

Though little had been achieved by their recent communications and the pitiful bear pools would undoubtedly remain, he had nevertheless managed to make one important change for the bears. At the back of their new enclosure, a separate room for Marla had been built. It would be dark and quiet, with a soft bed, privacy, and calm. This, he hoped, would encourage her to produce more successful offspring. Her daughter Darling would be paired off, in the move to the Carnivore Department, with Mushi, the bachelor male, and a similar privilege afforded her. Surely then, reasoned Sami, at least one of the bears would come up with another thriving cub.

Dr. Motke had been less impressed with the plan.

"You have four bears, Sami."

"This is right. Mother, father, daughter," Sami pointed to one cage, "and daughter's future husband." Mushi sat on his haunches and watched them closely.

"Two males and two females."

"Yes, that is right."

"What are you going to do with four bears of the same species?"

"Breed new bears."

"But why?"

Sami frowned. "I do not understand the question."

"Why do you need so many examples of just one species?"

Sami stared at him.

"Look," said Motke, "I know of a zoo in Israel that's looking for a breeding pair of Syrian bears. It's a very nice place. Maybe you could give them one of yours?"

"Give them away?"

"That's right."

"For money?"

"No."

"You mean swap them, for another kind of bear?"

"No. Give them away. As a gift."

Sami eyed Motke, then nudged him sharply and laughed out loud. "Dr. Motke!" he exclaimed. "You're a very funny man!"

◆   ◆   ◆

Bears, like lions, have always been a prized possession, feared, revered, and subdued in equal measure. In Russia, the bear is a symbol of strength and courage. Sixteenth-century czar Ivan Groznoj, Ivan the Terrible, owned bear pits close to where the Kremlin stands today. His favorite pastime was to pit peasants, armed only with pitchforks, against his best fighting bears.

Ancient cults across northern Europe worshipped bears as physical manifestations of long-dead ancestors. The Ainu of Japan believed them to be visitors from the spirit realm. They reared their bears lavishly by hand, suckled them at the human breast, and then accorded them the honor of a prolonged ritual sacrifice.

Saint Romedius subdued a bear and had it carry him from his hermitage, across the mountains to Trento. Karol Radziwill, an eccentric eighteenth-century Polish noble, trained his to pull a carriage. In 1784, he took Stanislaw August Poniatowski, the last king of the Polish-Lithuanian Commonwealth, out for a drive, pulled by eight magnificent brown bears.

The awe inspired by bears has been matched with cruelty. The Emperor Nero allowed his bodyguard the pleasure of killing four hundred with a javelin. For four centuries in Britain, bears were baited in bear gardens, tied down with chains, and set upon by dogs. In Pakistan, they still are. In the Balkans and in India, dancing bears, kidnapped from the wild as cubs, have plied the streets for ages. They are beaten, iron rings forced through their palate to keep them from misbehaving, and taught to dance on scorching metal plates.

At Qalqilya, the four bears were the most taunted and teased of all the zoo animals, second only to the lions. Stones were thrown at them by little boys; even adults could sometimes be spotted jeering and aping their gait. So Sami had had their new enclosures raised up to about a yard from the floor, waist-height to a human. It was an old trick to instill respect among zoo-goers for the animal on display. The visitor had no choice but to look up to them.

♦   ♦   ♦

At last, parts of the Carnivore Department were almost complete. Sami had been forced to cede his Crocodile Island, but had compensated for the loss by slotting a new crocodile enclosure into a roomy space at the far end of the building site. There, an ellipse of a pool was slowly being constructed along with a wide sandy area complete with palm trees.

Municipal threats, meanwhile, had succeeded. Abu Shir had sprung into unprecedented action, barking orders at stooped workmen and occasionally quitting the comfort of his office in favor of the muddy building site. Soon there were fences, floors, and fully tiled quarters for the leopards. His workers fitted doors and began landscaping the lion enclosure, though the reptilian Nidal Bakir, protector of regional plants, had not been seen since his visit many moons ago.

By the time the manager's attentions turned from feline to ursine, he had run into trouble. The budget for the project was exhausted. Materials had all been used up, and there were no bars left for the bears. Necessity called for invention, and in his new and competent capacity, it was Abu Shir who insisted upon a solution.

He would, he said, have the bears' sleeping quarters finished and fitted out with stout padlocks. Dr. Sami would anaesthetize each bear in turn, after which each one would be hauled in fishing nets to a new bedroom and secured inside. A team of workers would, with speed and efficiency, dismantle the bears' old iron fence panels and re-erect them along the line of the new cages. The manager believed it would take, at most, two days.

Sami foresaw a spectrum of complications but let them pass. He was too concerned with matters of his own.

Outside, the rain poured on. "And here I am, still waiting," said Sami to Mr. Salaa, who had come by to take tea. Since Abu Shir had commandeered the Carnivore Department and his Museum of Everything remained at an impasse with Abu Khaled, Sami had resorted to sprucing up his office. He had painted the walls, put up new curtains, and arranged a bouquet of peacock tail feathers in a vase in the corner. Rambo and Bussi delighted in scattering them until the feathers made them sneeze.

"I do my very best," he said. "If these people care about my work, they will want to reward me. But if they do not. . . "

Sami turned to a cork board on the wall behind him and unpinned an old, faded photograph, curled at two edges. It showed a much younger Sami Khader, some twenty years before, smart in a beige safari suit, smiling and waving next to a trumpeting elephant. Sami regarded it closely.

Abu Shir, he continued, glancing up, seemed to have forgotten entirely about the Jerusalem giraffe. The keen young zoologist's initial enthusiasm, too, appeared to have waned. No date had been set, no permits to travel sought. Neither had telephoned to talk further. Sami suspected the zoologist had been waiting for the management at Qalqilya Zoo to show some small signs of enthusiasm.

"No time," the manager had told Sami flatly.

"He does not care," concluded Sami. Mr. Salaa grimaced. "Giraffe or no giraffe—it's the same to him. He is happy if he can sleep without problems. Perhaps I should learn from this. I can do my duties and other things besides, or, like him, I can do nothing. I will get my salary all the same."

Mr. Salaa nodded.

"A giraffe is like a person," added Sami. "She cannot go on forever all by herself."

The two friends sat in silence.

"What do you see, in your future?" asked Mr. Salaa suddenly, as Sami gazed out of the window, watching Ruti graze through a pile of hay.

"When I first came here, long ago now," Sami reflected, "I thought nothing would ever change. I thought that the old mayor would be mayor forever. I could not imagine a war. Things can change in an instant. Perhaps I must leave." He rubbed the old photograph gently between his fingers. "Perhaps one day there will be an elephant."

"In sh'Allah," said his friend.

Once Mr. Salaa had departed, Sami settled down to the reconstruction of a former raccoon, which had recently died of old age. So far, he had completed only the body, and it leaned forward, spine bent, as if looking for its head. Whenever his soul was ruffled or he found himself waiting against his will, Sami concentrated on a skeleton, the perfect, exquisite framework to life itself.

It instilled in him a cool sense of repose. It gave him something to pass the time. His family, his friends, and his keepers had learned, over the years, that it was better to leave Dr. Sami alone if he was engrossed in bones.

A few minutes later, the telephone rang. Rambo screamed and ran for cover, dragging Bussi and a jeweled peacock feather with him. Sami picked up the heavy receiver. It was the mayor.

"Hello, Dr. Sami Khader."

"Hello, Mr. Wajeeh Qawas."

"I believe you have been waiting for my call."

"This is right."

The line fell quiet.

"I would like to inform you," said the mayor, speaking slowly, "that we have come to a conclusion."

"I see."

"And our conclusion. . . "

Sami held his breath.

". . . is that we have not yet had time to consider."

Sami felt the wind leave him.

"Dr. Sami?"

"I am here," Sami managed.

"Good. There is more to discuss. I have been speaking to Abu Khaled, and he says you have a problem."

Sami gritted his teeth. "This is right."

"I believe you do not require his help or advice on the new museum you are planning."

"Yes."

"I see," the mayor said.

Sami waited, his heart pounding. He heard murmured voices at the end of the line.

"Abu Khaled says that in this case, he does not wish to be involved. He only wishes to work on a fruitful cooperation, without trouble."

"I see. As he pleases." Sami allowed himself the hint of a smile.

"However—" There was another long pause. Only the crackle of static could be heard and the faint echo of sweet secretarial voices, somewhere along the crisscrossing wires. "We have been discussing other plans for zoo renovations and have some plans we would like to share with you."

"Please," said Sami.

"First, we have decided to expand the Friends' Restaurant into the vacant space behind the picnic garden. It will become deluxe, five-star, with very good food for important guests."

Sami's aviary, the place reserved for his owls, peacocks, pigeons, and pheasants, and a flock of parakeets. The vet nodded but could not speak.

"Also, we will extend the amusement park. It is very popular with the children. We will buy more rides and more entertainments. It is very good for income."

More noise, thought Sami. More music, screaming, flashing lights.

"And last, we have decided on a system for visitors to better enjoy their sightseeing tour of the zoo."

"Yes?"

"We intend to purchase a *téléphérique*."

"What is this?"

"A cable car. So that visitors can ride around the zoo. Their feet will never even have to touch the ground."

Sami was stunned.

"What was that?" he heard the mayor ask from far away, as his head filled with static. "Ah yes, Doctor. Abu Khaled is pleased you approve of his plans. Good day."

Slowly, Sami replaced the receiver and picked up the raccoon's skull. He brushed it down with a soft squirrel-hair paintbrush, removing dust and detritus. His hand, he noticed, was trembling.

"I have to kill myself one day," he told the skull shakily. The raccoon's empty eye sockets stared back, aghast. "Or change my clinic to a falafel shop. You wonder why?" The skull nodded its head. "Because maybe then, I have a chance of promotion."

◆　　◆　　◆

People from the outlying villages, the farmers, shepherds, and smallholders that made up the majority of a Qalqilyan vet's business, usually brought their animals to town for treatment early in the morning, taking circuitous routes over ancient goat paths to avoid the checkpoints, roadblocks, and inspections. Sometimes, when Sami had occasion to stop off at his clinic on his way to the zoo, he would find an owner waiting on his front step, an ailing ram or pony hitched to a lamppost. If the matter could be quickly resolved, he would treat the animal and send it home. If not, much as it pained him to do so, he would direct the animal's owner to one of his competitors. There, he believed, they would receive an inferior, expensive, and potentially disastrous service.

Early one morning on the last Thursday in January, Sami was tucked away in his Natural History Museum, busy screwing a skeletal raccoon in place, when a desperate farmer arrived at the zoo. He was soaked to the bone and hammered hard on its gates. Abu Shir emerged beneath an umbrella.

"Please," breathed the farmer, "I need to see Dr. Sami Khader."

"Why?" asked Abu Shir.

"My mare is in labor. A vet came to examine her, but he said that the foal has no head. He told me he cannot help my mare, and that she will die. She's the only one I have. Another came, and he also couldn't help. He said the only person who might be able to save her is Dr. Sami Khader, and that I would find him here at the zoo."

"Dr. Khader is busy with his duties," replied Abu Shir. "He can't come out to help you."

"But sir," pleaded the farmer, "if she dies, I will have nothing."

"Then you must ask the mayor."

The farmer turned and rushed away. Abu Shir took a cigarette from his breast pocket and felt for his lighter.

At the municipality building in the center of town, the dripping farmer dashed up five flights of stairs. He burst into the mayor's office before the alarmed secretary could stop him. The mayor looked up from his newspaper in surprise, as the farmer sank weeping to his knees.

"I cannot refuse," he said, having listened carefully. "Go back to the zoo and take the doctor to tend to your mare."

The farmer, between sobs, thanked him profusely.

"May Allah be with you," said the mayor as the farmer departed, leaving a wet patch on the carpet.

Less than half an hour later, Dr. Sami stood in a low, shabby shelter at the edge of town, watched by the farmer and his ashen son. Outside, the storm raged around them.

"We will have to go swimming in there," joked Sami, pointing to the rear of the mare. The two men stared back.

Sami sank one arm deep inside the mare and felt around.

"We must go right up to this baby and ask him very nicely to come out."

He picked up a length of rope, and with a grunt, inserted a second arm. The mare shied and stomped her feet. The farmer traced the star on his horse's forehead and blew gently into her nose.

Sami screwed his eyes tight shut in concentration, as he manipulated the rope, tying it firmly around all four legs of the unborn foal. "Now," he said, "I need you to pull."

Ten minutes later, three men heaving hard on the end of a rope delivered a heavy foal to a snorting chestnut mare. "Why,"

Sami panted, wiping blood and mucous from his upper arms and shoulders, "did the other vets say they could not help you?"

"They said," replied the farmer, flushed with gratitude, "that the baby had no head."

The foal whinnied and struggled to its feet. Lightning forked, illuminating the shelter. Sami accepted a cup of steaming tea and shivered. It was time to get back to the zoo. His animals needed him. Now, even the mayor knew it too.

"Some people," Sami said, the teacup hiding his smile, "look for the head at the wrong end of the horse."

Chapter Thirteen
February 2007

The pillar of a people's hope,
the centre of a world's desire.
—Eulogy for Jumbo the elephant,
London Daily Mail, 1885

It was early in the morning, the beginning of February, and despite fierce winds and a threatening sky, Sami marched brightly to the zoo's front gates. He had been to see a man about a car—a newish model, just two decades old, red, and running well. Though he wasn't yet sure how he would pay for it, it would, eventually, be his.

More exciting still had been the installation of Bussi and Rambo, exactly a week ago, into what was once the quarters of a sad silver fox. Their new home had a tree trunk in the middle for clambering, and a little wooden box filled with hay, into which they could retreat at night. The floor was littered with chicken legs for Bussi to chew. Rambo occasionally enlisted them as genuine drumsticks, tapping rhythms on the cage bars. Once, as Sami crouched in the cage teasing his young friends, two ladies and their children pulled up to stare. They watched as the monkey cackled, shinned up the tree trunk, and then fell, squawking, onto the little cat.

"A shame," one lady said, leaning in close to the other. "Such a sweet cat, to end up as dinner for that ugly brute."

Sami considered putting up an explanatory sign.

His office had been treated to a thorough cleaning, and though the scent of monkey lingered, Sami's belongings were back in their rightful place and remained so from day to day. His wife, too, had returned to her old doting self. Uzhdan missed the clownish animals but had buckled down with resolve to her studies, which made her father happy.

Sami stopped beneath the signpost at the zoo's entrance and craned his neck, gazing up. All that was left of its old animal parade were faint, peeling remnants. Bolted at its center, a large new shield bore the cornfield emblem of Qalqilya Municipality, framed in government green. On either side, the broken neon signs had been replaced by shiny metal panels. Each panel, some thirty feet high, depicted a dazzling array of creatures. Two trumpeting elephants, a moose, shiny tigers, a rhino, a grinning koala, a cockatoo with crest erect.

Sami let himself in through the side gate. He strode the avenue, humming lightly, and tripped up the steps to his office, depositing his briefcase on the plastic chair in front of the desk. It was nice to be alone. He ran a stream of water into his old tin kettle and set it to heat on the stove. A peacock called outside the window. Today was a half-day holiday, and he would leave at one o'clock to open his clinic earlier than usual. He took a pencil and paper, closed the office door, and swung back down the steps to begin his morning rounds.

All was well, noted Sami, with the ostriches. Wahib the dromedary, browsing hay, rolled his eyes and foamed at the mouth. It was mating season, and though his female was old and barren, Wahib's instincts could not be subdued. The camel, during this frantic, aggressive period, signaled his virility by puffing up his tumescent palate, which lolled out of his mouth like a half-inflated red balloon. He issued low, tempting gurgles, saliva frothing white and bubbly between his front teeth. Had Wahib lived as part of a herd, his efforts would have rendered him irresistible to all but the most frigid females.

The zebras snoozed against each other's flanks. Dubi was submerged in his pool. Sami performed a quick headcount on the Cameroon and Berber sheep, satisfied that all were well.

As he reached the next enclosure, he knew straight away that something was wrong. Only three of Sami's four addax stood tall atop their customary boulder. All three were transfixed by something in one corner. Sami pressed his nose against the fence to get a better look. Sure enough, there lay an inert white form, two chiseled horns excavating the dust. Sami frowned and pulled his keys from his pocket.

"Who can say," asked Charles Darwin, "what cows feel when they surround and stare intently on a dead or dying companion?" It was clear, even before Sami approached the animal, that the others knew it was dead. There had been no signs of illness, but now, when Sami glanced at its teeth, he saw that the creature was quite old. A shame, he thought, that it hadn't troubled to secure a legacy before it passed away. He took out his pencil and noted the death on his report. "Cause: Old age," he wrote. He would have Yail Misqawi remove the corpse later in the morning. Perhaps the skinning and stuffing could wait until after the weekend, so that he might still get away on time today. The three remaining addax regarded him levelly as he stepped out of the cage and locked the door behind him.

Sami remembered the kettle, which by now was likely whistling away to itself in the corner of his office. He would leave the remainder of the tour for later and treat himself to one quiet cup of tea before anyone could arrive to spoil his solitude. Tucking his pencil and paper into his pocket, he headed back to his office.

"Good morning, Fufu," he said, as he reached the little ibex waiting for him at her corner post. "How are you today?" Fufu cocked her head expectantly. Sami stopped and uprooted a clump of grass, scratching her nose as she munched.

He tore off a second handful and walked to Ruti's gate. "Ruti!" he called, and waited. There was no response from within the giraffe house. "Ruti!" he called again. Nothing. Sami walked along the perimeter fence and peered into the enclosure. "Ruti?" But still no gentle, loping giraffe appeared to claim her breakfast treat.

Sami retrieved his keys and fumbled with the stiff enclosure lock. His feet crunched over gravel as he made his way toward the entrance to the night shelter, stepping carefully over hard capsules of dung. "Ruti!" he called and rounded the corner.

"Ruti?"

Against the far wall of her night quarters lay a huge crumpled marionette. Beneath it, four dinner-plate hooves protruded awkwardly. A fancifully patterned neck stretched out straight against the back wall, beneath a feeder filled with grass. A liquid eye, framed with thick lashes, gazed into the distance. Sami stepped back. He looked away. He closed his eyes and rubbed them.

It took the vet time to convince himself that what he was seeing was real. He paced back and forth for a minute before walking over to the fallen giraffe and touching her neck. Cold. He checked her eyes, felt her nose for a whisper of warm breath, but there was none. Her two stubby horns had grazed the wall on the way down, leaving thin parallel trails of blood. Ruti was dead.

He knelt down and gazed into her face. He tried hard to breathe. Tears pricked his eyes and misted his glasses.

The kettle had boiled dry by the time Sami returned upstairs. He turned off the gas and pulled a blue workman's jacket from a cupboard. He took a pair of latex gloves from a box on the sideboard and pushed them into his pocket. He left the office, locking it behind him, and set out to find Abu Shir.

◆　　◆　　◆

As the plastic Kabaa clock in the ticket office trilled nine, a group of men assembled at the entrance to the giraffe enclosure. First, they would have to saw off the hinges of its main gate. Then they would need a tractor with a shovel to scoop up Ruti's body and transport her across to the zoo to the slaughterhouse. There, Sami would perform his autopsy.

Abu Shir stood limply beside the gate.

"Fifteen thousand dollars," he muttered. "Gone."

Heels dragging, he walked to Dr. Sami, who stood staring at the dead giraffe. The manager crouched, picked up one wide hoof, held the ankle as if checking for a pulse, and then dropped it to the ground.

"We must move her as soon as possible," said Sami.

"Not yet," replied Abu Shir, his eyes scanning the corpse. "There are people who wish to see."

The first to arrive was dapper chief engineer Nabil Baron. He appeared in a pinstriped suit and picked his way carefully across the enclosure. He stopped and studied the form for several seconds. "Why did it die?" he asked, turning to Sami.

"Perhaps a liver abscess," replied Sami, "or heart failure. From the way she fell, it seems she was dead before she reached the ground."

"How interesting."

"Now," said Sami, "I must work like a detective, to find out what went wrong. I estimate, from the state of her body," he waved one gloved finger at Ruti, "that it happened at around 4 AM." He glanced up to see four earnest young men in black leather jackets crunching toward them.

"Press," said Abu Shir. "Municipality photographer. Newspaper reporter. Local TV."

They had firm, vigorous handshakes. The youngest carefully extracted a large video camera from a bag slung over his shoulder and removed the lens cap. The second squinted around the enclosure and headed for a vantage point on the opposite side of Ruti's body. Another took out a Dictaphone. The shortest pulled a tiny spiral notebook from his inside pocket. He licked the tip of his pencil. Nabil Baron stepped forward.

"It is very sad," he announced, once a red light glowed on the Dictaphone. He paused to allow the other reporter time to note down his words. "We worked so hard to bring a male for this giraffe, and now we have lost everything."

Abu Shir gaped. Sami's eyes widened. They glanced at each other, then back at Nabil Baron. The reporter turned a page and looked up expectantly.

"I think," Baron continued, "that the giraffe is the main attraction of this zoo, the one that people have always come to see. Now we must try to bring a new animal as quickly as possible to cover this problem. A giraffe is not easy to acquire."

"So you have," the reporter addressed the whole group, "tried before to bring a new giraffe to the zoo?" The young cameraman shouldered his video camera. Nabil Baron coughed and straightened his tie. Sami opened his mouth to speak.

"Oh, yes," said the chief engineer. "Our efforts are unstoppable. But the problem is not with us. For one year already, I have tried to bring an elephant here, but sadly I have failed." Sami shot him a poisonous glance and went back to staring at Ruti.

"Israel, you see," Baron continued, "has forbidden us to bring such an elephant. But now we must make a big effort to try even more seriously. We must talk to other zoos and build cooperation. This is a political problem."

"Is there," asked the reporter, "any hope for the future?"

"Animals are culture. For the people. We must always be optimistic," said Nabil Baron. He shot a winning smile at the camera. A sleek black car slid up the avenue and came to a halt outside the giraffe paddock. "Gentlemen," he said, "if you'll excuse me."

The reporters wandered off. Dr. Sami and Abu Shir watched the black car speed away.

Abu Shir lit a cigarette. "Why is she suddenly dead like this?"

"Don't ask me this question," snapped Sami. "Animals die. This is from God, not from us. But," he considered for a second, "when we open her up, I believe we'll find it is heart failure."

"She died," said Abu Shir bitterly, "of a broken heart."

Sami noticed one of the reporters kicking idly at the corpse. "Excuse me," he called. "Please do not do that."

"What will you put here to replace her," the reporter shouted back, "if you can't get another one?"

"If one man or one lady dies in a family, the first thing to do is cry and be sad," replied Sami icily. "Only after that, we start to think about how they will be replaced." He turned to Abu Shir. "Are we ready to begin yet?"

"We are waiting for one more man," said Abu Shir.

◆   ◆   ◆

News of Ruti's death had hopped like a flea from the manager to the chief engineer, across the municipality to the mayor, then out of his window and across the road to the souk, where it had bitten the deputy's veterinarian brother. He wished very much, came the return message, to attend the autopsy.

At the zoo, another familiar face was now progressing up the avenue. Nidal Jaloud, international relations officer, was accompanied by three representatives of the United Nations on an inspection tour of their workers whose labor was slowly assembling the Carnivore Department. Jaloud wore a smart gray suit, a red necktie, and gold-framed glasses. He had another cold, and in one hand grasped a spotted handkerchief. He wished to demonstrate to his visitors the zoo's professionalism in the face of adversity and had promised that they would see a hippopotamus and feed a giraffe.

"Quoi?" hissed Jaloud, as word of the demise was whispered to him. "Ce n'est pas vrai! What will my guests feed now?"

Back inside the enclosure, Abu Shir was deep in an animated discussion regarding which hinge should be sawn first and whether the tractor ought to enter forward or in reverse. A municipality car arrived carrying the deputy's brother and promptly crashed into a concrete post. Everyone froze at the sound of creasing metal and crackling plastic. The car turned clumsily, deposited its passenger, and rolled away. Across the avenue, the ostriches watched with interest, their heads bobbing up and down like a line of pistons.

At ten o'clock, a large yellow mechanical digger chugged into the zoo and through the two demolished gates of the giraffe enclosure. It disappeared into the night shelter, from which shouts and scrapes soon emanated, then reappeared, fifteen minutes later, its wide mouth filled with the inverted form of a dead giraffe. Ruti's head hung over the side. Her front legs stuck stiffly into the air. The digger lurched back across the enclosure and turned right onto the zoo's top avenue. It was followed closely by Dr. Sami and Abu Shir, along with a troupe of zookeepers, the deputy's brother, and a few accumulating spectators. The cameraman brought up the rear, capturing the convoy for posterity.

In the distance, Nidal Jaloud was being interviewed by a member of the press. His eyes followed two young women passing by.

"The giraffe is something eccentric, something beautiful," he sniffed. "This is a great shock for the municipality. This zoo is an income-generating project. People come here to waste time and money. It is the only facility for fun."

He glanced up, and his eyes widened at the macabre procession.

"Ce n'est pas jolie!" he spluttered. "I must find my guests. Excuse me." He scuttled away.

At the top of the avenue, a little girl in a sheepskin winter coat clung to her younger brother's hand and watched as the digger turned sharply through the corrugated iron gates leading to the slaughterhouse.

"They will see worse," muttered Abu Shir, as their mother shielded their eyes and dragged them away.

The machine ground to a halt and, with a jerk, lowered its jaws. Ruti tumbled to the ground. A small crowd gathered around her. Abdel Raouf Joadi arrived with a fistful of knives in one hand, a saw and a hammer in the other. Somebody else brought a big blue cooler. Dr. Sami silently inspected the array of tools, setting them out carefully on an old upturned oil barrel. Yail Misqawi smoked a cigarette. The deputy's brother carefully donned a pair of latex gloves. The municipal photographer, journalist, and videographer attempted professionalism and strong stomachs. Abu Shir, working alone, tried in vain to maneuver the first of the giraffe's long legs through the slaughterhouse door.

In a stable at the back of the slaughterhouse, a black horse, with open sores on its flank and a knotted ankle, shied weakly away from the sound of machines and human voices, its eyes wide with terror. Peacocks clattered on the tin roof overhead.

Yail Misqawi started up a motorized winch, which ran a heavy chain through an eye attached to the ceiling. The motor whirred as the winch wound the chain, from which a rusty hook dangled, slowly upward. Yail yanked on it, testing its strength, then reversed the motor, sending the chain steadily down to the ground. Dr. Sami took a length of rope and tied Ruti's forelegs together at the ankle. He made a deep incision into her back right leg, at the knee, peeling the skin away like a ripe peach, and forced the hook through the joint. The motor squealed as the giraffe was pulled steadily into the slaughterhouse, until only her head remained outside. Her tongue dragged across the muddy floor.

Sami set to work. With a butcher's knife he cut a jagged line along the center of Ruti's upturned belly. The deputy's brother hovered just behind Sami's shoulder, eager to join in. Sami dug his fingers into the cleft and pulled apart the skin. Yail Misqawi set to work with the axe, with a series of wet, cracking thuds. The keepers gathered closer. Abu Shir took a step away, turned his back, and looked up at the sky.

Within minutes, Sami had opened a sizable hole in Ruti's abdomen. He tugged and wrestled, his arm plunged deep inside her. Occasionally, he passed a piece of matter to the old cross-eyed keeper, who carefully tucked it into the cooler.

From the wings, the cats moved in, scenting death. A fluffy white female seated herself close to Ruti's head and gazed intently into the giraffe's face for several minutes. Blood dripped from Ruti's nose and the tip of her tongue.

Over the course of the next three hours, Sami worked away at the giraffe's corpse, examining her stomach and its contents, prodding her vital organs, and feeling his way along snaking veins and arteries. He could not, as yet, see any clear reason for her death. An analysis of tissue would be necessary.

"Though," he muttered to Yail Misqawi, as the deputy's brother encroached further on his operating space, "this is only for procedure. Dead is dead. It does not matter now why."

As pieces of Ruti were peeled away, one keeper heading off with a lump of leg dangling from a hook, a tasty afternoon treat for the lions, her familiar form began to vanish. Dozens of buckets of murky liquid dotted the floor.

"This is the end of the story," said Sami to Abu Shir, placing Ruti's head into a metal pail. It no longer mattered that a giraffe from Jerusalem would never arrive. "They will be one family, finally together again."

Across the zoo, most visitors were oblivious to the catastrophe. Two ladies with little girls in pink cardigans collided in brand-new bumper cars. The Ferris wheel spun, though no one was aboard. A handful of tiny children perched atop the toy electric train as it trundled around the tracks, and a small half-day holiday crowd watched Rambo and Bussi at play.

◆　　◆　　◆

Across the world, statues and plaques, books and memorial services pay tribute to those creatures who captured the public's heart or the spirit of the age. Guy the Gorilla is honored by a statue at the gates of London Zoo. A. A. Milne's immortal Pooh bear is a memorial to a real black bear named Winnipeg. In Japan, zoo animal ceremonies regularly pay tribute to the dead.

When Jumbo met his untimely end in front of an express freight train, the indefatigable Barnum milked the tragedy for all it was worth. In 1886, at regular intervals, huge parades took place in honor of the elephant. Jumbo's stuffed carcass, along with his skeleton, was driven by black-clad mourners on carriages pulled by black horses. Barnum purchased, from London Zoo, Jumbo's old widow, Alice. She joined the procession in funereal dress. Barnum's other elephants brandished black handkerchiefs and were taught to dab their eyes.

In private, Barnum showed less decorum. He ordered a gala dinner for dignitaries and reporters, who consumed jellies set with gelatin of Jumbo's powdered tusks.

The giraffe who had once walked from Marseille to Paris at night, clothed in finery and protected by a holy talisman, slipped away more quietly. Opponents of her owner, King Charles X, used her as an object of ridicule. She became first a caricature, then a target of mockery, and finally was forgotten. Balzac prophesied that her decline in popularity presaged the deposition of the king, and he guessed correctly. In 1845, the giraffe died, aged twenty-one, and met her taxidermist. She remains today in the seaside town of La Rochelle, preserved inside a dusty Museum of Natural History.

Ruti's parts, arrayed around a hot and exhausted Dr. Sami, formed a giant jigsaw puzzle. A serpentine neck, the longest in the animal kingdom. A spindly leg, bandaged at one end; at the other, a prehistoric hoof. Her big heart, twenty-five pounds in weight, that once had pumped blood at the highest blood pressure of any mammal, through veins an inch wide in places. The rough, blue, eighteen-inch tongue that had chewed its way through seventy pounds of cud each day, and the four-chambered stomach that contained it all, gray, sleek, and shiny. The elaborate skin, now a discarded fur coat.

The giraffe as we know it today is the only surviving member of the genus *giraffa*, of which there were at least three dozen prehistoric species, some the size of Shetland ponies, others much larger than the modern breed. In the wild, only 25 percent of baby giraffes survive to adulthood, falling prey to disease, big cats, or poaching. "It looked so helpless," noted hunter Percy Madeira in 1909, "and tumbled over as if a church steeple was falling." Ruti had survived more than most.

It was evening by the time the autopsy was complete. Sami would have to wait a month, or more, for the results. Another journalist, sent by one of the national dailies, had surfaced and was doing the rounds. "How do you feel, Doctor, about the loss?" the journalist asked, removing the lid from his ballpoint pen.

"Take this down," said Sami, gray-faced and sweating. "It is a bad day. A very bad day." He glanced at his watch and summoned a smile. He would do his grieving in private, at home. "Because it is a half-day holiday, and I am still here. And because," he shook his hands free of blood, fat, and half-digested grass, "I have had no time for lunch."

Chapter Fourteen
March 2007

The last straw breaks the camel's back.

—Arabic proverb

D
r. Sami had a favorite joke. A baby camel, it went, once asked his mother why camels have such long eyelashes. "So that we can shield our eyes from the desert sands," she replied. "And why," he looked over his shoulder, "do we have this big hump?" "To store food for our long journeys through barren lands," she answered. "And why," he asked, glancing down, "do we have cloven hooves?" "So that we may walk more easily across the endless dunes," she explained. The baby camel considered this. "Then what," he demanded, "are we doing in a zoo?"

The dromedary, or Arabian camel, is known to the Bedouin as *Ata Allah,* God's gift. It is the most tenacious of all mammals. Its hump is a great lump of fat, a secret store on which it can draw when times are harsh. It possesses unparalleled skills of survival in hostile environments, capable of living with little food or water for a week and raising its internal body temperature to avoid wasting vital fluids through perspiration in excessive heat. It can lose 40 percent of its own body weight in water and still march on, but will slurp twenty-six gallons, fresh or brackish, in just a few minutes. It derives sustenance from whatever it can find or forage and has very thick skin.

The camel has thirty-four sharp teeth, which can be used, when necessary, against its enemies, though more often they are employed harmlessly in chewing the cud. It possesses a remarkably sharp sense of hearing but does not always choose to listen. Many mistake the camel's groans under the strain of load bearing for expressions of anger or aggression. An experimental camel corps in the U.S. Army, just years before the Civil War, found the creatures difficult to handle. The camels, they said, bore grudges against those who treated them harshly and waited patiently for the right moment to retaliate.

In the wild, the camel is unterritorial. Large, close-knit herds may number a thousand or more individuals, even more in times of hardship when the herd closes ranks. Together a herd will migrate in search of food, water, and better conditions for living. Camels once roamed free across the hills of the Middle East, but today exist almost exclusively in captivity. It is said they were first domesticated by frankincense traders plying the long route north from southern Arabia to the uppermost reaches of the Middle East. In some Shi'ite accounts, Muhammad spared a talking camel from execution by its owner. Napoleon crossed Suez on board a "ship of the desert," which was later stuffed and displayed in the Natural History Museum next to Charles X's equally journeysome giraffe.

Only one population now lives in freedom, in Australia. Its half-million feral camels are the legacy of those transported in the nineteenth century to help tame the territory's vast hinterlands. The first, sent from the Canary Islands in 1840, was named Harry. His owner, John Horrocks, saddled him up on several expeditions into the barren interior of southern Australia. In August 1846, Harry lurched unexpectedly, causing Horrocks to detonate the rifle he was loading. The gunpowder blast was huge, blowing off two fingers and a mouthful of teeth. Horrocks died a month later of gangrene and Harry was duly destroyed, at his owner's express wishes.

◆　　◆　　◆

Spring had finally come to Qalqilya. Three men were hard at work, bricking out a wide promenade between the new banks of Carnivore Department cages, and at the end, the crocodile pool had been waterproofed. A vast area behind it was filled with sand, bigger than the entirety of their current cage, and offering both sunshine and shade. It would be the only enclosure uncovered on top. It was farthest from the boys' school windows, and Sami felt it an unnecessary expense. "The man who tries to climb into here," he said, "is not my responsibility." Sami had also finally vetoed Abu Shir's unusual plan for completing the bear enclosures. The money had been found and duly spent on new iron bars.

Dr. Motke, on learning of Ruti's death, had offered Sami a solution. Since the elderly vet saw little hope of procuring a new giraffe or even another carnivore or two, he was willing to collect up surplus herbivores of different varieties from the various parks and zoos of his country. With these, Sami could fill Ruti's vacant lot. The weather had turned balmy, and Israeli zoos were busy, but as soon as the initial tide of visitors receded, he would start thinking about expanding the collection.

"Anything's better than an empty cage," Sami told Abu Shir.

"These animals will not be good for business," the manager glowered.

The lions' new cage was the first to be finished. It had a wooden platform, perched six feet high on thick stakes. There were boulders and grass, and a rash of saplings, protected with wire.

"Two months?" laughed Sami, as he proudly showed Mr. Salaa around. "Two years!"

The lions were moved on a warm Wednesday afternoon, quietly and with Motke in attendance. As a precaution, the zoo's westerly and northern avenues, along which the lions would progress, were cordoned off with rows of plastic chairs. The sleeping creatures were moved on large claw-snagging nets and hauled onto the back of a municipal truck. Even Mr. Eesa had decided to attend. Fat Mr. Sherif sneaked from the museum to snap a photograph for his mother.

The next morning, Sami watched Rabir standing proudly atop a boulder, surveying his new, broad domain. Sami grinned to himself. Later, he moved the old hyena. By the end of the day, the stray cats had come to find him.

◆　　◆　　◆

One afternoon, Sami received a telephone call from a laboratory in Ramallah.

"We have the results of the autopsy, sir," said a polite female voice.

"I see," said Sami.

"Shall we send them, or would you like them now?"

"Now, please."

"The cause of death," he heard a shuffle of papers, "was Diazonol."

"Diazonol?"

"That's right."

Sami was speechless.

"Sir?"

Sami struggled to find his voice.

"Are you still there?"

"Yes."

"I will put the full report in the mail."

"Thank you. Good-bye."

"Good-bye, sir."

Sami's brow furrowed. Diazonol was a cleaning product; cheap and strong smelling, it repelled cockroaches and, like any chemical, was lethal in large doses. It was used at the zoo for attacking the dirtiest of cages, but never in the giraffe's enclosure.

Ruti, it seemed, had been poisoned. But why, how? By an outsider or by a member of staff? He rubbed his face with the palms of his hands. It was impossible to think it had been one of his own keepers, but who else could have done such a thing? Whether Ruti's death had been intentional or not, he had no way of ascertaining.

Sami looked down at his desk and at his half-written daily report. The telephone rang again. Wearily, he picked up the receiver. It was, a voice announced, a government man from the Gaza Strip, with grand designs and the blessing of the municipality, for reopening a zoological facility in the area. Sami did not feel like offering encouragement. "It will be very difficult for you. There are international standards that are hard to meet," he warned.

"One day we will get our baby lion back."

"Good luck," said Sami, and hung up.

The week before, a similarly bothersome query had arrived at Sami's office from Tulkarem, twelve miles to the north of Qalqilya.

The visitor was a fellow veterinary surgeon who had been charged, without choice or warning, with the post of head veterinarian at the newly established Tulkarem Zoo. Sami eyed him with intense suspicion.

"Good morning, doctor," said the thin, balding vet nervously. "I have come for your advice." Sami nodded as the vet explained that he knew nothing outside the realm of common livestock.

"I hear that you are the most knowledgeable man on this subject," said the vet, "and that everyone comes to you for advice. So I wondered if you might help me."

Sami smiled and set the kettle on to boil. He seated himself behind his desk.

"Tell me," he said, "what do you have over there in Tulkarem?"

The new zoo had as yet just a handful of specimens.

"We have some baboons," the vet began.

"Everyone has some baboons!" scoffed Sami. "But this does not make it a zoo. They are not rare and are not difficult to treat. If," he added, "you know what you're doing."

"We also have some ostriches."

"I see."

"Some small birds."

"What type?"

"I—" the veterinarian blushed. "I'm not sure."

Sami smiled. "Go on."

"Several donkeys."

Sami raised an eyebrow.

"Some cats and dogs."

"And?"

The vet looked down. "This is all. So far."

Sami beamed and clasped his hands behind his head. "So, what do you want to know?"

"Well," the vet hesitated, looking about the room. "How do I administer anesthetic to a sick baboon?"

Sami drummed his fingers on the desk. "I can explain how to deliver an anesthetic. But," he paused and leaned forward, "what will you do then? How will you diagnose his disease when you have no experience?"

The vet tugged at his shirt collar. Fine beads of perspiration appeared on his brow.

"And if you receive a lion and the lion becomes sick, how will you know what is wrong? He is not going to tell you himself." Sami rose from his chair. "It is good for you," he concluded, "that you only have domestic animals at your park. These, you should be able to manage. Mostly. Would you care for sugar in your tea?"

◆　　◆　　◆

Abu Shir remained unhappy with Dr. Motke's plans for the old giraffe enclosure. Since his late involvement in the Carnivore Department, the manager had found that decisive action served to lift his habitual boredom. He would, he concluded, take the matter into his own hands. One day, with inspiration brought on by two strong coffees before breakfast, Abu Shir came upon the idea of transferring Wahib the dromedary to fill the gap.

The morning of the move began badly. "I have been trying to call you. Where have you been? Why did you forget your telephone?" Abu Shir demanded when he finally caught up with Dr. Sami, at eight o'clock, at the zoo gates.

"If I had remembered I had forgotten," Sami retorted, "I would not have forgotten to remember."

"I have a boy here waiting for you," said Abu Shir. "Today, we move Wahib."

Sami would say, in retrospect, that he had known all along the day would end as it did.

"If something will happen, it will happen," he would remark, time and again, as his preface to a retelling of the day's events. "If you try to escape it, it will come for you again. This is a very important point."

Wahib had never been tamed for load bearing, so he could not be ridden through the zoo as other camels might. He was as willful and unpredictable as the old she-camel was agreeable and slow, but Abu Shir felt he would make the livelier exhibit. It had all been arranged. In preparation for the move, the manager had enlisted the services of a young boy whose father kept camels for meat. Since the boy could barely crawl, he had played between their hooves; they trusted him, and he handled even the most unbiddable fearlessly.

At the boy's command, Sami and Abu Shir managed to herd Wahib halfway across the zoo, past the Carnivore Department and toward Ruti's enclosure, with the help of two hefty wooden sticks. They tapped sharply at either flank, and the camel progressed at an even gait along the avenue. All went well until the giraffe enclosure came into sight. Then, with Fufu on one side and the Berber sheep on the other, Wahib stopped. Sami and Abu Shir tapped on, but Wahib did not appear to notice. He yawned, considered, then turned around. The camel wanted to go home.

"But he has a better enclosure, a bigger one, this way," protested Abu Shir.

"He is a camel," said Sami irritably. "He does not know this. Perhaps he likes his own home."

Abu Shir turned to the camel boy. "What shall we do?"

The boy was busy knotting a rope. "Don't worry," he replied, and flung one end at Wahib. The lasso slipped neatly around the camel's neck. The boy adjusted the rope. He pulled, and Wahib responded. Together, they walked calmly to Ruti's roomy paddock.

The boy dropped the rope at the enclosure gate, and Wahib wandered away. Near the fence, he found a mound of hay, grumbled to himself, and took a noisy mouthful.

"Leave the rope until I come back," said the boy.

Abu Shir thrust him a crumpled bank note. "There's breakfast for you at the cafeteria."

The boy set off to claim his culinary reward, and Sami and Abu Shir stayed behind, watching Wahib.

"I think we should take off the rope," said Abu Shir, as soon as the boy had gone.

"He told you to leave it alone."

"No, it should be removed. It looks untidy. I will do it myself."

Yail Misqawi strolled up to join them. "Bring me a knife," Abu Shir commanded. "I will release the camel."

The keeper hurried off and returned with a steel kitchen knife. Abu Shir tucked it into his waistband and stepped with the air of a buccaneer into the enclosure.

"All right," said Sami, "nice knife. We'll see what happens now." He shrugged and stepped away.

Abu Shir got as far as the spot where an overhanging branch had once made lovers of a pair of giraffes. There, Wahib stood placidly chewing hay. As the manager pulled the knife from his trousers, the camel awoke. His eyes rolled in horror. Abu Shir advanced.

In one nimble swoop, Wahib was on top of him, snorting and spitting. The camel emitted a loud bellow and caught Abu Shir's head squarely between his teeth. The knife thudded to the ground. Abu Shir let out a shrill scream, and Wahib hollered back; Abu Shir slipped from his grasp. The camel lunged again, grabbing fast, this time, at the manager's right arm. His jaws locked. Abu Shir screamed.

"Save me!"

It took several minutes for the camel boy and Abdel Raouf Joadi to join Sami and Yail Misqawi in the struggle against Wahib. Meanwhile, Abu Shir writhed in agony. The camel held on tight, feverishly shaking the zoo manager's arm. Abu Shir shrieked as his knees buckled. He sank to the floor, suspended by his trapped hand. Instantly, Wahib collapsed on top of him and began to roll and writhe, his teeth still clenched tight around his victim's forearm. Blood trickled between Abu Shir's white knuckles, mingling with froth from the camel's mouth.

Wahib seemed prepared to fight to the death. Sami broke three wooden sticks across his skull, and yet he continued to rage. After ten minutes, without releasing Abu Shir's flesh, he had twisted the screaming man around, pinioning him to the ground between his two front legs. The boy tossed Sami an iron bar. Wincing, Sami clouted Wahib again across the head. Wahib reeled. Together, Sami and Yail Misqawi prized open the dizzy camel's jaws just long enough to extract Abu Shir's mangled right arm.

Immediately, Wahib sprang back into action. He went for the manager's left arm, then lost his grip. Abu Shir struggled free. As the manager lurched toward the gate, Wahib attacked again. He managed one good nip at Abu Shir's back, tearing away most of his shirt. The camel ignored the keeper, the vet, the little boy, and their manifold blows.

His arm was bloody and his hand already blue and ballooning by the time Abu Shir was finally safe. Yail Misqawi disappeared to call an ambulance as the manager, faint and moaning, was carried hastily from the mouth of the enclosure and deposited on a patch of grass.

Sami was unimpressed.

"What stupid work," he whispered. "It is not Wahib's fault."

Yet Sami had to admit that Wahib's sudden ferocity was inexplicable.

The manager let out a thin wail, closed his eyes, and turned his head into the grass. He slipped into unconsciousness. The ambulance pulled silently in through the gates, so as not to alarm the zoo's morning visitors.

That night, Sami telephoned an old friend in Saudi Arabia to determine what might have caused the outburst.

"There are three possible explanations," said his friend, an expert on camel husbandry. "The first is that the camel believed the rope to be a snake. Camels are very frightened of snakes. This might have made him lash out at your manager. The second," he theorized, "is that he was scared of the man's knife. Perhaps, long ago, he saw another camel slaughtered. Or perhaps," he paused, "there is something in the history of this man and this camel. Camels do not forget. If he behaved badly toward it in the past, it might have waited for its chance to take revenge."

Abu Shir survived the camel attack, battered and bruised, and doctors managed to save his crushed arm. Wahib had bitten off most of his old, heart-shaped tattoo. He had lost blood and would need repeated surgery, but the fractures were clean and would heal.

The scars on his back, head, and hands would serve as a reminder of the angry dromedary forever.

News reached the zoo next morning that he would survive relatively unscathed.

"How is he?" asked Amjad Daoud, arriving at the ticket office as the clock struck nine.

"He is concussed but will recover," replied Sami. "We moved him back to his home. In case he bites a visitor."

Amjad Daoud stared at him.

"Ah," said Sami. "He is alive. But he is an old man, not a young man. I believe he will be in bed, at home, for a long, long time."

◆　　◆　　◆

The zoo was buzzing as Sami set about his rounds. Entry had been declared free to students for a fortnight, and school groups were flocking in. On Monday and Wednesday, girls arrived; on Sunday, Tuesday, and Thursday, boys. Dozens of ancient buses were parked in untidy rows outside the gates. Today was the turn of the girls. Young ladies from the universities strolled the avenues in close groups. Small girls clambered across the playground's monkey bars.

The students had come from all around, braving long, uncertain journeys from Nablus, Ramallah, Tulkarem, and even from as far as Jericho. One bus, all the way from Jenin, a thirty-mile journey of well over three hours, was filled with boys. They had come on the wrong day. Distraught teachers pleaded with Amjad Daoud, who had no choice but to let them in.

"Just keep them under control!" he yelled to a harried mathematics teacher.

Sami had attempted to show several school groups around his museums, but their attention waned, and they wandered away.

"I am glad," he said, as the last teacher slipped out into the sunshine. "I did not want to continue the tour in any case. These are stupid people."

Uzhdan was among the throng, excited to be the important daughter of Palestine's sole zoo veterinarian. It was the day before her final exam, and she had been granted a half-day reprieve from her studies. She posed for pictures with Rambo and Bussi and showed her friends knowledgeably around the museums. She was proud when a classmate quizzed Sami about an ailment afflicting her pet cat.

"Bring him to the clinic for investigations this evening," said Sami, "free of charge."

An unsettling number of ladies had come in full religious garb and sat talking in tight, impenetrable circles.

"They are nice girls, mostly," said Uzhdan, when her father pointed them out.

"They are extremists, and they are trouble," he replied. "Be careful and stay away."

Despite her love of animals, Uzhdan had decided not to pursue veterinary science. Instead, she would study English. She loved literature—Jane Austen and George Orwell—and hoped, one day, to become a famous novelist or, at least, a translator.

Sami could not have been more pleased.

Since the swift departure of Abu Shir, Sami had heard no more from the mayor of cable cars or five-star restaurants. Though the manager dropped in occasionally, he seemed feeble, showing off his scars and then returning home to bed. Abu Khaled had not come to call, and the municipality, with the issues of Sami's status and salary still unresolved, was keeping its distance.

Plans for the Museum of Everything were coming along well, and Sami had sent an optimistic letter to the manager of Giza Zoo, of his own accord, enquiring after future spare animals. As yet, he had not received a reply.

Sami walked past the new gift shop that had opened in the wake of the amusement park. It sold sweets, soft drinks, a strange selection of general groceries, and a few souvenirs bought in from China: Toy machine guns emblazoned with the logo "Soldier Force Irresistible," and little wooden arks painted with mottos "Happy to You" and "Forever Friend."

He might skip the report today, Sami thought, whistling softly, and work instead on measuring out his new aviary, though funds, so far, were unforthcoming. A zebra looked up from its breakfast of alfalfa as he passed.

As Sami unlocked the door to his office, a terrible hoarse screeching pierced the air. Inside a cardboard box in one corner, five large orphaned owl chicks opened their beaks to the heavens and demanded lunch.

"All right, all right!" Sami shouted down at them. "Please shut up! It is coming soon." Yail Misqawi would be along shortly with their second daily ration of raw meat. Meanwhile, he had preparations to make. Fufu was pregnant, expecting in a month or so. He was preparing a nice stall, tucked away behind the Slaughterhouse, for her comfortable confinement.

"Are you here, Dr. Sami?" came a lazy voice on the stairs.

"Come in, Mr. Eesa," said Sami. "Tea?"

The day after Abu Shir's bloody departure, Mr. Eesa had reluctantly taken the helm.

"You are free," he had told Sami without interest. "You can do what you like."

Mr. Eesa, thought Sami, would make a very nice replacement.

Soon, Sami moved a new cardboard model into the manager's office, clearing the wide desk and placing it in the center. It portrayed his aviary in all its glory, its ceilings lofty and slung with nets, its walkways, bridge, and pool borrowed from his original plans for Crocodile Island. He had made trees of multicolored streamers and bright water out of cellophane.

Mr. Eesa, slack-jawed and smoking, squinted at it for a full twenty minutes.

Mr. Eesa did not often come to the zoo. Sometimes he was absent; other days he simply wandered, watching as Sami went to work. He did not care whether Sami handed in his daily reports on time. On the day that Wahib attacked the manager, Sami had failed to pen one at all.

The following afternoon, sunshine had dappled the pavement ahead as Sami went to work, combining two days' reports into one. He took a pencil from his pocket and made a note. "Tuesday, Camel attacks manager. Both survive. Wednesday. Nothing happens. A very good day."

Postscript
May 2007

Two months after Wahib attacked Abu Shir, a young man arrived at the zoo. It was late, an unusual chill in the air, and he entered unnoticed. His coat collars were tucked close around his face, and a woolen hat was pulled down over his eyes.

He stole up the main avenue to an enclosure near the top and looked inside. There, Wahib quietly chewed his cud. The young man took out a small, blunt object wrapped in checked cheesecloth. He opened the cloth and glanced around. No one was about. With trembling hands, he took aim. Crack. Crack. Two bullets hit the camel squarely in the jaw. Wahib swayed and collapsed.

The visitor replaced his pistol and turned to leave. On his way out, he was spotted by Amjad Daoud at his ticket desk. "Mansur! Hello!" he called. "How is your father?"

"Better, now." Mansur was startled.

"Would you care for coffee?"

"No," he replied, and hurried away.

Amjad Daoud scratched his head and went back to counting up his cash register.

◆　　◆　　◆

No one is certain whether giraffes really mourn, whether hippos feel lonely or donkeys despair, or whether camels experience fear at the flash of an errant blade. Many scientists have shunned the study of animal emotion, fearing accusations of anthropomorphism. One affirmation is repeated throughout much scientific literature on animal emotion: "They are not, and could never be, like us."

But animals have often been held culpable for their crimes, of passion or otherwise. In the fifteenth century, a sow was put on trial and hanged in France for murdering and partially eating a human baby. Her half-dozen piglets were pardoned, since they were under the influence of a poor maternal example. Another pig was sent to the scaffold for gobbling up a communion wafer.

In England, in the sixteenth and seventeenth centuries, witches' familiars—cats, dogs, goats, or toads—were murdered with their mistresses as devils incarnate who bade witches to do their terrible deeds. Beetles, voles, weevils, and locusts were excommunicated, cursed in the name of God, and banished from the lands they were destroying.

In the seventeenth century, a Russian billy goat was sent to a Siberian prison camp for a year for injuring a child; in the eighteenth, a parrot was guillotined for treason. In the great wars of the twentieth century, dachshunds, or "liberty pups," were killed on the streets of England and America, symbols of the dreaded Hun.

In 1993, an Afghan man crept into the cage of Marjan the lion, Kabul Zoo's most famous resident, hoping to impress his friends.

He was promptly dispatched by the great cat. The next day, the dead man's brother appeared and threw a hand grenade into Marjan's cage. Marjan survived but lost an eye and his hearing.

◆   ◆   ◆

Mansur was spotted the next day in Ramallah, where he now held an unimportant job at the water board. Though the police would not pursue the crime, the rumors Sami had once heard of a pistol in a playground were confirmed. Abu Shir, deeply ashamed, disowned the boy and refused to return to work.

Weeks later, Sami found his Berber sheep dead in their enclosure, and an autopsy again identified Diazonol. Immediately, the zoo reinstated Bassam Bogdadi, the couple catcher, as head of animal security. As a precaution, Sami decided to keep Fufu and her spirited young daughter in their quarters behind the slaughterhouse and went about discrete investigations. It was not, he concluded after lengthy snooping, the work of one of his keepers. Instead, a rumor he snatched on the breeze suggested that the poisonings were politically motivated, a silent gesture against Hamas by a particularly inventive and vitriolic protestor. Dr. Sami decided to put an end to the problem by removing Diazonol altogether from his cleaning inventory and investing in a stout padlock for the cleaning cupboard door.

At the borders of the city, restrictions on movement were tightening. Arrests increased. A citizen of Qalqilya, reported the press, had packed a car with one hundred tons of explosives and traveled undetected across the checkpoints to the other side of the Wall. He drove as far as Tel Aviv, then turned and headed home. Once back inside the city, he motored to an open field and detonated the device. Nobody would ever know why.

"I hear Africa is nice at this time of year," said Sami, shaking his head over a cup of Butterfly Brand tea with Mr. Salaa in his laboratory at the back of the zoo. They gazed at the wobbly figure of a stuffed dromedary.

"It is a strange life," remarked Mr. Salaa, taking a sip of tea.

Rambo and Bussi galloped past, then collapsed in a gleeful heap at the camel's feet.

"This, Mr. Salaa," agreed Dr. Sami, lighting up his narghile, "is a very important point."

*   *   *

In the final days of 2007, the same Hamadryas couple that produced Rambo gave birth to a second, equally unwanted baby. Again, Sami leapt to the rescue and named the baby Robin. He was quieter and gentler than Rambo—though this was of little comfort to Sami's wife—and he flourished. Days later, Sami was thrilled to welcome his very first kangaroo, donated by a small animal park in Israel. Dr. Motke meanwhile continued about the task of locating spare herbivores for Ruti's old enclosure, though as the new year was ushered quietly in, they had yet to arrive.

Sami's precautionary poisoning measures had, it seemed, succeeded. The animal murders had ceased, and Sami could finally remember Ruti fondly. On the first day of 2008, he proclaimed himself optimistic that an International Zoo would prove just a matter of time, though pay rise, promotion, and new inhabitants for the empty Carnivore Department cages all remained forthcoming.

Author's Note

Many thanks to the people of Qalqilya Zoo, who allowed me into their lives, enclosures, and meetings to tell their story. Some of their names have been changed. The story's events were either witnessed first-hand or related to me by one, or more, of its principal figures—often several times over—along with exhaustive accounts of their thoughts and feelings.

My deep gratitude goes to Lindsay Jones at PublicAffairs for her tremendous support, expertise, and wise guidance. Thanks, too, to the animals of the zoo, and especially to Ruti, who provided encouraging nuzzles even when life at Qalqilya seemed most desperate.

Finally, my love and thanks to the inimitable, indomitable, inscrutable Dr. Sami, who made Butterfly Brand tea—and very important points—throughout.

PublicAffairs is a publishing house founded in 1997. It is a tribute to the standards, values, and flair of three persons who have served as mentors to countless reporters, writers, editors, and book people of all kinds, including me.

I.F. STONE, proprietor of *I. F. Stone's Weekly*, combined a commitment to the First Amendment with entrepreneurial zeal and reporting skill and became one of the great independent journalists in American history. At the age of eighty, Izzy published *The Trial of Socrates*, which was a national bestseller. He wrote the book after he taught himself ancient Greek.

BENJAMIN C. BRADLEE was for nearly thirty years the charismatic editorial leader of *The Washington Post*. It was Ben who gave the *Post* the range and courage to pursue such historic issues as Watergate. He supported his reporters with a tenacity that made them fearless and it is no accident that so many became authors of influential, best-selling books.

ROBERT L. BERNSTEIN, the chief executive of Random House for more than a quarter century, guided one of the nation's premier publishing houses. Bob was personally responsible for many books of political dissent and argument that challenged tyranny around the globe. He is also the founder and longtime chair of Human Rights Watch, one of the most respected human rights organizations in the world.

·   ·   ·

For fifty years, the banner of Public Affairs Press was carried by its owner Morris B. Schnapper, who published Gandhi, Nasser, Toynbee, Truman, and about 1,500 other authors. In 1983, Schnapper was described by *The Washington Post* as "a redoubtable gadfly." His legacy will endure in the books to come.

Peter Osnos, Founder and Editor-at-Large